Framed Horizons:

Student Writing on Nordic Cinema

eds. Marita Fraser, Melissa Powell, Rose-Anne Ross,
Anna V. Strauss, C. Claire Thomson

Norvik Press
2012

© Linda Blank, Martin Butcher, Pei Sze Chow, Kitty Clark, Daniel Fredriksson, Clare Glenister, Lauren Godfrey, Elisa Jochum, Ville-Matti Kervinen, Colin Leventhal, Melissa Powell, Rose-Anne Ross, Rebecca Spaven, Anna V. Strauss, C. Claire Thomson, Essi Viitanen, 2012.

Norvik Press Series C: Student Writing, no. 1

A catalogue record for this book is available from the British Library.

ISBN: 978-1-909408-00-5

Norvik Press gratefully acknowledges the generous support of UCL Enterprise Knowledge Transfer Champions scheme towards the publication of this book.

Norvik Press
Department of Scandinavian Studies
University College London
Gower Street London
WC1E 6BT
United Kingdom
Website: www.norvikpress.com
E-mail address: norvik.press@ucl.ac.uk
Managing editors: Sarah Death, Helena Forsås-Scott, Janet Garton, C. Claire Thomson.

Cover illustration: Cecilia Larsson/imagebank.sweden.se
Cover design: Marita Fraser
Layout: Marita Fraser

This book was produced using Booktype from Sourcefabric.
Special thanks to Adam Hyde and Johannes Wilm from Sourcefabric for their generous support and assistance.

Printed in the UK by Lightning Source UK Ltd.

Contents

INTRODUCTION

Introduction: 'I wish I had written that!'   1
Reflections on Student Scholarship and Publishing Possibilities
C. Claire Thomson

PLACE AND SPACE

Tracking Nordic Cinema: 5
The Films of Carl Th. Dreyer and Ingmar Bergman
Colin Leventhal

Bergman's Fårö: 31
Inhabitation Remote from Modern Society?
Elisa Jochum

Aki Kaurismäki's Postcards   63
Kitty Clark

Bourgeois Space and the Post-Ideological Cinema of   83
Dogme 95 and Desplechin
Ville-Matti Kervinen

LOOKING AND TOUCHING

Sensuality and Gesture in Sjöström's *Körkarlen*   99
Daniel Fredriksson

Gazing at the Gaze: 113
Scopophilia in Ingmar Bergman's *Sommaren med Monika* and *Persona*
Melissa Powell

Hands as Icon and Symbol of Touch 139
Lauren Godfrey

INNI: Embodied Spectatorship 161
Rose-Anne Ross

AUTEUR AND STYLE

Tancred Ibsen and the Norwegian Film Industry 179
Clare Glenister

Dreyer, Dogme and the Real 199
Martin Butcher

'It is Too Beautiful': 223
Accidents and Auteurship in Lars von Trier's *Antichrist*
Pei Sze Chow

NATION AND IDENTITY

Alternative Endings in Early Danish and Russian Cinema 249
Anna V. Strauss

The Unknown Soldier in Finnish History 283
Essi Viitanen

Globalisation and National Identity in Transnational   321
Nordic Cinema
Rebecca Spaven

The Father Figure in Swedish 'Immigrant' Films   341
Linda Blank

Introduction: 'I wish I had written that!' Reflections on Student Scholarship and Publishing Possibilities

C. Claire Thomson

Earlier this year, a meme took hold amongst academics on Twitter. The exhortation to 'Tweet Your PhD' circulated for a few days, challenging researchers to sum up their project in 140 characters. It quickly transpired that it was indeed possible to encapsulate 100,000 words and three or four years of work in a tweet - but the task demanded absolute clarity on the part of the author as to what his or her project was about. Since that mass experiment, I've found that asking students to describe their essay projects in a tweet can be a useful exercise in forcing them to distill their ideas in terms of coherence and scope. And yet, the notion of assessing learning by Tweet sounds faintly ridiculous. Those 140 characters are just the beginning of a journey of 2000, 5000 or even 10,000 words. In the course of that journey, the student is expected to demonstrate not just what has been learnt during a course, but also that s/he has mastered the skills central to an education in the Arts and Humanities: marshaling, synthesising and critically engaging with a range of sources, constructing a sound argument in response to a question or statement, substantiating claims with evidence, drawing well-founded conclusions, expressing ideas clearly and accurately. It is obvious that many students devote a great deal of time and energy to mastering these skills and to researching their essays. A very few of them are awarded an elusive mark of 80 or above, reserved, in the peculiar marking scheme of Arts and Humanities in the UK, for work that is of publishable quality. And yet, in an era when untold millions of words are spewed daily into the blogosphere, the accepted fate of high quality student essays is to languish in a filing cabinet, rarely emerging even to function as successful exemplars from which student peers can learn.

This book celebrates the good old-fashioned Arts and Humanities essay, both as a tool for developing key skills, and as a form of narrative whose strengths and weaknesses are suddenly thrown into sharp relief in an era of proliferating communication platforms. The present book represents a pilot project which we intend to develop further within the School of European Languages, Culture and Society at UCL. Running over the academic year, the project will provide students with experience in proof-editing, peer review, graphic design, collaborative working, marketing, and training in emerging publishing technologies. It is one of these emerging technologies that has made *Framed Horizons* possible: SourceFabric's online publishing platform BookType enables groups of writers and editors to work together on a text in real time, and to publish it both as print-on-demand and e-book. Ultimately, the aim is to integrate practical skills in the use of new technology into the tried-and-tested pedagogical process of essay-writing, so as to equip students in flexible ways to function in the communication environment into which they will graduate.

The essays in this book were all written over the last six years by students who have taken my BA- or MA-level courses in Nordic Cinema, or who are now studying with me as PhD students but wanted to return to MA work on Nordic cinema

Introduction: 'I wish I had written that!'

they had written elsewhere. The essays thus span the gamut of coursework types: they include first-year BA projects, short essays testing second-year students' grasp of film analysis, year abroad projects, and MA essays by Film Studies students. Some authors are specialists in Scandinavian language and culture; others have no background in Scandinavian Studies (and thus no access to the original language dialogue) but are studying film or fine art. Around twenty former students who had achieved a mark at least in the high upper second range were invited to contribute; the selection published here is by those who chose to do so. The chapters are therefore, inevitably, on a fairly random range of topics within the area of Nordic Cinema, are of different lengths, and display different levels of scholarly maturity. Thus, it must be made absolutely clear that these essays are not presented here as academic research. Most of them have been revised for publication on the basis of my feedback and additional comments from a team of student peer reviewers, but we make no claims that they have all attained a standard of scholarship typical of an academic peer-reviewed journal. Apart from some minor revisions for clarity and accuracy, the style of individual authors -- several of them writing quite beautifully in English as a second or third language -- has been allowed to breathe.

In the commentaries written by the authors, they reflect on the context in which each essay was produced, and what they might have done differently in hindsight. These commentaries have been included as a reminder to the reader that this book is not a standard academic source. I would, in fact, suggest that it can usefully be used not just as a collection of interesting perspectives on Nordic cinema, but also as a set of exemplars of what a BA or MA essay can be. Students -- as well as, I would venture, more advanced scholars -- can learn a great deal by pondering the strengths and weaknesses of the writing of others. Moreover, evaluation of sources, and their judicious use, is one of the most important skills a student can develop, in an era in which communication platforms are proliferating at bewildering speed. Assessing the status of these essays could be compared as an exercise to puzzling out how and when to cite a newspaper article as a source, or Wikipedia, or a blog, or, for that matter, an article in a peer-reviewed journal. A grasp of the implications of the material and media instantiation of any source is essential, as well as the ability to discern a robust argument or sniff out a dubious statistic.

I would maintain that there is something to be learnt from all of these essays: a distinctive approach to an aspect of film theory adopted by a student approaching cinema from the perspective of another discipline, for example; tenacious use of fast-developing Scandinavian language skills to research a filmmaker ignored by anglophone scholarship; sparky insights gleaned from the unlikely juxtaposition of disparate filmmakers or films. To varying degrees, they all feature attentive and original readings of films, imaginative approaches to the subject matter, and engagement with different types of resources. All of them, for one reason or another, have caused me to stop, think, and exclaim: 'I wish I had written that!' -- one of the greatest pleasures of academic life.

Tracking Nordic Cinema: The Films of Carl Th. Dreyer and Ingmar Bergman

Colin Leventhal

Carl Th. Dreyer (1889-1968) and Ingmar Bergman (1918-2007), the two great auteur filmmakers of Nordic cinema, are, arguably, better known for close-ups of human faces than for tracking shots. However, in this essay I argue that the use of camera movement, particularly tracking shots, to explore interior and exterior spaces, objects and characters, plays a distinctive function in the construction of narrative and representational meaning in their films. I analyse and discuss this use in two late films directed by Carl Th. Dreyer, *Vredens Dag* (Day of Wrath) (1943) and *Ordet* (The Word, 1955), with a critical comparison to two key films directed by Bergman, *Sommaren med Monika* (Summer With Monika) (1953) and *Persona* (1966).

An Introduction To Camera Movement and Tracking Shots

Since the early days of cinema, filmmakers have used movement to represent the world visually in a way that differentiates the medium of film from other media such as still photography or the live theatre. Camera movement helps to construct the meaning of a film by providing information about the spaces in which images are being filmed and the people and objects in those spaces. Raymond Carney (1989:120 footnote) has suggested that by using camera movement 'Dreyer creates a heightened spatial and temporal awareness

Place and Space

The camera tracks Monika as she delights in her freedom on the island.
Sommaren med Monika, Ingmar Bergman, Sweden, 1953.

Anne moves through the cloisters, and the tracking camera turns to reveal the space behind her.
Vredens Dag, Carl Th. Dreyer, Denmark, 1943.

in the viewer. The moving camera communicates the fact that meaning is enacted, worked, performed into existence within the particularities of specific spaces and times'.

The impact of a moving image is greater where the framing is not stationary, as the image can focus on or highlight particular people and objects, and also provide greater appearance of three-dimensionality, which draws the audience into the visual experience. Corrigan and White (2009: 116) add that 'when the film frame begins to move, a film shot recreates a quality of vision that has always been part of the human experience'.

A frame or several frames of an image, recorded on film, shot by a camera moving backwards, forwards, sideways, circularly or in any direction along the ground, is known as a tracking shot. The title derives from the movement of the camera which was originally mounted on a platform with wheels to run on parallel tracks like a train. Subsequently, specially made, very manoeuvrable camera vehicles with rubber wheels, called dollies, were developed. Tracking shots are also referred to as dolly shots or travelling or trucking shots.

Tracking shots may be combined with other camera movements such as tilts or pans (in which the camera, stationary on a single vertical axis, moves up or down, left to right or right to left) or crane shots (in which the stationary camera moves above the ground on a mechanical arm or crane) to achieve complex sequences which have appealed to many creative filmmakers including Dreyer and Bergman. Since the 1970s, it has also been possible to attach the camera to the operator using a balancing camera mount patented as the Steadicam. This enables the operator to walk with the camera with fluid, even movements, thereby marrying the use of handheld camera techniques to conventional tracking shots.

Tracking shots are used to change the framing of an image of an object or character, or explore space. To do so, the camera moves towards or away from one person or more, moves in parallel to or between them, moves in front of them, or follows behind them. For example, in the iconic final scene of *Les 400 Coups* (The 400 Blows, Francois Truffaut, France, 1959), the camera films the protagonist, Antoine Doinel, as he escapes from the reformatory, following him, tracking parallel to him and finally zooming to close-up on him on the beach.

Tracking shots explore space by altering the way the image is framed. By moving the camera in relation to the mise-en-scène, the scale, size, shape and depth of the on-screen image is changed and redefined. This is exemplified in *Cabiria* (Giovanni Pastrone, Italy, 1914), which is regarded as the first use of a tracking shot in a major popular film. The film uses slow, long, diagonal tracking shots, moving the camera both forwards and backwards from mid-shot to extreme long shot, to show the size and scale of its huge sets, including the marketplace at Carthage, the Temple of Moloch and Hasdrubal's Palace. Nowell-Smith (1997:127) comments, 'the tracking shots of *Cabiria* perform a crucial narrative and descriptive function, and were filmed on a sophisticated system of tracks which allowed for remarkably complex camera movements'.

Cabiria influenced the work of many early directors including, famously, D.W. Griffith and F.W. Murnau, and early tracking shots were called 'Cabiria movements' (Salt 2009:138). *Sunrise* (F.W. Murnau, US, 1927) was particularly lauded for its use of the 'unbound' moving camera in scenes in both the country and the city. An example of this takes place in the country where the Man leaves the family home to meet the City Woman at night, with the camera following him in long shot and then moving parallel to him before moving forward through bushes to settle on the City Woman playing with a spring flower in her hand.

The introduction of sound inhibited the moving camera (as they were positioned in cumbersome soundboxes) until the development of more lightweight cameras in the 1940s. Since then, filmmakers have increasingly demonstrated their cinematic virtuosity with combination tracking shots in a wide range of films. It seems that every cineaste has their favourite tracking shots and my own nominations include the party scene in *Notorious* (Alfred Hitchcock, USA, 1946) (where the camera tracks down from the top of the stairs to find the cellar keys in Ingrid Bergman's hands) to the opening scene in *Touch of Evil* (Orson Welles, USA, 1958), (which starts with an bomb planted under a car and ends with its explosion) to *Boogie Nights* (Paul Thomas Anderson, USA, 1997) (where the opening shot picks up the movie title outside a cinema and then tracks down a street following a car to a nightclub which Burt Reynolds and Julianne Moore enter, introduces several characters including a waitress on rollerskates before ending in a mid-shot on the protagonist).

Each of these scenes heightens the visual experience of the

viewer by showing that movement is not just an integral part of the narrative but also a compelling and distinctive quality of the medium of film; not only is film a moving medium (that is, a succession of moving images) but what is shown on the images is itself moving.

Carl Th. Dreyer

Dreyer's own interest in camera movement was summarized by him as follows:

> The eye absorbs horizontal lines rapidly and easily but repels vertical lines. The eye is involuntarily attracted by objects in motion but remains passive over stationary things. This is the explanation why the eye, with pleasure, follows gliding camera movements, preferably when they are soft and rhythmic. As a principal rule, one can say that one shall try to keep a continuous, flowing, horizontally gliding motion in the film. If one then suddenly introduces vertical lines, one can by this reach an instantly dramatic effect – as, for instance, in the pictures of the vertical ladder just before it is thrown into the fire in *Vredens Dag* (Dreyer, in Skoller, 1973:129).

I have chosen the following examples of Dreyer's use of 'continuous, flowing, horizontally gliding motion' from three sequences in *Vredens Dag* (1943), which tells the story of Anne, the young and beautiful wife of an older pastor, Absalon, who falls in love with her stepson, Martin, with disastrous consequences. Against a background of village life in seventeenth century Denmark, the elders use the fear of witchcraft and its religious condemnation to maintain their male power over the moral and ethical behaviour of women.

First, early in the film, Anne enters the village church through a door on the left of the screen, and in a parallel tracking medium long shot from left to right, walks and then runs through a colonnade to a double row of steps up to the sacristy. The camera tracks round to face her as she looks about her to check that nobody is there, before walking up the steps to open the door. She appears youthful in her hurry, compared to the sombre, slow-moving environment in the previous scene in her house with Absalon and Merete where Herlof's Marte is found hiding. Anne has come to overhear, through the open door, Absalon questioning Herlof's Marte to obtain a confession that she is a witch. In response, Herlof's Marte asks for his help to spare her life as he did for Anne's mother, who was a witch. Herlof's Marte has already told Anne that her mother was spared because of her so this comes as confirmation of Absalon's involvement. She knows that Absalon could save Herlof's Marte's life but he does not, and she is taken away for torture.

The second example takes place on a stormy night with Anne consumed by her love for Martin. Absalon is away administering to a congregant who is dying, and Merete has just told Martin that she regrets the day that Absalon brought Anne to live in their house. Again, Anne enters the main living room of the house from the left of the scene. She has an almost seductive look on her face and her hair is flowing and uncovered in contrast with the first example, in which her hair is tightly covered by a mobcap. She walks from left to right in a flowing parallel tracking shot, passing behind the chair in which Martin is sitting, across the room to the door on the right of the screen which she locks with a hook before the camera moves with her walking back towards Martin. She does not take her eyes off Martin throughout this movement, drawing the viewer's attention to the intense sexual and emotional passion she feels for Martin. She no longer hides her feelings for him, and by locking the door to what is presumably her mother-in-law's room, she indicates that she wishes to make love or share physical intimacy with Martin.

The third example is taken from the famous last scene of the film where a ceremony is taking place in the sacristy of the church to honour the death of Absalon, who lies in his coffin. It is the same location in which Anne saw Absalon questioning Herlof's Marte in my first example and it is here that Anne will be forced to confront her own fate as a consequence of her relationship with Martin. In this complex scene, the camera moves in a swinging action between Anne and Martin on the left of the coffin and Merete on the right and ends with Martin and Merete on the right, with Anne isolated on the left, finally sitting next to the coffin. This swinging camera action is intercut with still close-up shots of Anne responding visually with her eyes and facial expression to her denunciation as a witch by Merete and to the consequent request by an elder that she deny the charge. Dreyer (in Skoller 1973:132-3) describes the rhythm of the camera movement in this scene as follows:

> Instead of using short, quick, moving pictures, I introduced what I call long, gliding close ups that follow the players in a rhythmic way, feeling their way from one player to another just as the action is taking place with one then the other. In spite of – or perhaps, more correctly, I should say because of – this almost wave-formed rhythm, the scene with the two young people by Absalom's coffin is one of the parts that touches the

public most strongly.

Anne 'confesses' to the murder of Absalon and the seduction of Martin whilst under the influence of the devil, 'the evil one'. She says of Absalon 'you have your revenge, after all'. So the camera movement indicates Martin's desertion of Anne to the 'side' of Merete, leaving her isolated and her passion for Martin destroyed. Her confession suggests that her life is no longer worth living. Her passion, and adultery, is a threat to the social order of village life and she sacrifices her life by admitting to Merete's accusations. Camera movement serves to explore and open up the tight confines of the sacristy, showing not just the change of allegiances but also the wider significance of the issues of life and death dealt with in the film.

Dreyer's *Ordet* (1955) is concerned with the life, death and subsequent resurrection of Inger Borgen, the loving wife of Mikkel and mother of young Maren. The first tracking shot in the film introduces us to the Borgen family who live together in Borgensgaard farm. The patriarch of the family, old Morten Borgen, has three sons, Mikkel, Anders and Johannes, who has gone insane. The camera starts with a long shot on Anders waking in the bedroom he shares with Johannes, and pans right to show his parallel empty bed. Anders gets up, looks out the window, lifting a blind, with a cut to Johannes walking up to the top of the dunes outside the house. The camera cuts back to a point of view long shot from the main living room of the house, showing Anders getting dressed in his bedroom and then walking through the bedroom door back into the main living room. The camera tracks in front of him as he moves left towards and into his father's bedroom, where he wakes him to tell him that Johannes is missing again. The camera tracks further left to show Anders going through a door to the outside of the house and then with nobody in vision continues to track left to discover Inger in her nightgown coming out of her bedroom to find out what is going on. She then goes back into her bedroom where he wakes her husband, Mikkel. So with minimal cutting, Dreyer has introduced us to the Borgen family and shown the family together, focusing on the disappearance of Johannes out onto the dunes again in the middle of the night. It is a scene of family intimacy with its members in their nightwear, but it also explores the interior of the house, showing us that although sparsely furnished it is elegant, sizeable, well laid out and belonging to a well-to-do family of farmers.

In the next example from the film, Inger seeks the support of Morten Borgen for the marriage of his youngest son, Anders, to Anne, the daughter of a tailor who belongs to a different religious group. The sequence takes place in a large, well-furnished, almost elegant, living room and has a duration of nine minutes, with only two very short cuts: a jump cut to Johannes entering and leaving the room, and a point of view shot of the new vicar walking into the church outside the window of the living room. For the rest of the sequence, the camera glides around the living room, following the movements of Inger and Morten as they walk about, sit down and stand up whilst discussing family activities, love, the proposed marriage, and how Anders is asking for Anne's hand in marriage without consulting Morten. At the end of the sequence, Morten still refuses to consent to the marriage despite being offered a bribe by Inger of fried eel for dinner on Sunday, and a son as her next child.

This is a gentle scene of family intimacy between a loving daughter-in-law and the head of the family, with the simple activities of drinking coffee, smoking a pipe and winding wool serving as precursors to a discussion of a key family issue. The appearance of Johannes reminds us that life is far from perfect in the Borgen family despite the apparent affluence of their lives and the impending birth of a new sibling for Inger's daughter, young Maren. The camera movement in this scene is slow and rhythmic, emphasizing the dance-like dialogue between the two characters, delicately skirting around and then directly discussing an issue that has been dividing the family.

In my last example from *Ordet*, the centrality of Johannes in the film's narrative is underlined in a 360 degree tracking shot which focuses on Johannes and Inger's daughter young Maren. The scene begins with the child entering the room, with Johannes sitting on a chair in the middle holding a reed rod, and asking him whether Inger will die soon (Inger is having a difficult labour). Johannes asks her whether she wants her mother to die and she replies that she does so that Johannes will raise her from the dead. Maren stands by Johannes' side as the camera tracks in a mid-shot in a slow circle around them whilst they talk about her mother, Inger's possible death, and her going to heaven rather than staying on earth. Maren asks him again to raise her from the dead and she kisses him on the cheek. Johannes then picks her up to take her to bed, she kisses him on the cheek again and he walks right, out of frame. The sustained tension of this tracking shot heightens the contrast between the naïve faith of the child and the irrational faith of the unbalanced religious believer.

Edvin Kau (2011) describes Dreyer's camera style thus:

> In Dreyer's work, the camera moves freely in all dimensions of space – around people, back and forth between them, and everywhere in the scenery, and in this way, that which is recorded from all these angles and positions is located in relation to the picture surface.
>
> The totality of the experience is mainly achieved through the free, mobile camera, which is not a camera that continually tracks, pans, shakes or tilts (although these movements are naturally present) but rather one that is weightless, privileged to take up any position and present its image from the chosen viewpoint – and in the next moment, an entirely different side of this.

For Dreyer, the moving, 'weightless' camera was central to his filmmaking, and in these examples, the use of combination tracking shots was at the core of his narrative and representational storytelling.

Ingmar Bergman

Ingmar Bergman, regarded by many as one of the greatest film directors of all time, towered over Nordic and world cinema during his lifetime. The films he made in the 1950s and 60s established his worldwide reputation and made his name synonymous with Swedish cinema. Philip Kemp (1997: 572-3) perceptively comments that 'the austere beauty of Bergman's images seemed to match his high seriousness of purpose – qualities for which, when fashions changed, he would be mocked and parodied as the prime purveyor of Nordic gloom'.

It is not known whether Bergman and Dreyer talked or discussed filmmaking but it would be surprising if Bergman had not seen Dreyer's films. It would be interesting to speculate on the influence which Dreyer's work may have had on Bergman's films particularly those early films dealing with metaphysical issues such as *Det sjunde inseglet* (The Seventh Seal, 1957). Contrasting with the exploration of interior space and characters in *Day of Wrath* and *Ordet*, Bergman uses tracking shots to focus or highlight exterior space in the Swedish summers featured in *Sommaren med Monika* (1953) and *Persona* (1966).

Jean-Luc Godard (1972), perhaps overexuberantly but with reason, described *Sommaren Med Monika* as

> The most original film of the most original of directors. It is to the cinema today [1958] what *Birth of A Nation* is to the classical cinema. Just as Griffith influenced Eisenstein, Gance and Lang, so *Sommaren Med Monika*, five years before its time, brought to a peak that renaissance in modern cinema whose high priests were Fellini in Italy, Aldrich in Hollywood and (so we believed, wrongly perhaps) Vadim in France.

It may be that Godard overstates the importance of Bergman's film but it is nevertheless an extraordinary depiction of teenage angst and sexuality. I would disagree with Robin Wood (1969: 39) who downplays the film's significance in the context of Bergman's earlier films, saying:

> It is a less personal work than *Sommarlek*, and relatively minor; it never achieves the generalizing significance of the earlier film, being in a more restrictive way a study of character and of a particular relationship.

The relationship featured in the film is between Monika, a young, troubled, delinquent teenager, and Harry, a conservative young man by comparison, with whom Monika escapes from their dreary lives and jobs in Stockholm to spend the summer on an island in the archipelago. As in several Bergman films of this period, their relationship, which starts at the beginning of summer, disintegrates as summer gives way to autumn. Bergman introduced us in this film to Harriet Andersson who plays Monika with animal vitality, powerful sensuality, and a real sexual allure; Melvyn Bragg once told me (and repeats the anecodote in his 1993 book on *The Seventh Seal*) that he remembers her even today as the first woman with whom he fell in love. In an iconic and much discussed sequence late in the film, just before the couple break up, Monika sits in a café with another man and stares out at the camera in a way which has been variously described as 'contemptuous' (Mosley in Hubner 2007: 45), 'ashamed and defiant' (Wood 1969: 42) and 'the saddest shot in the history of the cinema' (Godard 1971). This ambivalence and ambiguity is described by Laura Hubner (2007: 45) as 'an anticipation of elements in Bergman's later, more reflexive films such as *Persona*'. She adds that it 'also signifies a defiant female response to the heterosexual male gaze long before Mulvey's influential article on the subject' (45).

In my first example, Monika and Harry on their first date walk, arm in arm, along the street in Stockholm at night in a parallel tracking mid-shot after their visit to the cinema. Monika articulates the sort of good life she would like to lead, with kind friends, a nice house, going to clubs and dances in motorcars, in effect identifying with the actress in the movie they have just seen. The couple stop to admire a blouse in a shop window.

This seems to be a very different girl to the sensual, young woman, in my second example, who stretches her full-bodied frame on the roof of the boat in which Monika and Harry have sailed the day before from Stockholm to the island in the archipelago. Its their first morning on the island and Monika wakes early at ten past five in marked contrast to her life in her family's slum tenement in the city. After stretching in the warmth of the early morning sun in shorts and skimpy top, she jumps off the boat and walks along the seashore with primus stove and kettle in hand, tracked by the camera in a parallel long shot. The water sparkles and the viewer can almost smell the freshness of the sea and coastline as Monika settles on a rock to boil some water. Laura Hubner (2007:42) describes this sequence which starts with Monika waking as 'voyeuristic, almost predatory'. She adds that 'the felt authorial presence of the camera hints at Bergman's relationship as lover with Harriet Andersson' (42) but in my view, the viewer is privileged to see Monika's real excitement on her own for the first time in a natural habitat.

In my third example, at the end of the summer, the couple have run out of food and go foraging at a summer house on the island for something substantial to eat. Monika is caught by the couple who own the house but is offered food by the wife whilst the husband telephones the police. She sits at the dining room table looking disheveled, dirty and angry next to the well-dressed daughter of the house who regards her with snobbish disdain. Monika responds by stealing a joint of meat prepared for the family dinner and runs out of the house. In a tracking shot, she crawls through the undergrowth near the house with the meat in her hand tearing bits off it with her teeth. She is tracked by the camera in close-up resembling a feral animal fighting for survival, the niceties of bourgeois life epitomized by the family in the summer house far behind her. In this sequence, Laura Hubner (2007:43) says, 'Monika seems to represent a repressed rawness'.

These three sequences from *Sommaren Med Monika* show different aspects of her character and personality i.e. wanting a better life, enjoying the freedom of outdoor life and fighting for survival in tracking shots which draw the viewer into her experiences with greater intensity than if shot by a stationary camera. The tracking shots contribute to the narrative continuity which leads to Monika, now pregnant, returning with Harry to Stockholm, their marriage, the birth of their child and their subsequent breakup.

Marilyn Johns Blackwell (1997: 133) refers to *Persona* as 'occupying a singular position in film history, long acknowledged as one of the "great" films of the Western tradition. She adds:

> Bergman creates a film that opposes dominant cinematic convention and seeks a new form of representation that is attuned to complexity and difference and is more open to a meaning that is not structured by the male symbolic order and that argues the simultaneous impossibility and necessity of discourse. (134)

To the 60s generation, it was Bergman's most avant-garde and influential film, shot in black and white, although in my view its reputation today may have become diminished through parody, plagiarism and postmodern experimentation. In the film (which nevertheless remains a remarkable tour de force about womanhood and identity seen through the relationship between two women) Bergman articulates, using a wide range of stylistic devices, the story of an actress, Elisabet Vogler, who loses the ability to speak, as a reaction to her perceived role in the world around her; her alienation is characterized by a rejection of the desire to communicate. She is treated in hospital at the beginning of the film but her doctor suggests that she goes with her nurse, Alma, to the doctor's summer cottage on an island in the Swedish archipelago to convalesce.

In the first sequence on the island, Elisabet and Alma walk in a parallel long tracking shot behind a wall and trees near the summerhouse collecting mushrooms. It is a beautiful, idyllic, warm summer's day, and for the first time in the film Elisabet seems happy and engaged in activity. It is an exterior shot showing the countryside at its welcoming best, fecund and felicitous, but the wall and trees serve to hide the protagonists from public gaze as they bend down to pick mushrooms. Elisabet smiles as Alma talks away, but we do not hear what she says as the voiceover tells us that the move to the country is good for Elisabet. They look at the different mushrooms in their bags before the action cuts to the two sitting outside at a table trying to identify the mushrooms with the help of a book. Patient and nurse develop a relationship in which the nurse would like to be the actress; Bergman has underlined this motif, the convergence of the two protagonists' personalities, by casting actresses who look like each other, and with whom he was involved, one before and the other during and after the making of the film.

Alma reveals intimate details of her emotional and sexual life which she has never told anybody before, seeking to create an even closer bond with Elisabet. Elisabet puts her down in a letter to her doctor which she leaves open, perhaps deliberately, for Alma to read, by revealing some of those details and also suggesting that Alma is attracted to her. Alma reacts to this seeming rejection by accusing Elisabet of using her, and of abusing her friendship. The film seems to rupture at this point to emphasize the change in the protagonists' relationship and when the narrative resumes, the mise-en-scène has changed, with both protagonists dressed in black. A fight ensues, Elisabet slaps Alma, whose nose begins to bleed, and Alma threatens to throw a pan of boiling water at Elisabet. Finally, Alma's insults cause Elisabet to rush out of the cottage.

The second sequence is a long parallel tracking shot from left to right, which begins with the camera following Alma running along the seashore after Elisabet, who is not immediately in shot. The sky is dark with clouds and the summer seems to be coming to an end. Alma is calling for Elisabet to forgive her as she catches up with her, now in shot, walking quickly along the rocky beach. Both are dressed in black, with Elisabeth in trousers and Alma in a dress. The camera is moving quickly to keep up with the protagonists. It moves in parallel with bushes between it and the sea. They walk through an unseen gap in a low brick wall running down to the sea, with the camera now moving ahead of the women walking. Alma is trying to explain to Elisabet why she felt so let down by her. Taller bushes and some trees occasionally hide the women from the camera as they walk. Elisabet walks more slowly as the camera slows and comes to a halt, with Elisabet turning around to face or confront Alma.

In both films, Bergman shows the relationships starting optimistically at the beginning of summer and deteriorating as the summer changes into autumn, the mood of the characters reflecting the growing gloom of the season as the happiness of the early summer changes to despair and desperation. He uses tracking shots in both films to trace the shoreline of the islands of the archipelago, the sea and the surrounding rocks and vegetation. The focus is on the protagonists' relationship with this natural environment and its effect on their feelings towards each other.

Conclusions

I would draw the following conclusions from this analysis of tracking shots in these four films of Dreyer and Bergman, perhaps cornerstones of their work, which deal predominantly with female protagonists and their relationships with family, lovers and the world around them:

First, Dreyer is more deeply concerned with metaphysical issues in his films (the nature of existence, life, death and resurrection, good and evil) than Bergman, for whom they are intrinsically tied to the human experience. Bergman moves from metaphysics in his earlier films to give greater focus in *Sommaren Med Monika* and *Persona* to the psychology of human relationships, with tracking shots being one feature in the bag of cinematic tricks he uses to explore the complexities of those relationships. Dreyer (in Skoller 1973: 127) believes that 'the soul is shown through the style, which is the artist's way of giving expression to his perception of the material'. His style is the so-called 'weightless' camera involving the use of combination tracking shots as an essential or overriding element.

Second, as I mentioned at the beginning of this essay, both auteurs are perhaps better known in their film style for close-ups of human faces, which they use to complement, and to contrast with, their use of the moving camera. I refer in particular to Dreyer's use of multi-angled close-ups of Marie Falconetti in *La Passion de Jeanne D'Arc* (The Passion of Joan of Arc, France, 1928) which were later featured by his great admirer, Jean-Luc Godard, in *Vivre Sa Vie* (My Life to Live, France, 1962), and similarly Bergman's use of close-ups in *Persona* imbued that film with an extraordinary intensity, which stands in marked contrast to the long shots, including tracking shots, in the film.

Third, both directors subvert conventional classical Hollywood continuity methods by using tracking shots to draw the audience into the spaces they have constructed. With Dreyer, interiors predominate, perhaps reflecting the greater torment of the characters in the narrative. Dreyer in particular uses tracking shots to slow the rhythm of the film in a way which serves no specific narrative purpose. Bordwell (1981:142) describes this 'as a process which we perceive in its own right'. Whilst we certainly perceive camera movement as a process which makes the viewer more aware of the visual medium of film, in Bergman, the use of tracking shots in exterior scenes opens the narrative to the outside natural world but also supports the narrative by enhancing the emotionality of the particular sequence.

Fourth, Dreyer's tracking shots, as well as following

characters, are used most effectively to film conversations or dialogue between people. The camera moves between them creating continuity whereas classical Hollywood continuity would favour the shot/reverse shot technique which Bergman often uses. Bergman is stylistically more complex than Dreyer, using many more devices than camera movement to serve his narrative. For example, with his background of work in the live theatre, Bergman also favours a richer, less minimalist mise-en-scène than Dreyer. Dreyer seeks, on the other hand, to simplify and 'abstract' his mise-en-scène to create an increased awareness in the viewer.

Author's Comment

I am a first year PhD research student in Film Studies in the Centre for Intercultural Studies at UCL. My research explores how the practices of conflict imagery have changed the way that recent wars from Vietnam to Afghanistan have been constructed and represented in film, television and photography.

I have been a great fan of Ingmar Bergman films since I first saw *The Seventh Seal* as a teenager. His engagement with and passion for metaphysical issues, since rather derided and parodied, chimed with my own interest in philosophy which I studied as an undergraduate at King's College, London in the mid-60s.

After working for many years as a entertainment lawyer at the BBC and later at Channel 4 Television, I decided to resume my academic studies with an MA in Film Studies at UCL. The module on Nordic Cinema taught by Claire Thomson introduced me to the marvellous films of Carl Th. Dreyer as well as more recent auteurs such as Lars Von Trier and Aki Kaurismäki whose films I had previously watched with a relatively uncritical eye.

My essay on 'Tracking Nordic Cinema' was written at the beginning of the second year of my part-time MA. Reconsidering it today, I realize that my ability to construct and put forward academic argument has improved considerably in the intervening eighteen months. More analysis and argument, fewer descriptive and illustrative passages would have benefited my basis thesis about how camera movement, and tracking shots in particular, serve to give meaning and focus to film.

References

Boogie Nights (Paul Thomas Anderson, USA, 1997)

Cabiria (Giovanni Pastrone, Italy, 1914)

Vredens Dag (Day of Wrath, Carl Th. Dreyer, Denmark, 1943)

Notorious (Alfred Hitchcock, USA, 1946)

Ordet (The Word, Carl Th. Dreyer, Denmark, 1955)

La Passion de Jeanne D'Arc (The Passion of Joan of Arc, Carl Th. Dreyer, France, 1928)

Persona (Ingmar Bergman, Sweden, 1966)

Les 400 Coups (The 400 Blows, Francois Truffaut, France, 1959)

Det sjunde inseglet (The Seventh Seal, Ingmar Bergman, Sweden, 1957)

Sommaren med Monika (Summer With Monika, Ingmar Bergman, Sweden, 1953)

Sunrise (F.W. Murnau, USA, 1927)

Touch of Evil (Orson Welles, USA, 1958)

Vivre Sa Vie (My Life to Live, Jean-Luc Godard, France, 1962)

Bergman, Ingmar (1973). *Bergman on Bergman:Interviews by Stig Bjorkman, Torsten Manns and Jonas Sima*. Tr. Paul Britten Austin. London: Secker & Warburg.

Blackwell, Marilyn Johns (1997). *Gender and Representation in* the Films of Ingmar Bergman. Columbia, SC: Camden House.

Bordwell, David (1981). *The Films of Carl Theodor Dreyer*. Berkeley and Los Angeles, California: University of California Press.

Bordwell, David (1997). *On the History of Film Style*. London: Harvard University Press.

Bordwell, David, and Thompson, Kristin (2008). *Film Art: An Introduction*, 8th ed. New York: McGraw-Hill.

Bragg, Melvyn (1993). *The Seventh Seal*. BFI Film Classics. London: BFI.

Carney, Raymond (1989). *Speaking the Language of Desire*. Cambridge: Cambridge University Press.

Corrigan Timothy & White, Patricia (2009). *The Film Experience*. Boston: Bedford/St. Martin's.

Dreyer, Carl Th. (1973). 'A Little On Film Style', in *Dreyer in Double Reflection: Translation of Carl Th. Dreyer's Writings About the Film (Om Filmen)*, edited with essays and annotations by Donald Skoller. New York: Dutton.

Godard, Jean-Luc (1972). 'Summer With Monika'. Originally published in French in *Arts 680*, 30 July 1958: 6, and published in English in Milne, Tom (ed.) (1972): *Godard on Godard*, London: Secker & Warburg. http://www.bergmanorama.com/film/summer_with_monika_godard.htm. Accessed 3rd January, 2011.

Henderson, Brian (1970): 'Towards A Non-Bourgeois Camera

Style'. *Film Quarterly* 24:2, 2-14.

Hubner, Laura (2007). *The Films of Ingmar Bergman: Illusions of Light and Darkness.* London: Palgrave Macmillan.

Katz, Steven D. (1991). *Film Directing Shot by Shot: Visualising from Concept to Screen.* California: Michael Wiese Productions.

Kau, Edvin (2010). 'Cinema and Space'. *Carl Th. Dreyer: The Man and His Work.* Danish Film Institute. http://english.carlthdreyer.dk/AboutDreyer/Visual-style/Camera-and-Space.aspx. Accessed 3rd January, 2011

Mosley, Philip (1981). *Ingmar Bergman: The Cinema as Mistress.* London: Marion Boyars.

Nowell-Smith, Geoffrey (1997). *The Oxford History of World Cinema.* Oxford: Oxford University Press.

Salt, Barry (2009). *Film Style and Technology: History and Analysis.* London: Starword.

Singer, Irving (2007). *Ingmar Bergman, Cinematic Philosopher: Reflections on His Creativity.* Cambridge MA: MIT Press.

Wood, Robin (1969). *Ingmar Berman.* London: Studio Vista.

Place and Space

Bergman's Fårö: Inhabitation Remote from Modern Society?

Elisa Jochum

> Few filmmakers have been, along with their work, so closely associated with a certain geographic location. The barren landscape with its wind-torn trees, meadows and sand and shingle beaches, and its harsh, white light are synonymous with a world class filmography. (Bergman Center)

The relationship described above is that between Swedish director Ingmar Bergman and the island of Fårö. Since his initial visit in 1960, searching for a setting for *Såsom i en spegel* (Through a Glass Darkly, 1960) (Bergman 1989: 207-8), Fårö has served as the location for five fictional films and two documentaries. Besides *Såsom i en spegel*, the fictional accounts encompass *Persona* (1966), *Skammen* (Shame, 1968), *En Passion* (The Passion of Anna, 1969) and *Scener ur ett äktenskap* (Scenes From a Marriage[1], 1973). *Fårö-Dokument* (1969) and its sequel *Fårö-Dokument 79* (1979) are the documentaries.[2] Also on Fårö, Liv Ullmann filmed part of the feature film *Trolösa* (Faithless, 2003) whose script Bergman wrote (Pizzello 2001: 28). As to his private life, Bergman constructed a house on the island in 1966 and 1967 and it remained his home till he died in 2007 (Bergman 1989: 208; Bergman Center). This extraordinary connection has received much attention in the scholarly discourse about the director. Yet, there is no analysis that compactly and exclusively inspects the island, the Fårö films and Bergman's biographical link. I intend to throw some light on this field – this, however, from a specific point of view and the concession given that *Fårö-Dokument 79* is currently unavailable. I shall approach the topic from the perspective that Bergman, the real people captured in his documentary, the fictional characters and even the actors playing them have something in common: the perspective of inhabitation and the relationship between human and space. Therefore, the argument of this essay is that Bergman's Fårö represents a territory that actual persons and imaginary film characters strive to interact with and live in. A central aspect of these relationships is the ambivalent role of modernity and (Swedish) society. In order to demonstrate this phenomenon, to begin with, I shall introduce facts about the island and define the terms 'territory' and 'modernity'. On this basis, I shall illustrate, first, that the factual Fårö inhabitants relish a harmonious attachment with the natural, unmodernised Fårö environment while, at the same time, certain modernisations by the Swedish welfare state have been necessary. Second, the actors in the fictional accounts interacted with the real island while performing their part on location or even constantly inhabited Fårö during the shooting periods. As a consequence, they themselves experienced the often barely modern conditions surrounding their characters. Since these circumstances had stressful effects while also increasing authenticity of experience, the issue of (absent) modernity again causes ambivalence. Third, many of the fictional characters hope to find refuge on the remote territories – partly from social and modern constraints – but fail to do so. As six fiction films are involved, this is not an universal statement equally valid for each of them. However, a tendency is traceable. While the films, in their problematization of modern society, tend to present a negative outlook, once more a contradiction appears when they are opposed, as hinted at by Birgitta Steene (2005: 40), to Bergman's own impressions of the island. Contrary to the characters in the films, Fårö provided the director with a satisfying and life-long home where he could withdraw from some aspects of modernity and society, whilst successfully incorporating others.

Erik Hedling's essay on post-utopian landscapes (2008) must be mentioned as a crucial inspiration for this essay. Hedling introduces the idea that Bergman, commencing with his 1960s fiction films, adopts a critical viewpoint towards Sweden's modern welfare society. The director does so, *inter alia*, by portraying landscapes that contradict the (in Hedling's opinion) 'chauvinist' Swedish ideal of their modern nation's idyllic natural environment (2008: 180-5). Hedling provides the expression of the 'profoundly anti-modern experience of the Fårö landscape' (2008: 186). The prefix 'anti' can either mean 'the opposite of' modernity, i.e. unmodern, or 'against' it (Wehmeier 2005: 56). Hedling implies both. His conclusions substantiate aspects of this essay. I will, however, put more emphasis on the ambivalent nature – instead of his purely negative outlook – of the relationships between people, space and modern society. I acknowledge in consensus with Hedling that Bergman has hitherto mostly been examined as a phenomenon detached from a wider social framework (Hedling 2008: 180-91). All the more reason to, as Hedling puts it, explore 'the dark corners of the history of Bergman country' (2008: 191).

Facts and Terminology

The small Swedish island of Fårö – with a length of 18 miles and a width that does not exceed 9 miles – is situated in the Baltic Sea and can be reached by ferry from the neighbouring and larger island of Gotland, meaning there is no non-stop link from the Swedish mainland. The island has the status of a nature reserve (Cowie 1992: 250; Steene 2005: 418; Ingmar Bergman Foundation). The official Bergman Center established on Fårö is one of many voices to declare the island to be 'one of Sweden's most distinctive landscapes.' Most notable is the occurrence of enormous *raukar*, which are limestone formations. Further, the island is often connoted with barrenness, crooked vegetation – trees and shrubs – shingle-covered shores, foggy weather and low, 'inhospitable' (Cowie 1992: 248) winter temperatures.[3] Susanne Kippenberger (2011) concludes: 'Schroff und kalt und mitten im Nichts' (Craggy and cold and in the middle of nowhere). In the fiction films, the territory is never explicitly named Fårö, but the remote or even insular nature of the setting is, for the most part, orally stressed and the distinctive appearance of Fårö is always audio-visually perceivable (see, e.g., the description by Cowie 1992: 330).

Having denoted Fårö as a 'territory', this term needs definition. According to Martin Lefebvre, 'territory is space seen from the "inside", a subjective and lived space' (2006: 53). As a premise, this life within an environment comprises ownership of land. It further includes the inhabitation, the sense of 'identity', i.e. of 'belonging' to a location[4] as well as human beings' labour on a ground, such as agriculture (Lefebvre 2006: 52-3). Lefebvre sees these characteristics concentrated in geographer Claude Raffestin's understanding as 'the "sum" [in the sense of totality] of the relations maintained by a subject [or a collectivity] with *their* environment' (Raffestin 1980: 145, n. 27, cited and translated in Lefebvre 2006: 53, Lefebvre's emphasis).⁵

We can reconcile the term 'landscape' in the Scandinavian languages with Lefebvre's concept: the term 'landscape' traditionally describes a territorial province, a 'landskap' disposing of its own administration. Nowadays, a large part of the population still refers to these historical territories instead of the contemporary broader regional divisions when asked for their spatial attachment. Even when used in a second sense, that of 'scenery', 'landscape' is thought of as the observable product of the interrelations between man and his surroundings (Olwig and Jones 2008: xiv-ix; Germundsson 2008: 161-2; Sporrong 2008: 146). In this sense, I go beyond Lefebvre's strictly binary distinction between ownership/territory and non-ownership/non-territorial space. Even if people do not materially own the land, they can attempt to inhabit or interact with it. Complementarily, I adopt Harri Kilpi's definition of nature (2007) which 'excludes everything man-made that is inorganic (e.g. buildings, cars, roads)'.

The second key term is 'modernity'. Don Hubert and Kenneth Thompson define it as 'a cluster of trends and institutions emerging from the Middle Ages' with the post-World War II era as its apex (1996: 231). According to John Tomlinson (2003), the task of these institutions is to formally and comprehensively organise processes that were earlier dealt with locally. Combining Tomlinson's examples with traits of modern societies given by Stuart Hall (1996), modern institutions encompass capitalism and the development of industrialised economies. Further, they comprise 'policing of social territory' in form of urbanisation and the secularly governed nation-state. Modernity implies the decay of the historical structures of society. Materialism and rational thinking replace religion's dominance. Tomlinson argues further that the relevance of local places has declined as mass media and communication devices such as telephones help to bridge spatial distances (Hall 1996: 3-8; Tomlinson 2003: 272-3).

Most of the stated features of modernity apply to Twentieth-Century Sweden. A fast-paced industrialisation process was accompanied by increasing urban agglomerations while rural regions faced huge losses of inhabitants. This trend intensified after 1945. Throughout the 1950s and 1960s, the nation-state was governed by Social Democrats and elaborated one of the globe's leading welfare states. Additionally, urbanisation in Sweden has made rural areas popular for tourism as city residents are attracted by the outdoor opportunities in natural surroundings (Jones and Hansen 2008: 558-9; Sporrong 2008: 152-4; Tortella 2005: 21-7/42).

Real Inhabitants of Real Fårö

In the following section, Bergman's *Fårö-Dokument* constitutes the film-textual basis. The documentary about life on the island was shot on location in spring 1969 (Steene 2005: 418).[6] I will demonstrate that, on the one hand, Fårö is not a modern area and the inhabitants live in harmony with their unmodern environment. On the other hand, the island is modern, but representing the other side of the coin of what is usually associated with modernity. In this context, Bergman and the islanders see themselves in need of more beneficial aspects of modernisation (see similarly Cowie 1992: 267).

The categorisation as unmodern applies to conditions that have not changed, which means conditions that have not been modernised. To begin with, it is depicted in the film that nature-related – as opposed to industrial – labour still plays an important role, for example small-scale farming and fishing. Second, these professions are at least in part not conducted with modern – meaning up-to-date – equipment. For instance, Bergman interviews farmer Ingrid against the backdrop of her farmstead which is characterised by old wooden barns as well as manually and animal-operated tools. Remoteness of human settlements is seen as emblematic in the history of the Nordic countries due to natural barriers such as fjords (Jones and Hansen 2008: 545). Hence, the visible spatial distance between houses on the island can be interpreted as a traditional feature. It parallels the 'insularity' of Fårö with respect to Gotland and the mainland, demonstrated on the maps at the beginning of the film.

Despite, or thanks to, these unmodern aspects, the all-year-round inhabitants – the actual owners of territorial stretches – live in harmony with 'their' island and manifest regional identity. According to Peter Cowie, '[t]he island yields a certain type of human being; and the inhabitants of Fårö dwell in a remarkable, inexplicable symbiosis with their environment. It is hard to imagine the place without the people' (1992: 329). The man-nature symbiosis is even conveyed when, amidst nature, a sheep is slaughtered by the farmer's bare hands, which allows him to have an immediate relation to his nutrition, a connection usually not sustained by city-dwellers anymore. Additionally, instead of feeling isolated in the anti-urban area, most of the residents interviewed enjoy loneliness, life within a small community and a sense of freedom, mirrored by the wide open spaces Bergman repeatedly captures in his frames. One islander points out: 'But if I weren't at sea or near it, then I just don't know [...]. In a city or large community, you're done. [...]. But freedom, that's what man is made for.' This declaration demonstrates a rejection of emblematic modernity, i.e. city life. Similarly, interviewees qualify tourism as a menace to the intact environment.

However, not all features of the island are entirely 'unmodern'. Rather, they do represent facets of modern times that are not likely to be connected to modernity. Peter S. Soppelsa clarifies:

> While Europe underwent fundamental social, spatial and technological changes (urbanization, industrialization and globalization), so the familiar story goes, European ways of life became more civilized, rationalized, standard, advanced, efficient, democratic, humane, or even universal. (Soppelsa 2009: 1)

Hedling also stresses this kind of ambivalent praise of modern processes in Sweden (2008: 182). Thus, when speaking of urbanisation as characteristic of modern times, low population density or depopulation is often assumed to be the contrary, whereas it constitutes just the other side of the same coin. Fårö, for instance, has always been sparsely inhabited, as Bergman's voice-over statements suggest. It is however, he continues, menaced by further depopulation. Among Fårö's youth, the intention to move away prevails.

Moreover, Bergman presents the island as threatened by certain actions of the modern welfare state as well as by its inaction in other domains. The actions mainly entail centralisation processes. An interviewed official explains that the formerly individual municipality of Fårö has merged with others. Institutions like schools and post offices face impending closure. Cowie thus reads Bergman's approach as an urgent 'political' appeal to make the islanders 'escape the leaden hand of central government' (1992: 266). The term 'political' puts emphasis on the fact that Fårö is treated as a territory in the original Scandinavian sense. On the other hand, the inactivity of the modern state, for instance the disregard for infrastructural maintenance, is criticised (Bergman Center). The interviewees unanimously advocate that a bridge – in other words, a technical modernisation – should be built which would simplify their connection to the 'outside world'. Bergman's voice-over advocates that, in 'this era of industrialised prosperity', the modern phenomenon of 'democracy' be applied to Fårö as much as it is to urban areas.

In conclusion, the island Bergman depicts is in Steene's words an 'outpost in a modern welfare state' (2005: 40) - geographically as well as with respect to (beneficial) aspects of modernity. Cowie describes the situation as a 'tension between past and future' (1992: 267). His words and his additional explanations can be paraphrased as ambivalence between cherished 'anti-modernity' and demand for modernisation.

'Performative Inhabitation'

When shooting his fictional Fårö films, Bergman's actors

interacted with the island as a territory. These inhabitations again entail an ambivalent relationship to modernity. While the fictional stories will be touched upon in the following section, it shall be stressed here, that they set the characters – partly or entirely – in remote, anti-urban territory.

The basis is provided by the concept of 'performative inhabitation' or 'performative attachment', discussed by Mark B. Sandberg in the context of Carl Theodor Dreyer's creative approach to sets (2006: 24). Sandberg suggests that Dreyer sought to provide credible sets in which the actors were potentially able to feel 'at home'. Dreyer aimed at integrating them personally and physically into the stories' spaces, a process described by Sandberg as *'mise-en-milieu'* (2006: 23-7). Dreyer used this method in constructed and pre-existing spaces, i.e. 'found locations'. Sandberg especially juxtaposes found locations that dispose of discernible traces of former inhabitation with three-walled spaces in the studio that appear artificial (2006: 26-9). Without arguing that Bergman was explicitly engaging in performance-space explorations comparable to Dreyer's, elements of Sandberg's concept are applicable to Bergman's and Ullmann's filmmaking process on Fårö.

Sandberg's notion is reconcilable with the term 'territory'. The actors temporarily 'lived' or, at least, 'performed' living on location, to experience the environment from the 'inside'. Without reference to Sandberg or Lefebvre, Wheeler Winston Dixon tackles the concept of performative and personal inhabitation when discussing *Persona*: 'In short, only by embracing the domestic sphere of his own habitation with Liv Ullmann was Bergman able to capture the spiritual essence of the conflict between the two women in *Persona*' (2000: 53).⁷ Yet, he is mistaken in his claim *Persona* came into existence in Bergman's and Ullmann's shared home. The domicile was erected on a nearby spot only after the production. Likewise, the relationship between director and actor apparently started during, not before, shooting (Bergman 1989: 208; *Bergman Island* 2004). Thus, Dixon takes the idea too far, too early. Still, his approach proves useful and can be expanded to the totality of the Fårö films: *Såsom i en spegel*, *Persona* and *Skammen* were partly made on Fårö. Each time, a complete house was constructed. The shipwreck, rocky coast and garden in *Såsom i en spegel* constituted 'found locations' exactly matching Bergman's ideas (Bergman 1989: 207-8; *Bergman Island* 2004; Cowie 1992: 250; Siemens 2011: 2; Steene 2005: 249-83). The acted inhabitation of real locations might have allowed the actors to literally put themselves in the environmental position of their characters. This notion is supported by Dixon. He recognises in the following quotation from Bergman that the attachment to Fårö had inspiring potential for the production of *Persona*: 'The filming [in Stockholm] dragged on, and the results were miserable. But when we went out to Fårö things went fine' (Björkman, Manns and Sima 1973: 202-3, cited in Dixon 2000: 53). Besides, *En Passion* was completely shot on Fårö and Max von Sydow and Ullmann played their lead roles within the stage house that had been built for *Skammen* – the film they also had acted the major parts in (Cowie 1992: 250; Steene 2005: 290). This 're-inhabitation' potentially reinforced intimacy. Furthermore, the exterior shots in *Trolösa* stem from the actual island. For the passages inside the protagonist's house, Bergman's own study was rebuilt in a television studio (Pizzello 2001: 26). It can be assumed that director Ullmann felt a bond with the replica of her former home. Also, as the crew was often invited to Bergman's domicile (Cowie 1992: 260-1), lead actor Erland Josephson, already starring in previous Fårö films, might have been personally connected to Bergman's house. *Scener ur ett äktenskap*, partly filmed on Fårö, constitutes a borderline case as a barn was turned into a film studio. It served as the setting for many interior scenes (Ingmar Bergman Foundation; Siemens 2011: 2; Steene 2005: 304). As an overall result, the productions on Fårö bear the potential of 'performative inhabitation' of various degrees of intensity.

In addition to general opportunities for 'performative attachment', the Fårö settings can be explicitly seen in the light of modernity. Instead of performing in a studio, that is to say in industrialised working conditions[8], the actors were able to live out the 'anti-modern experience of the Fårö landscape' (Hedling 2008: 186). Indoor scenes placed them in the same natural silence and window views. Outdoor scenes put them in the same conditions of climate, vegetation and spatial isolation as the characters they embodied. This might have enhanced their familiarity with the characters' space. However, Britt Hamdi's account of the shooting of *Skammen* also demonstrates the extent to which missing trappings of modernity hampered shooting, as harsh weather and temperature caused considerable strain (2007: 53-4).

It must also be taken into account that the inhabitation experience did not stop when the camera was switched off, since the cast and crew often spent the entire shooting period on Fårö. Thus the 'performative inhabitation' was extended to a real, similarly unmodern, inhabitation. Hamdi describes the living conditions during shooting *Skammen*: 'For the crew of forty, this means three months of hard work and almost uninterrupted isolation on Fårö' (2007: 53). For the crew's stay while producing *En Passion*, Cowie illustrates the restricted possibilities on the remote territory: 'in their free time they could play ping-pong, bathe in the icy sea, drink wine and eat cheese' (1992: 261). In particular, von Sydow may have achieved a profound understanding of how isolated and remote they – and their characters – were. While *En Passion* was being shot, he constantly had to make the wearisome ferry journey back and forth in order to meet his simultaneous obligations at the theatre in Stockholm.

In conclusion, the performative and real inhabitation of Fårö by actors involves a conflicting relationship to modern facilities. Shooting in this unmodern location posed climatic, logistical and organisational obstacles. At the same time, exactly because of this lack of modernity, the actors potentially gained greater access to their characters' 'island experience'.

Inhabitation by Fictional Characters

According to Steene, 'Fårö quickly became both a real and a symbolic place to Ingmar Bergman' (2005: 40). 'Symbolic' is the attribute she assigns to his fictional films summarised as 'island films' (2005: 40).[9] On the textual bases of the fictional Fårö films, I shall illustrate the relationships between the island and the characters it accommodates – including the role of modernity and society. In each paragraph, I will examine the more demonstrative examples of *Persona*, *Skammen* and *En Passion*, complemented by glances at *Såsom i en spegel*, *Scener ur ett äktenskap* and *Trolösa* yielding restricted evidence.

Applying the term 'territory', the characters attempt to make themselves at home or at ease in the settings provided by Fårö. In *Persona*, the actress Elisabeth Vogler, having renounced speaking, is sent with Nurse Alma to the doctor's house by the sea as temporary visitors for a therapeutic inhabitation: 'La nature comme [...] thérapie' (Nature as therapy) (Daudelin 2009: 20). In *Skammen*, the married couple Eva and Jan Rosenberg have settled in a farm on an island engaging in agriculture (Steene 2005: 281). Andreas Winkelmann in *En Passion* physically works at his new home on a Baltic island, to keep it inhabitable. In *Såsom i en spegel*, Karin, her brother and her husband live in a house by the sea where her much-travelled father returns for holidays. In *Scener ur ett äktenskap*, glimpses of Fårö are only granted in a handful of shots constituting the environment of a holiday home that is visited twice by the owners, the couple Marianne and Johan. In *Trolösa*, an aged writer is the solitary inhabitant of a house in a deserted coastal environment, leaving only for occasional walks in the landscape.

At the outset, the fictional territory mostly serves the purpose of a refuge – partly from modern and social threats. In *Persona*, Elisabeth is at the seaside to recover. One possible diagnosis why she needs recovery is the impact of modernity: Hedling refers to Leif Zern who contrasts the prevailing idea of the modern – materialistic, secular, confident, and healthy – Swedish citizen with the emotionally unstable Bergman characters who cannot come to terms with these aspects of modernity (Zern 1993: 25, cited in Hedling 2008: 183). The inner turmoil of Elisabeth – and Alma who is frequently interpreted as schizophrenic (e.g. Mosley 2010: 126) – is traced back by Hedling to 'a rationalist society gone berserk, or on the verge of a breakdown' (2008: 187). At the beginning of *Persona*, this modern world is represented by technology and sterile hospitals. The television horrifies Elisabeth with a display of modern warfare in Vietnam before their departure for the summer house.

The Rosenbergs in *Skammen* have escaped from war on the mainland (Steene 2005: 281). Although, as Leonard Quart points out, this war is not linked to concrete history (2004: 34), in my opinion, the bombs, parachutists etc. are an industrial form of warfare that according to Anthony McGrew has introduced unseen devastation (1996: 252). Cowie, initially stating Bergman refrains from addressing questions of society, concludes: 'Perhaps, despite his detractors, he was more shaken than many of his fellow countrymen by the impact of the Vietnam conflict' (1992: 255).

As far as *En Passion* is concerned, the protagonist Andreas has retreated from the world, a prison sentence and a broken marriage (Cowie 1992: 261; Quart 2004: 34). This might more generally be an escape from a failed attempt to live within a social context (whose framework, however, is modern Sweden). More clearly, for a very short moment, when modern television which links Andreas to the world outside displays cruel images of the Vietnam War, the living room on the silent island seems like a safe place beyond modernity.

Looking at schizophrenic Karin in *Såsom i en spegel*, there is no hint that Fårö is a chosen refuge from modernity. Yet, with reference to Zern's and Hedling's description of the modern Swede, she is not integrated in modern life and thinking, struggling with religious questions.

In *Scener ur ett äktenskap*, the married city-dwellers initially consider their lives devoid of complications, by which they in a very modern way mean the non-existence of 'material concerns' as well as professional contentment and good health. Marianne only complains about their entirely predefined everyday life. Their first sojourn to their holiday home can therefore (only) be qualified as a retreat from modern life to the same extent as many Swedish city inhabitants flock to the naturally preserved countryside for a counterbalance to urban life.[10] When they visit their summer place for the second time, the then divorced couple hides, not from modernity but generally from anyone who could betray their ongoing affair.[11]

Moreover, the withdrawn writer of *Trolösa* is plagued by distressing fantasies set in urban Sweden. One can only speculate whether he has specifically chosen the isolated natural territory as a refuge. But his thoughts are, according to Hedling, connected to a modernity exemplified by the unsympathetic social worker symbolising 'the absence of moral values' (2008: 189).[12]

Yet, the different efforts to find an inhabitable refuge described above predominantly fail. As for *Persona*, Dixon writes of 'domesticity gone awry' (2000: 53). In accordance with James Norton's claim that '[i]slands [...] encourage introspection' (2007: 24), Dixon sees emotional turmoil kept under the surface while Elisabeth and Alma are situated 'in the world' (2000: 56). He claims: 'Only in the zone of domestic intimacy will these long-suppressed emotions erupt with unexpected ferocity precisely because of the safety offered by the idyllic location' (Dixon 2000: 56). The emptiness of Fårö is opposed to the women's habitual 'social existence', reinforced by the absence of radio, television etc. (Dixon 2000: 56) – in other words, of modern technology. As a result, the setting becomes a catalyst of crisis.

When the isolated island of *Skammen* is invaded, modern destruction catches up with the Rosenbergs. Cowie mentions that the uncontrollable ringing of the phone – again a modern device – anticipates these events (1992: 251-2). Their house is physically destroyed. The island is not offering security but is 'as unfriendly and uncaring as a lunar landscape' (Cowie 1992: 255). Moreover, Jan, 'the artist as fugitive' (Cowie 1992: 242) does not use his violin. With reference to Cowie, this might indicate he does not feel sheltered enough to develop his creativity (1992: 242-52).

Similarly, in *En Passion*, Andreas' peaceful domesticity does not last either. Quart points out that, instead of a war, more subliminal dangers now threaten the territory (2004: 34), and, I would add, its hospitality. The menace from the outer (modern) world does not surmount the television screen, but violent attacks are due to an animal torturer running amok on the island (Cowie 1992: 261-3). This implies a distorted man-nature relationship and troubles the local community. The territorially rooted Johan, conducting nature-related labour throughout the film and stating to have no other place to go, is accused and tormented into suicide.

As Robert Daudelin puts it, the landscape presented in *Såsom i en spegel* poses a threat (2009: 20). In fact, Karin incorporates her surroundings – shipwreck and wallpaper – into her madness expressed by incestuous approaches towards her brother and hallucinations about God. Ironically, mentally trapped in her illness (Quart 2004: 30) and spatially trapped on the remote territory bordered by the sea, it is a modern means of transport, a helicopter, that needs to help her escape this prison.

Concerning *Scener ur ett äktenskap*, Johan announces his elopement with another woman in the summer house. The processes triggered by his confession are modern phenomena such as Marianne's female self-discovery[13] and their eventual divorce. Hence, their summer territory is no retreat from modern social problems; rather, these problems are exposed and debated there. When Marianne and Johan return decades later, too much suffering is connected to the summer place rendering it uninhabitable for them. Yet, they do find interpersonal and spatial harmony in a friend's unmodern cottage with a paraffin lamp and open fire. Jesse Kalin writes: 'They go away for a weekend to a friend's cabin, where for the first time they honestly talk' (2003: 154).

Such a slightly positive note also accompanies the ending of *Trolösa*. When succumbing to his thoughts, the writer is seen several times amidst the grey and gloomy Fårö landscape that seems incapable of pacifying inner turmoil. However, the writer comes to terms with his thoughts as he closes this chapter with an affectionate farewell from his imaginary character Marianne. In fact, *Trolösa* leads over to Bergman's own inhabitation. The film incorporates many (auto)biographical threads; the anonymous writer even bears the name 'Bergman' in the film script (Pizzello 2001: 24).

Before looking into Bergman's biography, it should be

mentioned that, instead of representing a refuge *from* modern society, Hedling interprets Fårö as 'the perfect spatial metaphor for the condition of man *in* the modern Swedish welfare state' (2008: 186, my emphasis). He sees desolate territory as an emblem of a malfunctioning Swedish society. In other words, unmodern Fårö with its distorted plant life, drabness and physical remoteness is, in the end, not used to show an inhabitable alternative apart from modernity. It becomes the inhospitable materialisation of many characters' inner or social disorder, emptiness or isolation which is – as has been shown above – partly connected to modernity (Bergman Foundation; Hedling 2008: 183-7).

In conclusion, the settings based on 'unmodern' Fårö largely fall short of offering a rescue from the struggles and complexities that are often, though not always, linked to modern society. The notion of modernity here is negative. An ambivalence is not inherent in the films themselves but can be established when comparing the characters to Bergman's life, as Steene notices: 'Fårö, while becoming Bergman's personal retreat and his "*smultronställe*" in life, also inspires, through its isolation, both the stark form and stern vision of Bergman's film work in the Sixties' (2005: 40). *Scener ur ett äktenskap* and *Trolösa*, the most recent Fårö films, however, assume a more positive outlook. This brings us to the next section of my essay.

Bergman's Inhabitation of Fårö

The ambivalence between Bergman's own and his characters' experiences can be illustrated by several aspects of Bergman's Fårö life. First, the term 'territory' is quite literally applicable here. Bergman owned the house he had had erected in the Sixties. He inhabited it as intensely as his profession permitted him to – except for his six-year stay abroad discussed below. Bergman further extended his buildings and plot of land. He sold his other residences in 2003 and was eventually buried in the soil of Fårö (Ingmar Bergman Foundation; Siemens 2011: 2-3; Steene 2005: 418). He betrayed a profound attachment to the island when he stated 'I had found my landscape, my real home' (Bergman 1989: 208). Furthermore, while local communities are rare and unhealthy in the feature films, Bergman's symbiosis included his harmonious relationship with the remaining islanders. They saw Ullmann during her years on Fårö as 'astumor', i.e. 'neighbour's wife' in their dialect (Hamdi 2007: 56). Bergman spoke of them as his 'seven hundred neighbours' (Cowie 1992: 266). He developed a regional identity and felt 'genuinely anchored' (Hamdi 2007: 56) in this territory.

Furthermore, Fårö also proved to be a genuine 'refuge' from the implications of modern life. Daudelin uses the term to express that Bergman, on Fårö, successfully withdrew from the busy capital and hearsay about him (2009: 20). In this sense, Fårö was, first, an escape from a city emblematic of urbanisation as Bergman never felt comfortable in urban areas. Second, it was an escape from the pressure put on him when accused of tax evasion – the tax system being one pillar of the modern welfare state (Cowie 1992: 248; Steene 2005: 45; Tortella 2005: 27). At the time, Berman became aware 'that anyone in this country could be assailed and degraded by a special kind of bureaucracy that grows like a galloping cancer' (1989: 101). Within Sweden, he felt bereaved of his sense of 'security' (Bergman 1989: 100). Although he left the country in 1976, Fårö did not cease to offer him shelter; when he got 'homesick', as he put it, it was Fårö he travelled to. He fully returned in 1982 (Cowie 1992: 329; Bergman and Donner 1998: 184; Steene 2005: 418). Further, the phenomenon of tourists has been shown to be connected to modern developments. On the distant and hardly accessible Fårö, Bergman managed, even though not completely, to avoid their visits (Cowie 1992: 247; Hamdi 2007: 56).

Moreover, whereas the landscape cannot offer relief or, instead, even stimulates the inner suffering the characters experience, Bergman emphatically stressed how his contact – more precisely, his walks in the open, barren Fårö environment – helped him ease his inner turmoil: 'The demons don't like fresh air. What they like best is if you stay in bed with cold feet' (Bergman Island 2004). (Maybe a similar feeling is achieved by the writer in *Trolösa*.) Thereby, as far as Bergman himself is concerned, the isolation bound to this refuge does not become a negative metaphor for an inner state. Instead, in conversation with Hamdi, he expressed his appreciation of it (Hamdi 2007: 60).

Although he appreciated the lack of modernity, Bergman positively integrated emblems of modernity to the island world. Indeed, as Hedling illustrates, the non-existence of completely modern equipment was deeply cherished by Bergman. Hedling points to a statement from the director's autobiography where the latter romanticised the dependence on 'fires, paraffin stoves and battery radio' (Bergman 1989: 95; Hedling 2008: 186-7). But Bergman was able to reconcile this inclination to non-modernised nature with the benefits of devices such as television. Whereas, in *Persona* and *En Passion*, it is negatively connoted as bringing the menacing world closer, Bergman was, in his own words, 'incredibly excited at the thought that here, on this little island, in the middle of this great ocean, we had the whole world within our reach' (Hamdi 2007: 58). The phone, hostile in *Skammen*, was, according to Marie Nyreröd (2009), the aged Bergman's 'contact with the world'.

Lastly, one might argue Bergman felt such homeliness on Fårö that his creativity could flourish, in contrast to Jan in *Skammen*. The fact that Bergman was inspired to direct seven films on the island, and to productively keep amending his oeuvre during his residency, allows to call it 'his artistic base' (Bergman Center). This creative or productive inhabitation has not come to a halt with Bergman's death. The Bergman estate on Fårö invites artists to stay and create on the island, i.e. to inhabit and be imbued by 'the same environment that inspired Ingmar Bergman in his own artistic pursuits through forty years' (The Bergman Estate on Fårö). Kippenberger (2007) concludes: 'Fårö ist insofern eine mehr als ungewöhnliche Bergman-Geschichte: Sie hat ein Happy End' (Fårö is thus a more than unusual Bergman story: it has a happy ending).

Fårö functioned as a home and retreat from modern society while Bergman simultaneously managed to integrate advantageous modern elements. His success in this regard contrasts with most of his Fårö characters. As the title of Nyreröd's documentary puts it, Fårö is 'Bergman Island'.

Conclusion

To sum up, in this essay, I intended to examine Bergman's

Fårö from the point of view of inhabitation and man-nature interactions. During Bergman's life and work, the Fårö islanders, Bergman's actors, the characters they played and Bergman himself attempted to live on the Fårö territory. With its unmodern features, as well as the particular relationships between people and (natural) space, the island is imbued with a certain ambivalence towards modernity. The real inhabitants in *Fårö-Dokument* live in harmony with their traditional surroundings, but request certain modernisations by the state. Bergman's actors, performatively or really inhabiting the island for some time, were hampered by a lack of modern transport and facilities. However, experiencing these same conditions their characters have to cope with, the performances might have felt more authentic. Though it is not equally applicable to all fiction films made on the island, one can interpret some of the characters as fleeing to the island for refuge from modernity and society. However, with the exception of the later films, *Scener ur ett äktenskap* and *Trolösa*, the characters' efforts fail. Thus, their Fårö experience conflicts with that of Bergman as a person: to him, the island was home and refuge. It protected him from unpleasant facets of modernity, but he successfully integrated others. I leave the final words to the director himself who summarises: 'This is your landscape, Bergman' (1989: 208).

Author's Comment

I read Communication Research/Media Studies and Film Studies at the Johannes Gutenberg-Universität Mainz, Germany (2008-2011) and am currently completing the MA

Film Studies at UCL (2011-2012), where I took Nordic Cinema in my first semester. Prior to studying, I undertook placements in the media and film industries of Sydney and Paris, going on to work as an online film critic during my undergraduate degree. The Nordic Cinema course was a chance to enjoy the primary promise of cinema – the promise to take you places. The films and discussions allowed me to explore intriguing cultures and their cinematic heritage and approaches. When you think about Nordic cinema, you cannot bypass Ingmar Bergman. Countless works examine his life and large body of films. Yet, fascination has no expiry date, and the vivacity of a conversation lives in the ongoing expression of comments, new ideas and changes of perspective. In this essay, I hope I have shared my fascination with space in cinema and with Bergman's films, and to spark more thoughts, contributing to the liveliness of these discourses. If I were to write the essay again, I would like to shed some more light on the actual aesthetics of the films, on how the territory is captured and conveyed to us.

1. The feature film is a compact version of Bergman's homonymous 1972 TV series comprising six episodes of 50 minutes each (Steene 2005: 302/424).
2. Information stems from the Bergman Center. The original titles are taken from Steene (2005).
3. The information about the island can be found in: Bergman Center; Cowie 1992: 248; Ingmar Bergman Foundation; Steene 2005: 46.
4. For further elaborations on 'place identity', see Olwig and Jones (2008: xi).

5. Lefebvre has italicised 'their' to emphasise that ownership is a premise for a location to be seen as a territory. He does not provide the original quotation in French (2006: 53-9, n. 52).
6. It needs to be kept in mind that, in contrast to a representative survey, the 'real' inhabitants and conditions presented here are mediated through Bergman's lens and look at them.
7. Dixon later partly contradicts himself when praising the quality of Fårö as an 'uninhabited space', but then clarifies he thereby means a location free from 'ordinary social commerce' in the studio environment (2000: 56). It seems he is thus referring to the high rate of social interactions and conventions bound to the studio rather than to the question of home.
8. Dixon equals 'in the studio' to 'in the world' (2000: 56). Besides, here, it becomes evident that *Scener ur ett äktenskap* is a problematic case in between studio and real location.
9. In this category, Steene also includes *Vargtimmen* (The Hour of the Wolf, 1967) and *Beröringen* (The Touch, 1970). The first is set on an island, the latter is partly filmed on Gotland, but none is made on Fårö. On the other hand, she excludes *Scener ur ett äktenskap* and *Trolösa* from the 'island films' (2005: 40/276/293).
10. Note, that Marianne, in an outburst of fury, declares holidays to be even more pre-structured.
11. Kalin, speaking about the television version of *Scener ur ett äktenskap*, notes the interview on the outset is a report about modern couples, an information stressing the contextualisation of the film as modern, but not given in the feature film itself (Kalin 2003: 152).
12. A further ambiguity is very well expressed in Hedling's description of *Persona* as 'anti-modern, yet modernist' (2008: 187). Artistically, this film and Bergman's other films in the Sixties manifest an utterly modern approach. *Inter alia*, he

reduced his aesthetics to the crucial. Fårö being a void landscape, the ambiguity stated in the first sentence seems less harsh (Dixon 2000: 44-52; Steene 1970: 25; Steene 2005: 142/291).

13. Kalin states that Marianne's 'growing sense of having to be someone else (and a new awareness of her own sexuality)' mirror 'concerns of the times', i.e. modernity and feminism (2003: 152-3).

References

Bergman Island: A Documentary by Marie Nyreröd (2004 [on DVD])

En Passion (The Passion of Anna, Ingmar Bergman, 1969)

Fårö-Dokument (Ingmar Bergman, 1969)

Persona (Ingmar Bergman, 1966)

Såsom i en spegel (Through a Glass Darkly, Ingmar Bergman, 1960)

Scener ur ett äktenskap (Scenes From a Marriage, Ingmar Bergman, 1973).

Skammen (Shame, Ingmar Bergman, 1968)

Trolösa (Faithless, Liv Ullmann, 2003)

Bergman Center http://bergmancenter.se/en/. Accessed 9 January 2012.

The Bergman Estate on Fårö http://www.bergmangardarna.se/en/. Accessed 9 January 2012.

Bergman, Ingmar (1989). *The Magic Lantern: An Autobiography.* Translated from the Swedish by Joan Tate. New York: Penguin.

Bergman, Ingmar and Jörn Donner (1998): 'Demons and Childhood Secrets: An Interview'. Translated from the Swedish by Joan Tate. *Grand Street* [n.vol.]:66, Secrets, 180-92.

Björkman, Stig, Torsten Manns, and Jonas Sima (1973). *Bergman on Bergman*. Translated from the Swedish by Paul Britten Austin. New York: Simon & Schuster.

Cowie, Peter (1992). *Ingmar Bergman: A Critical Biography*. London: André Deutsch.

Daudelin, Robert (2009). 'Entre la mer et le coin aux fraises: la nature chez Ingmar Bergman'. *24 Images* [n.vol.]:144, 20-2.

Dixon, Wheeler Winston (2000). '*Persona* and the 1960s Art Cinema.' In Michaels, Lloyd (ed.): *Ingmar Bergman's Persona*. Cambridge: Cambridge University Press.

Germundsson, Thomas (2008). 'The South of the North: Images of an (Un)Swedish Landscape.' In Jones, Michael and Kenneth R. Olwig (eds): *Nordic Landscapes: Belonging on the Northern Edge of Europe*. Minneapolis: University of Minnesota Press.

Hamdi, Britt (2007). 'Ingmar Bergman Is Making a Film on Fårö again.' In Shargel, Raphael (ed.): *Ingmar Bergman: Interviews*. Jackson: University Press of Mississippi.

Hall, Stuart (1996). 'Introduction [of Part I: Formations of Modernity].' In Hall, Stuart et al. (eds): *Modernity: An Introduction to Modern Societies*. Malden: The Open University.

Hedling, Erik (2008). 'The Welfare State Depicted: Post-Utopian Landscapes in Ingmar Bergman's Films.' In Koskinen, Maaret (ed.): *Ingmar Bergman Revisited: Performance, Cinema and the Arts*. London: Wallflower Press.

Hubert, Don and Kenneth Thompson (1996). 'Introduction [of Part II: Structures and Processes of Modernity].' In Hall,

Stuart et al. (eds): *Modernity: An Introduction to Modern Societies*. Malden: The Open University.

Ingmar Bergman Foundation. *Ingmar Bergman Face to Face* http://www.ingmarbergman.se/. Accessed 9 January 2012.

Jones, Michael and Jens Christian Hansen (2008). 'The Nordic Countries: A Geographical Overview.' In Jones, Michael and Kenneth R. Olwig (eds): *Nordic Landscapes: Belonging on the Northern Edge of Europe*. Minneapolis: University of Minnesota Press.

Kalin, Jesse (2003). *The Films of Ingmar Bergman*. Cambridge: Cambridge University Press.

Kilpi, Harri (2007). 'Green Frames: Exploring Cinema Ecocritically'. *Wider Screen* [n.vol.]:1 www.widerscreen.fi/ 2007/1/green_frames-exploring_cinema_ecocritically.htm. Accessed 9 January 2012.

Kippenberger, Susanne (2011). 'Ingmar Bergman: Gestrandet auf Fårö.' *Der Tagesspiegel* 17 April http://www.tagesspiegel.de/ kultur/ingmar-bergman-gestrandet-auf-froe/4066826.html. Accessed 9 January 2012.

Lefebvre, Martin (2006). 'Between Setting and Landscape in the Cinema.' In Lefebvre, Martin (ed.): *Landscape and Film*. New York: Routledge.

McGrew, Anthony (1996). 'The State in Advanced Capitalist Societies.' In Hall, Stuart et al. (eds): *Modernity: An Introduction to Modern Societies*. Malden: The Open University.

Mosley, Philip (2010). *Ingmar Bergman: The Cinema as Mistress*. London: Marion Boyars.

Nyreröd, Marie (2009). 'Bergman and I'. Booklet (Criterion Collection) accompanying *Bergman Island: A Documentary by Marie Nyreröd* (2004 [on DVD]).

Norton, James (2007): 'Mortalities: Antonioni and Bergman'. *Vertigo* 3:7, 23-4.

Olwig, Kenneth R. and Michael Jones (2008). 'Introduction: Thinking Landscape and Regional Belonging on the Northern Edge of Europe.' In Jones, Michael and Kenneth R. Olwig (eds): *Nordic Landscapes: Region and Belonging on the Northern Edge of Europe*. Minneapolis: University of Minnesota Press.

Oxford Dictionaries *http://oxforddictionaries.com/ definition/modern?q=modern*. Accessed 9 January 2012.

Pizzello, Stephen (2001): 'Through a Glass Darkly: Ullmann Analyzes Bergman'. *American Cinematographer* 82:1, 24-8.

Quart, Leonard (2004): 'Ingmar Bergman: The Maestro of Angst'. *Cineaste* 29:4, 30-5.

Raffestin, Claude (1980). *Pour une géographie du pouvoir*. Paris: Librairie technique.

Sandberg, Mark (2006). 'Mastering the House: Performative Inhabitation on Carl Th. Dreyer's *The Parson's Widow*.' In C. Claire Thomson (ed.) : *Northern Constellations: New Readings in Nordic Cinema*. Norwich: Norvik Press.

Siemens, Christof (2011). 'Ingmar Bergman: Insel der

Dämonen.' *Zeit Online* 14 February http://www.zeit.de/ 2011/07/Berlinale-Bergman-Faroe/seite-1, 1-3. Accessed 9 January 2012.

Soppelsa, Peter S. (2009). 'The Fragility of Modernity: Infrastructure and Everyday Life in Paris, 1870-1914'. Doctoral thesis. University of Michigan.

Sporrong, Ulf (2008). 'The Swedish Landscape: The Regional Identity of Historical Sweden.' In Jones, Michael and Kenneth R. Olwig (eds): *Nordic Landscapes: Belonging on the Northern Edge of Europe*. Minneapolis: University of Minnesota Press.

Steene, Birgitta (1970). 'Images and Words in Ingmar Bergman's Films'. *Cinema Journal* 10:1, 23-33.

Steene, Birgitta (2005). *Ingmar Bergman: A Reference Guide*. Amsterdam: Amsterdam University Press.

Tomlinson, John (2003). 'Globalization and Cultural Identity.' In Held, David and Anthony McGrew (eds): *The Global Transformations Reader*. Cambridge and Oxford: Polity Press and Blackwell.

Tortella, Gabriel (2005). 'Sweden and Spain – Different Paths towards Modernity?' In Jerneck, Magnus et al. (eds): *Different Paths to Modernity: A Nordic and Spanish Perspective*. Lund: Nordic Academic Press.

Zern, Leif (1993). *Se Bergman*. Stockholm: Norstedts.

Place and Space

Aki Kaurismäki's Postcards

Kitty Clark

The world of Aki Kaurismäki is loaded with a kind of mysterious liminality, continuously wavering on the edge of many contradictions. Helsinki is the core location, but not Helsinki as we know it. Transformed by a carefully constructed mise-en-scène bursting with nostalgia and artifice, it becomes a so-called 'Kaurismäkisinki' (Louvish 2002: 25). Temporally confused, melancholic yet absurdly droll, within this ambiguous space between reality and fantasy Kaurismäki is able to create a vision of his culture that is both seductively evocative and critically engaged.

This recurrent theme of nostalgia, of melancholic longing for a lost era that is incredibly apparent throughout Aki Kaurismäki's *Ariel* (1988) and *Mies vailla menneisyyttä* (The Man without a Past, 2002) seems to be important in understanding why these films have resonated so strongly with global audiences. Why does Kaurismäki imbue his films, set in a supposedly contemporary Finland, with such a loaded 1950s Americana aesthetic? Perhaps the saturated, evocative visuals of these films are not just visually similar to the aesthetic qualities of nostalgic ephemera of vintage photographs, films, and postcards, but the films themselves act as transnational postcards to a global audience. In the same way that a typical souvenir-shop postcard uses exaggerated, condensed and loaded imagery to communicate a message between nations, Kaurismäki's films send out a highly stylised understanding of his own nation to the world, with his message against modernisation and consumer-driven culture.

Despite the countless traumas and depressions his characters face, it could be argued that Kaurismäki's nostalgic depiction of Finland is actually fairly idealised and romantic, clinging on to the remnants of an era in the face of modernisation. It is behind the preservation of an ideal that a futile, perhaps even regressive attitude lingers, and perhaps in this futility lies the melancholy. In several interviews Kaurismäki openly admits his dissatisfaction with the modernisation of Finland, mourning the loss of his favourite bars and cafés across Helsinki. By setting *Ariel* and *Mies vailla menneisyyttä* in and amongst the remnants of his preferred old-fashioned locations he is memorialising these places on film. As Satu Kyösola (2004: 50) suggests, this desire to preserve is a kind of urgent archive, and Kaurismäki is quoted lamenting, 'Not very many good places remain because the modern world is everywhere. I showed each bar I loved. I poked my camera into every nook in Helsinki.' The filmmaker uses nostalgia to preserve his own perfect vision of Finland, and by condensing and filtering the history and culture through this method of nostalgia, the films become perfectly suited to a international rather than domestic audience, who can absorb the richness of loaded visuals, characters and narrative without the understandably critical eye of a native Finn. By closely examining formal elements in *Ariel* and *Mies vailla menneisyyttä* it is possible to recognise Kaurismäki's skill in utilising nostalgia in order to portray an idealised Finland in a global context.

Kaurismäki's use of colour is incredibly stylised, with a small palette of colours that dominate visually in almost every scene. Typically, an eggshell blue, a pale tan brown, and a strong blood red are composed like paint across the screen, with vivid strength of colour. The lighting he implements accentuates the palette, bringing in subtle, yet brilliant whites and expanses of blackness, allowing the colours to burn through the darkness like neon lights. In an article on contemporary Scandinavian cinema Anders Marklund (2008: 54) discusses the use of such warm and bright colours, and highlights Sirpa Tani's suggestion that 'This glow transforms ugliness into beauty, elevates everyday life, and brings marginal life into the center'. Tani appropriately brings to light one of Kaurismäki's most prominent talents, his ability to transform what could be seen as the everyday gloom and mundanity of 'real-life' into a beautiful and poetic depiction of humanity, simply in his carefully composed visual elements. According to Kaurismäki these vivid glowing colours are attempts to revive the evocative colours found in the golden age of American cinema: 'I am in love with colours that remind me of Hollywood films of the 50s. But Technicolor has disappeared, so I cannot make the same thing anymore.' (Cardullo 2006: 7) Often associated with classic musical films such as *The Wizard of Oz*, Technicolor's luminous hues can certainly be found in Kaurismäki's films. While the content of the two films couldn't be more dissimilar, perhaps some of Kaurismäki's more romantic moments are also influenced by the optimistic fantasy in *The Wizard of Oz*. The end sequence of *Ariel* suggests this might be the case, as the most famous song from the film, *Somewhere Over the Rainbow*, plays out as Taiso and his loved ones sail off into the metaphorical sunset, but perhaps most significantly, the song is sung in the Finnish language. This clever device recalls the glory of Technicolor and Hollywood of the 1950s, while remaining culturally removed and re-contextualized.

The vivid Technicolor hues throughout the film also constantly recall the primary colour schemes of comic books and vintage postcards, and this comic book reference seems to be reflected also in the narrative content and characters of the film. In the opening sequence of *Mies vailla menneisyyttä* the protagonist 'M' is badly beaten by thugs and left for dead. A close up of M's hand as he walks through the recognisable location of Helsinki Station on the verge of collapse reveals a gruesome amount of blood, yet the image seems somehow artificial and cartoon-like. The blood is thick and opaque, and the colour is an unrealistically exaggerated red, bearing a striking resemblance to the iconic paint-like blood used in Italian film maker Dario Argento's expressionist horror films. Like Argento, Kaurismäki's blood is intensified and exaggerated to become a horrific yet striking image, purely in its vivid colour. The violence itself, however brutal, is basic and immediate, much like a simplified comic-book version of reality. This caricatured depiction of blood could perhaps suggest that the strongly saturated colours in the shot replicate the low-resolution printing techniques in the comic books and vintage ephemera already mentioned. The simple, 'baddie' and 'goodie' characters in the films also recall the exaggerated stereotypes of old-fashioned adventure books and B-movie plotlines, yet in *Scandinavian Cinema* Peter Cowie (1990: 76) suggests that both Aki and filmmaking brother Mika 'must relinquish their childish jocularity and improve on their comic-book characterisations.' Though Cowie might be making a surprisingly blunt yet constructive criticism, this so-called 'childish jocularity' seems to be one of the most essential aspects of understanding Kaurismäki's oeuvre, not something that needs improvement. Instead, this exaggeration and nostalgic reference contributes to the films as a stylistic whole, and reiterates the idea of creating a fantasy version of Finland.

If Kaurismäki's aim is to preserve and almost museologically display the old style, pre-modernised Helsinki in his films, could his chosen colour palette reflect this intention more literally? The repeated use of bright blues and whites in close composition create an image of flag-waving nationalism, and while this could be seen as a quite oversimplified assumption, a sequence in *Mies vailla menneisyyttä* suggests this flag-like image quite plainly. By the waterfront in the community of shipping containers, a washing line has been strung across a balcony to dry some clothes, and a man plays a cheery melody on his accordion. It is a straightforward establishing shot that depicts the community as a simple, domestic place, run down but pleasant enough. It is the clothes on the washing line that seem so carefully constructed, alternating neatly in colour between white and blue in turn. Shot from a low angle, nothing but a blue sky can be seen behind the washing line, other than perfect white clouds. The image is only fleeting, but stands out significantly for its clearly precise choice of colour, which is echoed more subtly throughout the rest of the film. Perhaps the use of nationalistic colours is a mere coincidence, but the obviously constructed set up of the clothing seems intentional, as not only do the colours of blue and white stand out as representative of the Finnish flag, but the clothes flap on the washing line like a string of flags in the wind. In *Ariel* a similarly incidental shot of ice in the water around the docks also shows an uninterrupted blue and white colour scheme.

Alternatively, instead of intentionally using these colours in a reference to a prescribed national palette, Kaurismäki is just reflecting the colours that occur naturally in the city and landscape that surrounds his characters, bringing a level of reality and authenticity back into the otherwise increasingly fantastical environment he creates.

A sequence in *Ariel* that neatly depicts this spanning of reality and fantasy through a distinctive use of colour occurs after the lead character Taiso loses his job and resorts to selling his car. Mourning his losses, Taiso sits in a café bar attempting to smoke a discarded cigarette butt in an ashtray. The bar is awash with red, a colour that seems to crop up in places of retreat or comfort, not in domestic places, but the various bars and clubs that offer refuge in the city to the nomadic loner-stereotypes that Kaurismäki repeatedly focuses on. Taiso sits looking out of the window, and notices the man who first robbed him when he arrived in the city. Chasing him, Taiso leaves the warmth of the café until once again the screen is awash with blues and greys in the station underground. Here the lighting takes a significant role in dressing the scene in cold, repetitive shadows from a metal gate. The shadowed patterning of bars could perhaps pre-empt Taiso's imminent arrest as he beats the thief in revenge, and with the almost monochromatic colour scheme the whole scene is reminiscent of a 1950s *film noir*. It is then in stark contrast that the next shot in the courtroom appears in absolutely plain colour. No rich reds and yellows, blues or whites; suddenly the viewer is transported into what could be assumed is the 'real world'. The judge sits plainly in the centre of the shot, surrounded by law books and dreary purple-coloured chairs. There are no harmonious pastels or moody lighting, just natural light on plain walls. The contrast of these two shots wholly emphasises the extremely stylised qualities of scenes in the hostel rooms and bars of previous sequences, not allowing the viewer to become fully immersed in the dreamlike nostalgia. Kaurismäki notably said of himself 'I am a realist, but you have to be successful in making colours become surreal, or non-realistic. So I guess you could say I try to use colour poetically' (Cardullo 2006: 7). By suddenly introducing the stark, bare, characterless courtroom the filmmaker thrusts the audience into an uncomfortable reality, intentionally void of poetry, that perhaps represents the modernised Helsinki that Kaurismäki finds so hard to bear. From the second Taiso is sentenced to jail, we know there will be no more lingering in moodily lit bars or cruising around in a 1950s convertible. The joy associated with the nostalgic, timeless activities of freedom is cut short by cruel reality, marked clearly by the disparity of colour and atmosphere in the courtroom.

In her book *A Kinder, Gentler America: Melancholia and the Mythical 1950s* Mary Caputi (2005: 43) suggests that longing for past eras, most specifically the so-called 'Mythical' 1950s, is the result of dissatisfaction with modern life. This certainly could be said of Kaurismäki who maintains 'I must be a species of monster that was born too late. That is why I want to have everything from my old world around me. What happens outside horrifies me' (Kyösola 2004: 46). Such an idealistic, regressive attitude is perhaps dangerous, as we see in Taiso's story, as sometimes the horrific outside reality will find a way in. According to Caputi (2005: 43), such dissatisfaction with the modern world and melancholia go hand in hand: '[o]ne specific reading of modernity... argues that the more modern life offers a preponderance of material goods, the more immanent reality appears bereft of intrinsic, imbedded value'. This analysis certainly agrees with the characters' experience in Kaurismäki's films, but also seems very close to a potential reading of Kaurismäki's own psyche. The idea of material goods of the modern world also stands out as a significant factor when reading *Ariel* and *Mies vailla menneisyyttä*, as the carefully chosen objects that surround the characters are sparse, and defiantly out of touch with the modern world. Perhaps Kaurismäki's inherent interest in the working classes and down-and-outs of Finland is because their world is so far away from the materialistic, consumer driven lifestyle that has powered the economic changes in Finland towards modernisation. This could certainly be said of both *Ariel* and *Mies vailla menneisyyttä*, where the communities of the shipping containers and Salvation Army have no choice but to survive on the very minimum. While this might not be by choice, there is an admirable quality to the happiness the characters find in such minimal circumstances that makes the lifestyle seem quite surprisingly attractive and utopian. The few items that the characters do own become incredibly significant objects, as shown in a sequence in *Mies vailla menneisyyttä*, where M begins to furnish his new home. Driving in the electrician's van they stop where a number of pieces of furniture have been discarded on the roadside, a table, stool, fridge and jukebox. What would appear to be rubbish to most is treasure to M, who with the help of the electrician gets the jukebox working back in the shipping container home. The three men sit around the salvaged fridge, which has now become a table, making a picture of cosy domesticity with the jukebox glowing brightly in the background. Like cowboys around a campfire, the men share a meal cooked on M's small gas stove as a bluegrass record plays away on the jukebox behind them. By using these settings seemingly caught in a temporal bubble, Kaurismäki surrounds his characters, as he wishes to do to himself, with the trappings of an old fashioned era, dissolving the harsh reality of their circumstances with a warm nostalgia. The minimal aesthetic draws our attention to the fact that these people, whether they want for more or not, have everything they need in life. In later scenes this idea is reinforced: when Irma comes around to M's for dinner all that is needed is a stove, a chair and a jukebox to create an ideal romantic evening. Kaurismäki seems to be able to use this kind of minimalism to strip back the films to their core fascination of humanity. He believes in '[n]o ornamentation; the basis for all art is reduction, simplicity' (Cardullo 2006: 7). It is, then, the introduction of such heavily referential props, settings and costumes against the minimal, simplistic scenarios that creates such a stylised and evocative atmosphere.

Throughout *Mies vailla menneisyyttä* and *Ariel* there are certain objects that have a huge nostalgic significance, and upon which explicit importance is placed. Two icons of 1950s design, Taiso's convertible Cadilliac and M's jukebox, are clearly outstanding as objects that carry a great deal of importance within the films, and while they function as regular objects in the films' narratives, they are clearly carefully chosen for their vintage aesthetic. This is perhaps most true of Taiso's car, and as *Ariel* could be seen as a road movie, it makes sense for the car to be significant. However, it isn't just a vehicle for transport; the car itself is a striking image in the Finnish landscape as Taiso drives to Helsinki. Repeated shots of the car from every conceivable angle fetishise its design, showing close ups of the various dials and devices around the steering wheel. It is clear that Kaurismäki finds the car itself aesthetically pleasing. After visiting the bank, Taiso attempts to close the hood of the convertible, stopped by the roadside in front of a sign sponsored by Coca-Cola. The shot is composed very neatly, so the white car with its red interior sits in front of the infamous logo matching perfectly. The two iconic American designs agree with each other, but the contrasting snow-covered Finnish landscape behind creates a bizarre juxtaposition of imagery. Pietari Kääpä (2008: 211) describes this awkward setting as a 'space of transition', where traditional culture meets the new. This image sums up the way Kaurismäki designs his mise-en-scène, carefully arranging dominant stylistic elements against a backdrop of Finland that creates and beautiful, yet somehow uneasy and awkward setting, which articulates the uncomfortable, melancholic point at which Kaurismäki's dream-like idealised Finland is cross-cut with a modern reality.

The jukebox in *Mies vailla menneisyyttä* also represents a quintessentially American design, yet performs a secondary function that contributes much to the nostalgia in the film, as it neatly provides a soundtrack throughout. In both films the characters have radios that also provide the same function, but the jukebox with its records stuck in the past contributes greatly to the antiquated mood of the film. M's radio provides a powerful and emotive diegetic soundtrack as the thugs are beating him up at the beginning of the film. However, the music from the jukebox seems to be most significant; while a radio picks up music that is being transmitted in the present day, the jukebox's records are trapped in a bygone era. The soundtrack throughout the film is almost entirely music from the 1950s and 1960s, and is one of the most effective factors in creating the nostalgic atmosphere. The use of music is one of the aspects of the film that most successfully encapsulates Kaurismäki's vision of the past. A totally clichéd, yet wholly seductive longing for the past is evoked in the swelling melodies from the jukebox at moments such as when M and Irma kiss for the first time in *Mies vailla menneisyyttä*. One criticism of the soundtrack could be that while it is so successful in creating a nostalgic atmosphere, it is somehow more removed from the idea of Kaurismäki's national vision. Unlike the depiction of the Cadillac car that is so noticeably American driven through the Finnish landscape, the soundtrack is quite dominant and overwhelming, without providing such an eloquent transnational dialogue. Kaurismäki seems to be at his best when he's traversing the many contradictions he plays with, between reality and fantasy, the local and the exotic, traditionalism and modernity. Perhaps within the soundtrack there is a danger that his use of nostalgia can become less about condensing and exaggerating his characters to create an impression of his idealised culture and more about boasting a stylish taste in records.

A moment in *Ariel* balances out the soundtrack and context very successfully, as Taiso first drives into the city to stop for a hamburger. This sequence also introduces another aspect of Kaurismäki's carefully constructed rendering of Helsinki, in his use of cartoon-like character archetypes. From an extremely high angled long shot we see Taiso's distinctive Cadillac pulling into the car park of a roadside diner. While it is unclear whether the sound is coming from Taiso's car radio or the café itself, the speaker in the foreground of this opening shot makes a reference to the loud rock-n-roll music blaring out of the scene, perhaps implying that the menacing music in this sequence is a signifier of the trouble to come. The camera glides down, pulling in closer to the car and following it around the building in a smooth tracking shot, revealing two suspicious looking men talking together and noticing Taiso. As he pays for his food, the camera zooms into a close-up of his wad of money, a cartoon-like movement that evokes the image of the thieves' eyes out on stalks. The music continues to play; now the rhythm has even more of an ominous threat, as the viewer is already sure of what is about to happen. Totally unaware, Taiso chats innocently to the men, who once they have his back turned smash a bottle over his head and steal his money. The sound stops instantly, indicating Taiso's loss of consciousness and playing with the tension between diegetic and non-diegetic music. The music, in combination with the cool, calculated physical presence of the thieves, is evocative of a stereotypical 1950s gang of street thugs in a children's cartoon, entirely over-exaggerated but absolutely threatening. A similar situation in *Mies vailla menneisyyttä* also sees the protagonist beaten by thugs, yet this time they are even more caricatured, all dressed in black leather jackets and turned up denim jeans. This sequence is very evocative of an imagined yesteryear, but unlike the various bars and cafés that Kaurismäki films in as a preservation of an ideal Helsinki, it veers too far away from reality, and feels a little clichéd, perhaps just a little too accurately representing stereotyped 1950s America, rather than a flavour of an influence. The scene is perhaps somewhat alienating; as Anu Koivunen (2006: 134) suggests, 'the comic, ironic and violent tones of the narration create a distance, blocking or hindering rather than encouraging national sentiments and nostalgic pleasures'.

Could it just be nostalgia for the sake of nostalgia? Here again Kaurismäki remains in the in-between, somehow able to exist in the liminal space between genuine adoration of the old fashioned and almost parodic use of exaggeration. According to Koivunen (2006: 134), Kaurismäki 'fuses sentimentality with irony and resentment with melancholia' in *Mies vailla menneisyyttä*, creating an experience for the viewer that in all of its confusion and ambiguity is actually accurately emotional in its irrationality. Kaurismäki's repeated use of temporal dislocation and sometimes heavy-handed retro-reference do contribute to a strong feeling of alienation for the viewer rooted in the 'real', modernised world, but perhaps this is wholly intentional, as Kaurismäki transforms the viewer into one of his own marginalised, disconnected characters.

This feeling of transition, and the intentional uprooting of any sure sense of place and belonging that is evident in his films, is represented by the repeated references to journeys and transport within both *Ariel* and *Mies vailla menneisyyttä*. Perhaps the various modes of transport that are repeatedly depicted in both films - trains, cars and boats - go further beyond their natural narrative function by reflecting on the disconnected instability of their lives, as well as adding a self-reflexive nod towards the transnational mode of the films. *Mies vailla menneisyyttä* is clearly framed at the beginning and end of the film by such images. M arrives into the city by train in the opening sequence, and as Irma and M walk into the distance together in the final scene their image is interrupted in the foreground by a passing cargo freight train. In *Ariel* the film is established as a car-focussed road movie from the opening sequences in which Taiso sets out on his journey in the distinctive Cadillac, framed in stereotypically grand landscape and tracking shots that could be seen as essential to the road movie genre. In his essay 'Aki Kaurismäki's Crossroads: National Cinema and the Road Movie', Nestingen (2005: 286) suggests that as a genre, the road movie can 'be defined as a series of conflicts between fixity and mobility, belonging and marginality, attachment and emancipation', which seems to accurately describe the liminal status that Kaurismäki applies to the characters in the films and the transitional culture he creates around them.

When asked what he thinks of Finnish culture in general, Kaurismäki states that it is 'the most beautiful culture in the world. Its problem though, is the same as that of European culture in general: American culture, which remains the most important one in Europe, on the surface – meaning that it smothers, or tramples everything that exists at a deeper level' (Cardullo 2006: 7). Kaurismäki's references to American culture in his films certainly don't give off this negative impression, yet in other interviews he clearly states that his American obsession is with the times of Roosevelt's New Deal (Romney 1997: 14), not contemporary American culture. Perhaps even the golden age of American culture that Kaurismäki prefers to recall still has the power to trample on the deeper levels of his own films. Once again it seems as if Kaurismäki is most successful, in a holistic sense, when he is engaging the timelessness of nostalgia alongside a critical examination of Finnish culture.

As a non-Finnish viewer I can only experience Kaurismäki's films from the perspective of an outsider to the country. It is well documented that films such as *Mies vailla menneisyyttä* have been very successful on an international level, while receiving a much less glorious reception in their native Finland (Sundholm 2005: 215). Perhaps Kaurismäki's style of filmmaking will always be more successful internationally because the way he condenses Finnish culture into an overexaggerated representation can only be appreciated by an outsider to that culture. Is Kaurismäki an outsider in his own country? Like the marginalised outsiders that epitomise Kaurismäki's films, perhaps the filmmaker himself is speaking from a point of view that is different from most in his native land. Aspects of the film such as Kaurismäki's unconventionally formal use of the Finnish language may be deemed unnecessary and potentially irritating by a Finnish audience, yet to a non-Finnish speaking audience such choices translate differently and appear to be charming and idiosyncratic. Andrew Nestingen discusses this use of language, suggesting indeed that Kaurismäki 'seeks to create a space for himself as a dissatisfied outsider' (Nestingen 2007). Perhaps, then, Kaurismäki always intends for his films to be seen by a transnational audience from the beginning. John Sundholm articulates this idea as 'national content and international form' (2005: 215), which seems to support the analogy of Kaurismäki's films as 'postcards' from his version of Finland. They act as condensed, caricatured reflections of a nation, designed to resonate outside of the country itself. Kaurismäki's role as a representative of Finland provides an interesting contradiction to examine: his films are very distinctly marked and marketed as his own, and much of their content is derived from his personal experience and beliefs. Due to his singular success, Kaurismäki, however unwillingly, has had to take on the role of representing Finland in cinema throughout the world. It would make sense, then, that the domestic audience would be unhappy with any unrealistic portrayal perpetuating a simplistic stereotype of a stern, cold people, though Kaurismäki himself maintains contentiously that 'the country is full of them' (Cardullo 2006: 7). Nestingen (2004: 96) argues that Kaurismäki's films may offer the Finnish people what he terms a form of 'neo-kansankuvaus' (self-portraiture), with which the Finns may understandably uncomfortable, as it is an entirely unsolicited depiction. In this extreme self-portraiture Kaurismäki's films create an understanding of the Finnish culture through one man's vision that both caricatures the Finnish psyche and captures what he considers to be the ideal lost elements of their culture, creating a rich and condensed depiction of a country to be delivered to the rest of the world.

Author's Comment

It was while I was studying at the Slade School of Fine Art that the opportunity came up to take on a subsidiary subject for a term from elsewhere in the University. I was immediately drawn to Nordic Cinema, and after seeing a Kaurismäki film for the first time I was hooked and knew I wanted to study his work in more detail. It seemed fitting to try and make the most of my background in history and theory of art by making a formal visual analysis of his films for my final essay, and his distinct aesthetic seemed very suited to this approach. One aspect of the essay that particularly reflects my studies in Fine Art is the comment on Kaurismäki's use of colour in reference to printed matter such as comic books and postcards; a large part of the artwork I was making at the time involved printmaking, particularly screen printing. The appeal of screen printing to my own work seems to have parallels with some of the ideas I discuss in the essay, as a form of image making that simplifies and condenses ideas into a saturated and immediate visual matter.

References

Caputi, Mary (2005). *A Kinder, Gentler America: Melancholia and the Mythical 1950s*. Minneapolis: University of Minnesota Press.

Cardullo, Bert (2006). 'Finnish Character: An Interview With Aki Kaurismäki'. *Film Quarterly* 59:4, 7.

Cowie, Peter (1990). *Scandinavian Cinema*. London: Tantivy Press.

Kääpä, Pietari (2008). *The National and Beyond: The Globalisation of Finnish Cinema in the Films of Aki and Mika Kaurismäki*. Unpublished doctoral thesis, University of East Anglia.

Kemp, Phillip (2003). 'The Man Without a Past'. *Sight and Sound*, 13:2.

Kaurismäki, Aki (2007). 'On Bresson'. *Sight and Sound*, 17:11.

Kyösola, Satu (2004). ''The Archivist's Nostalgia'. *Journal of Finnish Studies*, 8:2, 50.

Louvish, Simon (2002). 'A Tale of Two Memories'. *Sight and Sound*, 12:12, 25.

Marklund, Anders (2008). 'Can Anyone Help These Men? A Portrait of Men in Successful Contemporary Scandinavian Cinema'. *Film International*, 6:5.

Nestingen, Andrew (ed.) (2004). *In Search of Aki Kaurismäki: Aesthetics and Contexts*, Ontario: Aspasia Books.

Nestingen, Andrew (2007). 'Aki Kaurismäki and Nation: The

Contrarian Cinema', *Wider Screen*, http://www.widerscreen.fi/2007/2/aki_kaurismaki_and_nation.htm Accessed 10th April 2009.

Nestingen, Andrew and Trevor G. Elkington (eds) (2005). *Transnational Cinema in a Global North: Nordic Cinema in Transition*. Detroit: Wayne State University Press.

Romney, Johnathan (1997). 'The Kaurismäki Effect'. *Sight and Sound*, 7:6, 14.

Soila, Tytti, Astrid Söderbergh Widding & Gunnar Iverson (1998). *Nordic National Cinemas*, London: Routledge.

Soila, Tytti (ed.) (2005). *The Cinema of Scandinavia: 24 Frames*. London: Wallflower Press.

Thomson, C. Claire (ed.) (2006). *Northern Constellations: New Readings in Nordic Cinema*, Norwich: Norvik Press.

Vincendeau, Ginette (2007). 'Lights in the Dusk'. *Sight and Sound*, 17:4, April 2007.

Von Bagh, Peter (1999). *Drifting Shadows: A Guide to the Finnish Cinema*, Helsinki: Otava Publishing Company Ltd.

Place and Space

Bourgeois Space and the Post-Ideological Cinema of Dogme 95 and Desplechin

Ville-Matti Kervinen

At a superficial level Arnaud Desplechin's feature film *La Vie des morts* (The Life of the Dead, 1991) and Thomas Vinterberg's Dogme 95 classic *Festen* (Dogme#1: The Celebration, 1998) seem to have a lot in a common: a splendid bourgeois house as the setting, a big family reunion as the initiator of events, and a suicide or a suicide attempt of a close family member as the lurking threat in the background, these taking the abstract but semi-spatial forms of ghost and death. These similarities offer a fruitful starting point to a more profound study of space in the films. 'My supreme goal is to force the truth out of my characters and settings' declare Vinterberg and Lars von Trier in their Vow of Chastity (Vinterberg and von Trier 1995: 7). I interpret this line, in which settings have been placed on a level with characters, as a demonstration of the immense importance of location, surroundings, set and space to the Dogme 95 filmmakers, and I choose to read the quotation as establishing a symbiosis between Vinterberg's characters and space. Desplechin is also renowned for his thoughtful use of space: 'space is an equally important signifying element in his work, all the more powerful for being virtually inseparable from the images themselves' (Warehime 2002: 62). In *La Vie des morts* and *Festen* the space that we are concerned with is remarkably bourgeois: both films depict well-to-do families surrounded by material wealth, all their problems stemming from personal relationships rather than socio-economic issues. Desplechin and Vinterberg take slightly different attitudes towards the bourgeois culture, but they both draw inspiration and influence from the (at least) initially anti-bourgeois French New Wave. In this essay I will explore space in the two films and the ways it has been represented, concentrating on how strikingly bourgeois the space seems to be, both in physical and ideological terms. Desplechin and Vinterberg appear to be adopting similar attitudes towards the bourgeois space, depicting the negative impact it can have on people's lives. However, I will start by mapping where the films stand ideologically.

Both Desplechin and Vinterberg are post-ideological filmmakers mainly representing bourgeois values, whether or not this was what they wanted. Ginette Vincendeau argues that *Le jeune cinéma français*, to which Desplechin is often said to belong, is political in a new way; not 'depicting organised, future-orientated action or being informed by well-defined ideology' (Vincendeau 2005: 35). Instead it concentrates on 'the local struggles of small groups or individuals' without the 'political language to name the wrongs done to them' (O'Shaughnessy 2005: 77), hence it is post-ideological. This is partly true for *La vie des morts* which shares with *Le jeune cinéma* the interest in the regional identity in the less glamorous provinces of France, and also stylistically shows the way to the boom of hand-held cameras and raw naturalism of the later 1990s. But rather than having a 'socially-conscious syntax' (Austin 2008: 222) like many of the films of the movement, Desplechin explores 'narcissistic personal relationships in bourgeois milieux' (Vincendeau: 34), a much criticized feature of the French auteur cinema. Desplechin's interests stem from the grand auteurs of the French New Wave, especially François Truffaut (Zagha 2005: 21), but the fetish to form, which is present in his 'postmodern attachment to intertextuality' (Powrie 1999: 15), has been criticized. So, while sharing many of the values of the emerging *Le jeune cinéma*, *La Vie des morts* is still very much a bourgeois auteur film, this being seemingly exactly the kind of filmmaking that the Dogme 95 movement tried to rebel against.

> The new wave proved to be a ripple that washed ashore and turned to muck . . . The anti-bourgeois cinema itself became bourgeois, because the foundations upon which its theories were based was the bourgeois perception of art. The auteur concept was bourgeois romanticism from the very start and thereby... false! (Vinterberg and von Trier 1995: 6)

Despite the harsh tone of these accusations in the Dogme 95 manifesto, Vinterberg and von Trier approve of what the French New Wave directors were aiming for; the influence of the likes of Truffaut and Jean-Luc Godard on Dogme 95 is undeniable. Vinterberg and von Trier claim that the reason why New Wave failed was the treating of the artist as a concept (Schepelern 2005: 82). Instead, they offer discipline and truth as solutions, but, according to Ellen Rees, even though Dogme 95 stylistically seems radical, it 'reveals what might perhaps best be described as a reactionary ideological core' (Rees 2004: 165). The only political exhortation seems to be the denunciation of the bourgeois form of cinema (MacKenzie 2000: 164), at the same time forgetting the content, thus demonstrating the post-ideology of the movement. Also, as Peter Schepelern points out, the core objective of Dogme 95 - the stripping down of all the superficial elements - in the context of the filmmakers having access to better equipment and more funds, seems to be 'a typical symptom of Western culture' (Schepelern 2005: 84). This leaves us with a bourgeois filmmaker depicting the life of the bourgeois in an anti-bourgeois style, which actually might be bourgeois as well.

After having mapped the auteurs and their films as post-ideological, it is logical to proceed inside the films, and examine the locus in which the events take place. Roubaix, the setting of *La vie des morts*, gained prosperity in the 19th century thanks to the textile industry, but after the factories closed in the 1970s, it became notorious as one of the decaying Northern cities (Plummer 2007). Roubaix, as portrayed in the film, is dead, empty and isolated. The only signs of life are a few industrial machines working outside of the family house, but not even the people using the machines are seen, arousing feelings of unease in the spectator. It is hard to locate and mentally map the house in which the Mac Gillis live because it is always seen in isolation from its environment, the camera only revealing the immediate surroundings. Most of the film takes place inside or just outside of the house, emphasizing the dominating role of the building. One of the only times the domestic space is exited is the sequence of the boys playing football in the end of the film, which on many levels works as a breath of fresh air in comparison to the oppressive atmosphere of the house. When the cousins first arrive, the family is seen waiting for them in the darkness in the porch with the only light coming through the open door, suggesting the depression present inside the house. But it soon becomes evident that the light symbolized a false hope. The front garden is as lifeless as the house; there is not even any grass growing. Desplechin seems to be suggesting that the reason for the family living as if they were already dead is the environment that surrounds them: the closing factories and the decaying economy have led to the realization of one's mortality and resulted in desolation and apathy. This is also the most political Desplechin gets, here representing the themes of *Le jeune cinéma*.

In *Festen* the villa is clearly Danish, yet is 'never visually connected to any mappable locus, and remains emotionally and topographically adrift' (Rees 2004: 168). This is an interesting paradox since the unity of the Danes is emphasized throughout the film: from the first shots of the house with the gallantly flying Danish flags to the traditional racist songs which everyone knows the lyrics to. Still, the house itself is disconnected from the surrounding Denmark. Rees goes as far as calling the space 'a magical transgressive realm separate from the realities of the physical geography of Denmark in the 1990s' (166). In this magical space, Denmark is a conservative patriarchy at whose expense Vinterberg makes fun. The opening sequence of Christian walking on the road in his 'fatherland' and then being picked up by his brother, who drives 'little' Mette and the children out of the car since there is no room for women in this space, is surprisingly aggressive, but also humorous. Another characteristic of the patriarchy is highlighted by how the ruler, Helge, wants to keep his family together in the same space, in the luxurious villa, just like in a bourgeois idyll. Therefore, after the transgression has been made public, Helge's punishment accordingly is the dispersal of the family when Michael declares that Helge will never see his grandchildren again. The illusory unity of the Danish space is broken by the unveiling of the transgression, which has taken place in a private space and results in the demolition of the patriarchy.

The living space has to be shared by the whole family, and this causes problems in both of the films. Especially in *La Vie des morts* the difficulty of living under the same roof arises as one of the major themes. The family Mac Gillis is a microcosm consisting of small groups - the mothers, the fathers, the boys and the girls - who each have their own space. The youth occupies the upstairs space, whereas the mothers are often seen in the kitchen and the fathers in the living room. Desplechin depicts the groups as entities between which there is little, if any, communication. In particular, the intergenerational communication has failed. A striking example of this is when Yvan's mother calls him from downstairs but he does not answer, despite hearing the call and being just above her at the top of the stairs. Every member of the family, but most clearly the children, feel trapped in the house and in the family. The daughters are afraid of becoming like their mothers, the mothers are guilty about the suicide of the children, and everyone is paralysed by mortality, hence mourning their own death. Being trapped in the family space becomes concrete when Yvan lies on the ground in the backyard and the camera takes his point of view, gazing at the surroundings, but all he is able to see is a massive repressive brick-wall and rotting garbage.

The villa of *Festen* is a hotel, carrying 'a tension between private family memory and the public economy' (Rees: 168), but simultaneously offering a range of different public and private spaces for Vinterberg to investigate. It seems like there are very few real private spaces on the premises because in the hotel the rooms are impersonal and transitory, and the

Bourgeois Space and the Post-Ideological Cinema of Dogme 95 and Desplechin

Helene and Lars inspect the bathroom where Linda killed herself. *Festen*, Thomas Vinerberg, Denmark, 1998.

guests carry their privacy in their luggage. However, the most obvious private space is the father's place, separate as it is from the hotel building, and thus marking a clear division between the public and the private. In the world of *Festen* the private space is dark, dangerous and locked so that it is inaccessible to others; a space where transgression takes place. It was in Helge's locked and darkened study where the twins were abused, and now again when Christian goes to visit him, a danger can be sensed: there is little light, the atmosphere is oppressive and the discussion feels like an interrogation. Also, bathrooms are private spaces because they are usually occupied by only one person, providing ultimate privacy. Here they function as places where the characters are able to show real and raw emotions as opposed to the roles they play in public: Michael becomes violent, Helene has a breakdown, not to forget that Linda killed herself in a bathroom.

The space in the hotel can be divided into the servants' and the masters' spaces, revealing the social inequality between the family and the staff. The straightforward division into downstairs and upstairs is further strengthened by the way the guests treat the staff. For example Michael shows arrogance towards the receptionist, and later hits Michelle in order to dispose of their old affair. Unlike Michael, Christian is sympathetic with the staff, who join 'the children of privilege in battle against a common enemy' (Rees 2004: 171). The unity of the working class is emphasized through editing, which ties together all the individual actions in the hiding of the keys sequence, creating an image of a group working together for common good. The ending of the battle is celebrated in the piano room by the servants, siblings and Gbatokai all dancing together. They cheerily hug each other in a group, forming a unity, while surrounded by the grandeur and emptiness of the huge room, creating a metaphor of solidarity in the bourgeois space. However, the next morning it seems like the old attitudes clinging to the class differences have returned as even despite Christian asking Pia to move with him to Paris, immediately afterwards he asks her to continue serving, accompanied by Michael's jokes. It also becomes evident that the public spaces are the only sphere where the servants can operate, whereas the family occupies the private spaces. Only the owners of the property have a right to their rooms, to their privacy, whereas the working class has to perform on a public stage – emphasizing the bourgeoisness of the space of the villa.

In *La Vie des morts*, Desplechin contrasts crowded and unoccupied spaces. Throughout the film, autonomous shots of rooms of the house are shown in no relation to the preceding or following sequences accompanied by menacing music. These dislocated entities show static rooms with absolutely no life in them, almost emitting coldness. The only movement comes from the hand-held camera, which in this way reminds the viewer of its presence. The room shots emphasize the role of the house in the misery of the people living in it, adding some responsibility and characteristics to the space, and possibly even suggesting a 'curse' associated with the space. The total opposite to the dead space are the sequences where the house and the frame are crowded. 'Desplechin also uses space to define the relationships among his characters. . . in the literal amount of space they occupy within a frame' (Warehime 2002: 73), an example of which is the sequence in which the youth smoke cannabis upstairs and the frame is always filled with torsos and heads. Also, the camera moves constantly, to the extent that, in addition to the walking and crawling people, it becomes comical. But it also has a serious meaning in that all the characters compete for the same space and there is no air to breathe; the family is suffocating itself.

The shaky camera imitating a home video style is everywhere in *Festen*, depicting the celebration from the most inventive angles. In the birthday conga sequence alone the camera is under a table, inside a fireplace, in the ceiling and in the middle of the conga line as a participant. The unoccupied rooms with curtains blowing in the wind and the feel of camera often hiding from the guests have been interpreted as the point of view belonging to Linda's ghost (Laursen 2000: 81). But I would like to take this interpretation further and suggest that the perspective is that of the haunted house, and thus explaining the presence of the camera in the most ridiculous places. Ellen Rees points out that 'the space itself influences the characters and their actions', and also notes that the sexual abuse started after having moved into the house (Rees 2004: 168-169), leading to the conclusion that the villa has a similar 'curse' as the house in *La Vie des morts*, affecting negatively the lives and actions of its inhabitants. The culpability of the house could be seen affirmed in one of the final shots where Christian looks at his father, who lies beaten on the ground and in surrender, while the house lurks in the background, soon again mirrored in the lake, singled out as the culprit. In obedience to the Dogme 95 rules Vinterberg searches the truth out of his settings and finds it: a corrupting bourgeois space.

How can the curse then be broken? In *La Vie des morts*, the only solution appears to be to escape and leave the family space in order to save oneself from suffocation. The escape can take many forms: Patrick has been driven to commit suicide, death functioning as the ultimate liberating act; one of Patrick's brothers lost his memory; another escaped to Lyon without ever contacting the family again; and, as Laurence comments: 'It's funny to have a priest in the family', suggesting that Uncle Lucien chose the church over the family. Whatever the means, the family space has to be left behind either physically or mentally. However, in *Festen* escape is not an answer. Christian has been escaping home for years, but in order to solve the matter the only answer is to bring the transgression from the private space to the public realm, as he does in his speech in the dining room (Rees 2004: 170). Eventually, after the truth has been revealed and accepted, Michael in his aggression takes it as far as trying to destroy the whole private sphere by breaking the windows of the father's building, demanding that he come out and leave the private space. Another more subtle way to fight the common enemy seems to be the solidarity between different classes and nationalities in the surrounding hostile space, but as mentioned before, this comes to a questionable end in the final sequence of the film.

Whereas Vinterberg namely holds a hostile attitude towards the bourgeoisie, Desplechin concentrates on depicting their life in a more neutral way. Despite the different approaches, they both discover a highly problematic bourgeois space, which seems to cast some sort of curse over its inhabitants. In *La Vie des morts* the death and depression come from the dying city, from the deep-frozen house and from the suffocating family. It enters the body (Pascale's ghost pregnancy) and the mind, poisoning them. In *Festen,* the villa functions as a 'safety net for the transgressions' of the family Klingenberg-Hansen (Rees 2004: 167), possibly even more as the corrupting bourgeois space can be seen as the initiator of the transgression, the rotten bourgeois values and ideals having caused the tragedy. However, in Vinterberg's case, the renouncing of bourgeois values is ambiguous because in the film 'the underlying message is elitist and troublingly disconnected from the real world' (Rees 2004: 180). Despite criticism of the bourgeoisie, it is difficult to identify any ideologies in these two films; the world-views offered are too ambiguous. Thus *La Vie des morts* and *Festen* must be seen to represent post-ideological filmmaking, concentrating on depicting life as it is, and, at the same time, challenging the spectators to make their own interpretations. One of the most interesting aspects of Vinterberg and Desplechin as filmmakers is how their films turn to space, rather than time or history as their organizing logic, and understandably so, after the struggles and achievements of those who have come before have lost their meaning to the masses of the post-ideological era.

Author's Comment

This essay was my first-year project as a student of Scandinavian Studies with Film Studies. It was one of the first film essays I had ever written and I enjoyed the process tremendously, mainly because I had the complete freedom to choose any topic that interested me, something that I was not used to in high school. I ended up choosing two very different kind of films that I greatly admired and found to be dealing with similar themes, but which now in hindsight seems like the biggest weakness of the essay, since they are a bit of a strange and forced combination. However, I do think that I managed to justify my choice of films to a certain extent and I am still quite happy with the final result. Looking back on the essay, I would like to develop the concept of post-ideology further, and link those ideas more strongly to the bourgeois values, and especially, to the concept of space as means of organization and communication in film. I would also concentrate more on actual physical/cinematographic spaces in the films, rather than mainly talk about space in ideological terms. At the moment I am very much looking forward to seeing both of the directors' new efforts, namely Vinterberg's Cannes nominee *Jagten* and Desplechin's mystery project *AKA Jimmy Picard*.

References

Austin, Guy (2008). *Contemporary French Cinema: An introduction*. Manchester: Manchester University Press.

Laursen, Thomas Lind (2000). 'The Agitated Camera: A diagnosis of Anthony Dod Mantle's camera work in *The Celebration*.' *p.o.v.* 10, 77-87. http://pov.imv.au.dk/Issue_10/section_3/artc2A.html. Accessed 10 April 2011.

MacKenzie, Scott (2000). 'Direct Dogma: Film Manifestos and the *fin de siècle*.' *p.o.v.* 10, 159-170. http://pov.imv.au.dk/Issue_10/section_4/artc6A.html. Accessed 10 April 2011.

O'Shaughnessy, Martin (2005). 'Eloquent Fragments – French Fiction Film and Globalization.' *French Politics, Culture & Society* 23:3, 75-88.

Plummer, Robert (2007). 'French town finds life after industry.' *BBC News*, May 2. http://news.bbc.co.uk/1/hi/business/6582681.stm. Accessed 20 April 2011.

Powrie, Phil (1999). 'Heritage, History, and "New Realism": French Cinema in the 1990s.' In Powrie, Phil (ed.): *French Cinema in the 1990s: Continuity and Difference*. Oxford: Oxford University Press.

Rees, Ellen (2004). 'In My Father's House Are Many Mansions: Transgressive Space in Three Dogme 95 Films'. *Scandinavica* 43:2, 165-182.

Schepelern, Peter (2005). 'Film according to Dogma: Ground Rules, Obstacles, and Liberations.' Translated by Rune Christensen. In Nestingen, Andrew and Elkington, Trevor G.

(eds): *Transnational Cinema in a Global North: Nordic Cinema in Transition*. Detroit: Wayne State University Press.

Vincendeau, Ginette (2005). *La Haine*. London: I.B. Tauris & Co. Ltd.

Vinterberg, Thomas, and Lars von Trier. 1995. 'Dogma 95.' *p.o.v.* 10, 6-7. http://pov.imv.au.dk/Issue_10/section_1/artc1A.html. Accessed 10 April 2011.

Warehime, Marja (2002). 'Politics, Sex, And French Cinema in the 1990s: The Place of Arnaud Desplechin.' *French Studies* 56:1, 61-78.

Zagha, Muriel (2005). 'In the Name of the Father.' *Sight & Sound* 15:6, 18-21. http://vnweb.hwwilsonweb.com/hww/results/external_link_maincontentframe.jhtml?_DARGS=/hww/results/results_common.jhtml.44. Accessed 4 April 2011.

Place and Space

Sensuality and Gesture in Sjöström's *Körkarlen*

Daniel Fredriksson

Victor Sjöström's *Körkarlen* (The Phantom Carriage, 1921), a screen adaptation of a Selma Lagerlöf novella which bears the same name, is a film which has achieved canonical status. In an essay entitled 'Victor Sjöström and the Golden Age', Bo Florin writes that both 'historians and critics are fairly unanimous that *Körkarlen* represents the apex of the Golden Age of Swedish Film' (Florin 2010: 83). Furthermore, the film has been linked to notable figures in the history of cinema such as Ingmar Bergman, who counted it as one of his all-time favourite films (Bergman 2007), and Stanley Kubrick, who is said to have been inspired by one of its scenes (*Den svenska filmens Guldålder*).

It could be argued that the film is also notable for the close resemblance it has to the novella on which it is based. Even elements such as lighting seem to have been formulated with close reference to the original text. Arguably the most notable example of this is the scene where David Holm takes Syster Edit to task for having mended his jacket. At this point in the novel Syster Edit is at first shocked but then she quickly recovers and her eyes are described as lighting up: 'men sedan lågade det opp ett klart ljus i hennes ögon' (but then a bright light burnt in her eyes) (Lagerlöf 1997). At the same point in the film's narrative, Astrid Holm's face is lit in such a way that her eyes actually shine (Sjöström 2007). Such attention to detail is certainly remarkable but it does not, I would argue, account for the film's enduring success. Florin credits 'the ability to reproduce the mood of Lagerlöf's tale' as one of the factors which has contributed to the film's prestige (Florin 2010: 83). The film definitely has a dark and gritty feel which does justice to the original novel, a ghost story with elements of social critique. However, although the film has a similar atmosphere to the novel, it does not, indeed, cannot, employ the same techniques to create that atmosphere. I would argue that in order to truly understand the innovative character of *Körkarlen* one must focus on the ways in which the text has been subtly transmuted by the process of adaptation; that is, those moments where the same mood is achieved as in the novel, but the means by which that mood is created are different due to the logistic problems of adapting from novel to film. Over the course of this essay I will examine some examples of this transition from novel to film.

One could argue that the very act of adapting the novel into a film has given the text a whole new layer of meaning. Bjarne Thorup Thomsen points to this in his essay 'Ibsen, Lagerlöf, Sjöström and *Terje Vigen*: (Inter)nationalism, (Inter)subjectivity and the Interface between Swedish Silent Cinema and Scandinavian Literature'. Commenting on the work of Sjöström, he writes that Sjöström is 'true to the concerns of silent cinema' in the sense that 'his work displays a recurring, sometimes self-referential interest in the phenomenon of visual perception' (Thomsen 2006: 199). He goes on to maintain that *Körkarlen* is a particular case in point as it 'celebrates the existential implications of showing and seeing and could be understood as a tribute to cinema itself' (Thomsen 2006: 199). The filmatisation of Lagerlöf's tale allows it to take on another meaning. In the novel, David Holm is compelled to change his life on the basis of conversations he overhears as a spirit. The living characters in the novella talk freely when he is in the same room because they are not aware of his presence. As a ghost he is invisible to them. He is therefore able to observe without being observed. In the film version of the story, the act of observation takes on a new significance. Not only does it act as a device by which Holm learns the error of his ways, but it also serves as a comment on the act of looking itself.

An added layer of meaning is not the only consequence of the novella's filmatisation. In his book *Novel to Film: An Introduction to the Theory of Adaptation*, Brian McFarlane maintains that a distinction should be made between 'what may be transferred from one narrative medium to another and what necessarily requires adaptation proper' (McFarlane 1996: 13). To address this issue McFarlane offers up his own working definitions of the words 'transfer' and 'adaptation':

> Throughout the rest of this study 'transfer' will be used to denote the process whereby certain narrative elements of novels are revealed as amenable to display in film, whereas the widely used term 'adaptation' will refer to the processes by which other novelistic elements must find quite different equivalences in the film medium, when such equivalences are sought or are available at all. (McFarlane 1996: 13)

McFarlane's definitions have important implications for this essay. It is implicit from McFarlane's definitions of these terms that certain novelistic elements are more amenable to transfer than others. In the case of *Körkarlen*, it is safe to assume that aspects of the mise-en-scène such as set design, props and costumes could have been drawn directly from Lagerlöf's novel without any major logistic problems. This is because the novella was published only nine years before the film was made. McFarlane notes how filmmakers adapting novels by authors such as Dickens and Austen are often distracted trying to recreate the spirit of the time in which the novel is set (McFarlane 1996: 9). He writes that what was 'a contemporary work for the author, who could take a good deal relating to time and place for granted, as requiring little or no scene-setting for his readers, has become a period piece for the film-maker' (9). As the film was roughly contemporary with Lagerlöf's novella, the filmmakers would not have encountered any major problems trying to set the scene. This would presumably have given the film a sense of immediacy, adding weight to its elements of social critique. Other aspects of the text would have proved more difficult to realise on film. In *How to Read a Film: Movies, Media and Beyond*, James Monaco writes that 'language systems may be much better equipped to deal with the nonconcrete world of ideas and abstractions (...) but they are not nearly so capable of conveying precise information about physical realities' (Monaco 2009: 179). Herein lay the challenge which would have been posed by the task of adapting *Körkarlen* from novella to film. Lagerlöf's novel provides the reader with an insight into the psychological torment faced by someone who is starting to realise the full extent of the pain and suffering their actions have caused. The novel is arguably a format better equipped than film to evoke this sense of torment which belongs much more to the 'nonconcrete world of ideas and abstractions'. Psychological information relating to characters belongs to the category which McFarlane, borrowing a term from Roland Barthes, refers to as 'indices' (McFarlane 1996: 13). According to Barthes, indices denote a 'more or less diffuse concept which is nevertheless necessary to the meaning of the story' (Barthes 1977: 89). Barthes further subdivides this category into 'indices proper' and 'informants' (96). McFarlane explains how the first category refers to more diffuse concepts such as character and atmosphere, while the second category refers to what Barthes calls 'ready-made knowledge' e.g. the names, ages and professions of characters. McFarlane notes that only the latter category can be directly transferred, whereas indices proper are more open to adaptation (McFarlane 1996: 14). A film which has been adapted from a novel must therefore invent strategies by which it can convey information which belongs within the category indices proper.

Some examples of these strategies can be found early on in the film, during the scene in which David Holm has died and he is about to lay eyes on the phantom carriage for the very first time. In the novella a whole chapter (albeit a rather short one) is dedicated to this episode, which also includes David's first encounter with the spirit of Georges. The first part of this chapter deals with David's attempts to try to come to terms with his seeming paralysis; he is dead, therefore he can neither move nor cry out for help nor experience cold (Lagerlöf 1997: 26-29). He tries to deny the reality of what has happened to him, reasoning that he cannot be dead because he can both see and hear (27). This section also deals with the unsettling effect which the creaking noise of the approaching carriage has on David Holm. It is referred to as 'det förskräckliga gnisslet' (the terrible screeching) and is said to be scaring him out of his senses; a real feeling of suspense is created in this part of the novel; as Holm is fixed in one position, he does not

David Holm covers his ears at the arrival of the phantom carriage. *Körkarlen*, Victor Sjöström, Sweden, 1921

immediately see the phantom carriage in its entirety. Rather, it slowly enters into his field of vision, bit by bit (29). At this point in the film's narrative, no attempt is made to convey the sensation of being trapped within a dead body. This is presumably because such a sensation would have been almost impossible to present visually. However, the film does manage to convey the traumatic effect which the sound of the approaching carriage has on David Holm. As it draws nearer, Holm claps his hands over his ears as if to try and drown out the sound. When the carriage draws to a halt, Holm lowers his hands from his head. This gesture clearly signifies that it is the sound of the carriage as it moves which has so distressed him. It could be argued that the arrival of the carriage does not create quite the same feeling of suspense as it does in the text, where it gradually appears before Holm's eyes.

However, the on-screen version of this episode is not somehow inferior purely because it does not seek to replicate the novella exactly. As McFarlane argues: 'There are many kinds of relations which may exist between film and literature, and fidelity is only one – and rarely the most exciting' (McFarlane 1996: 11). Indeed, it is a much more rewarding exercise to look at the ways in which the text has been enriched by the process of adaptation from one medium to another. While the scene in which the carriage arrives may lack the carefully constructed suspense which this episode has in the novel, this lack of suspense is masterfully counterbalanced by the sheer spectacle of the carriage realised on screen. The carriage and the spirits are not only eerie in a way which evokes the atmosphere of Lagerlöf's text, but they are also visually stunning and technically brilliant; they thus represent a feat which, for obvious reasons, cannot be achieved in literature. Commenting on the double exposures used to create the ghostly apparitions, Florin writes: '[t]he double exposures, often identified as the stylistic device most conductive to the magic of the film, are still stunning by virtue of their effectiveness and brilliant execution' (Florin 2010: 83).

Equally innovative is the way in which the film endeavours to engage the senses of the viewer through the use of simple gestures. An important example of this strategy can be found in the above-mentioned episode where a hand gesture is used to create the impression that Holm is unsettled by a disturbing noise. This represents an elegant solution to the problem of how to convey the idea of sound prior to the advent of sound films. The film obviously cannot stimulate the viewer's sense of hearing like an audiovisual film can, but it makes a heartening attempt to communicate the notion of sound *via* the visual. An author who has written widely on the role which the senses play in cinema is Laura Marks. In her book *Touch: Sensuous Theory and Multisensory Media,* Marks offers up a definition of the term 'haptic cinema':

> Haptic cinema appeals to a viewer who perceives with all the senses. It involves thinking with your skin, or giving as much significance to the physical presence of an other as to the mental operations of symbolization. This is not a call to wilful regression but to recognizing the intelligence of the perceiving body. (Marks 2002: 18)

Marks refers to more recent works in her survey of haptic cinema. She does, however, include a brief discussion of the early years of cinema. She notes that 'in its early years cinema appealed to the emerging fascination with the instability of vision, to embodied vision and the viewer's physiological responses' (Marks 2002: 7). She goes on to maintain that the 'early-cinema phenomenon of a "cinema of attractions" describes an embodied response, in which the illusion that permits distanced identification with the action onscreen gives way to an immediate bodily response to the screen' (Marks 2002: 7). Marks concludes her discussion of early haptic cinema with the assertion that as 'the language of cinema became standardized, cinema appealed more to narrative identification than to body identification' (Marks 2002: 7). Although *Körkarlen* belongs more to the realm of narrative cinema, it is important to note, as Tom Gunning does, that the cinema of attractions did not simply disappear with the advent of narrative cinema; rather, it found its place within that paradigm (Gunning 2004: 43). As Gunning points out, 'the desire to display may interact with the desire to tell a story' (Gunning 2004: 43). *Körkarlen* certainly does not go to the same lengths to elicit a bodily response from the viewer as films which belong within the cinema of attractions. Nor does the film's imagery 'have the effect of overwhelming and spilling into other sense perceptions' (Marks 2002: 133). What the film does do, however, is invite the viewer to imagine with the senses. It does this through the use of visual cues which, when properly decoded, intensify the viewer's understanding of the film's narrative. These visual cues not only transmit information pertaining to sensory perception, but they simultaneously convey information which belongs within the category of indices proper. The above-mentioned scene where Holm claps his hands over his ears is a particular case in point due to the fact that it communicates the fact that Holm is hearing a noise at the same time as it tells the viewer that he is experiencing anxiety. This gesture thus represents one of the strategies by which the film attempts to adapt that which cannot be simply transferred from the novel onto the screen.

Another instance of this strategy occurs later on in the film during a flashback sequence which reveals how Syster Edit came to fall in love with David Holm. It occurs in the scene where Holm arrives at the newly founded Salvation Army centre hoping to find a bed for the night. Holm quickly passes out in the room which houses the beds and Syster Maria goes to turn out the light, but with a simple hand motion Edit gestures for her to stop. At first it is difficult to understand what is meant by this gesture; surely Edit who is portrayed as being so caring would want the light to be turned off so that Holm could sleep in peace without it disturbing him. However, this gesture takes on a different significance if one considers the possibility that this could have been a gas lamp. Gas lamps produce an incredible amount of heat when they are left on in a room and they are for that reason invaluable during winter time. This action is therefore intended to signify that Edit wants to protect Holm by ensuring that the room where he is sleeping is as warm and comfortable as possible. The intertitles explicitly state that the room where Edit goes to sleep is dangerously cold. They do not however give the viewer any clue as to how warm Holm's room would have been by comparison. The ability to decode this visual cue is not vital to an audience's understanding of the film. Nevertheless, when it is decoded successfully, this cue intensifies the viewer's understanding of the story. Not only does it contain information relating to the senses but it also enhances the characterisation of Edit as charitable and selfless.

In *Körkarlen* the desire to evoke certain memories and sensations is not at the forefront as it is in the films examined by Marks, but rather it is integrated more discreetly into the narrative. To adapt a phrase by Gunning, the desire to engage the body interacts with the desire to tell a story. Sensory perception nevertheless provides an exciting new angle by which one can analyse this classic film. *Körkarlen* is fondly remembered by critics for its spectacular special effects and technical innovation. Such reverence for the film's special effects is undoubtedly justified. The text has also been enriched by its filmatisation in the sense that it has gained a whole new layer of meaning. I would argue, however, that the most innovative aspect of the film is the way in which it seeks to convey the non-visual elements of the original novel through the use of sensuality and gesture. Therein lays the true power of the film.

Author's Comment

I wrote this essay as my final piece of coursework for Nordic Cinema. I recall that it was with a great sense of excitement that I started writing this project in the last four to five days of the Christmas holidays; the rest of my holiday had been taken up with writing an essay for a history module (a task which had proven to be much more onerous than expected as history is not one of my strong points). I was eager to do a good job, not only because the marks for the essay would make up a large percentage of my final grade for Nordic Cinema, but also because I had enjoyed the course immensely and I wanted my enthusiasm for the subject to be reflected in my essay.

Looking back on this essay over six months later, I would have to say that I am fairly content with how it turned out. However, there is one thing which I would do differently if I were to rewrite it; namely, I would provide more examples of ways in which the film seeks to convey information belonging within the category 'indices proper'. The reason I did not do this is because I mistakenly believed that the maximum word count for the project was 3000 rather than 5000 words. Had I written more, I'm sure the finished piece would have been far more engaging. Nevertheless, I am proud that I managed to fit so much into an incredibly small space. Working with a smaller word count than necessary was a good exercise in learning how to be succinct and use clear, precise language.

References

Barthes, Roland (1977). 'Introduction to the Structural Analysis of Narratives'. In Roland Barthes, *Image-Music-Text* (trans. S. Heath). Glasgow: Fontana/Collins.

Bergman, Ingmar (2007, July 31). *Ingmar Bergmans utlåtanden om svenska filmer.* Retrieved January 5, 2011, from www.aftonbladet.se: http://www.aftonbladet.se/kultur/article558995.ab

Den svenska filmens Guldålder (n.d.). Retrieved January 5, 2011, from http://www.thorellifilm.com/sidaMedia/filmartiklar2_guldalder.htm

Florin, Bo (2010). 'Victor Sjöström and the Golden Age'. In Mariah Larsson, & Anders Marklund (eds): *Swedish Film: An Introduction and Reader.* Lund: Nordic Academic Press.

Gunning, Tom (2004). '"Now You See It, Now You Don't": The Temporality of the Cinema of Attractions'. In Lee Grieveson & Peter Krämer (eds): *The Silent Cinema Reader.* London: Routledge.

Lagerlöf, Selma (1997). *Körkarlen & Herr Arnes penningar.* Bra Böcker.

Marks, Laura U. (2002). 'Video Haptics and Erotics.' In Laura U. Marks: *Touch: Sensuous Theory and Multisensory Media.* Minnesota: University of Minnesota Press.

McFarlane, Brian (1996). *Novel to Film: An Introduction to the Theory of Adaptation.* Oxford: Clarendon Press.

Monaco, James (2009). *How to Read a Film: Movies, Media and Beyond* (4th Edition). Oxford: Oxford University Press.

Sjöström, Victor (Director). (2007). *The Phantom Carriage KTL Edition* [Motion Picture]. Tartan Video.

Thomsen, Bjarne Thorup (2006). 'Ibsen, Lagerlöf, Sjöström and Terje Vigen: (Inter)nationalism, (Inter)subjectivity and the Interface between Swedish Silent Cinema and Scandinavian Literature'. In C. Claire Thomson (ed.): *Northern Constellations: New Readings in Nordic Cinema*. Norwich: Norvik Press.

Gazing at the Gaze: Scopophilia in Ingmar Bergman's *Sommaren med Monika* and *Persona*

Melissa Powell

Where do we locate the filmic gaze? The question is more problematic than it first appears; one might assume that the viewer simply gazes at the film, but this is reductive. As Metz argues, 'there are several kinds of exhibitionism, and correspondingly several kinds of voyeurism'; the dynamic relationships between viewer and performer are far from as simplistic as this (Metz 1983: 58). When a spectator views a film, he gazes at the characters, the actors, and, according to Mulvey's argument that 'cinema satisfies a primordial wish for pleasurable looking, but it also goes further, developing scopophilia in its narcissistic aspect', he gazes at his self-image (Mulvey 2009: 17). The on-screen bodies, too, gaze at each other, and at themselves. Furthermore, as the notion of the film having a 'skin', and being therefore capable of a mutually responsive relationship with its viewer, has been enthusiastically adopted in recent scholarship, we might concede that the film can look back at the spectator. The plural manifestations of scopophilia (or, the love of looking) in film are complex, potentially troubling, but essential to the nature of cinema.

The filmic gaze has been defined as erotic, unsettling, mimetic, and 'crazy' (Mulvey 2009: 14; Barthes 2000: 13, 113; Bazin 2009: 8; Metz 1983: 66). But whether we want to understand the film as a screen, window, mirror, 'skin', or even a piece of life (or death), the gaze is paramount (Mulvey 2006: 16-17). Though it is often associated with early cinema, we have never got away from the 'cinema of attractions' (Gunning 2004: 42). Nor are we ever likely to tire of the bewitching pull of the film's ability to *show*. Cinema is a scopophilic medium, obsessed with the image, and with itself as bearer of the image.

In this essay, I intend to analyse two films by Ingmar Bergman in which I consider the obsession with looking, or 'scopic drive' to be central (Metz 1983: 58). I shall begin with a discussion of *Sommaren med Monika*, isolating three types of looking: looking *in* the film, *at* the film, and *out of* the film. Taking as a point of departure Mulvey's influential essay 'Visual Pleasure and Narrative Cinema', I shall explore how the film variously exemplifies and problematises her theory of 'woman as image, man as bearer of the look' in cinema (Mulvey 2009: 19). Subsequently, I shall discuss *Persona*, in which the issue of scopophilia becomes the driving force behind what is shown (I hesitate to use the term 'plot', as the film consistently resists narrative coherence). I shall explore how the film subverts convention, uses defamiliarising techniques and takes a decentralising approach to narrative in order to present itself as a film about film. It uses its two central *personae* (no word could be more appropriate – we cannot refer to them either as characters or actors with full authority) to explore the possibilities existent between the film and the viewer. Through this discussion, I hope to show that we cannot consider the cinematic gaze as monolithic; it is a profoundly complex phenomenon, and difficult to locate. This consideration is manifest in my chosen films; Bergman's exploration of the scopophilic impulse is thoughtful, pluralistic, and integral to the ontology of his work.

Monika has become an icon of European cinema; she was a 'new type of woman', both celebrated and infamous (Bragg 2008: 17). Her iconic status is seemingly inaugurated by her erotic appeal; she has even been called 'eroticism incarnate' (Cowie 1992: 102). However, is her appeal inextricably bound to her position as fetishised object of the look? After all, instrumental to Monika's allure is that she subverts stereotyped Hollywood 'womanliness'. In fact, Monika's relationship to the gaze is intriguing; she is object and subject, viewer and viewed; she is looked at, but she looks back. We would hardly call Monika a powerless object of the scopophilic impulse, yet we cannot remove her from her objectified appeal. Ultimately, Monika's approach to the look is 'challengingly ambivalent' (Hubner 2007:30).

I shall first discuss looking *in* the film. We instantly recognise Monika as an object of male desire in the film; we see from the scene at her workplace that men behave suggestively, even predatorily, towards her. Almost every time she is on screen, the camera is centred on her. This seemingly agrees with Mulvey's theory that 'pleasure in looking has been split between active/male and passive/female; [...women] connote *to-be-looked-at-ness*' (Mulvey 2009: 19, original emphasis). However, we might suggest that Monika enjoys being an object of the gaze; she is an exhibitionist. After all, Mulvey also argues that 'looking itself is a source of pleasure, just as, [...] there is pleasure in being looked at' (Mulvey 2009: 16-17). If we perceive Monika as aware of her potential identity as object, and as exploiting this potential, then we understand her as 'performing' her gender role, and her self-consciousness allows her to an extent to control her own image. And the image that Monika wants to convey is inspired by cinema. As Hubner argues, '[h]er identification with the female star suggests an absorption in the illusion of what she might be and that her role as a woman is constructed' (Hubner 2007: 41).

We understand from the scene of Harry and Monika in the cinema how deeply affected Monika is by the on-screen couple, and how she admires their glamorous lifestyle; her attraction to Harry also derives from the fact that she imagines him as a film character. When Monika wishes to seem appealing, her behaviour, dress and speech suggest glamorous Hollywood stars. This mimicry has a meta-cinematic dimension; when Monika is most obviously 'performing', she seems to present herself well to the camera. When the couple kiss in Harry's home, for instance, the shot is initially poorly composed; Harry is in the foreground, and Monika obscured behind him. Monika reorders the shot so that she, the scopophilic object, replaces Harry in the foreground, and appears pleasingly to the camera. Furthermore, in such moments the aesthetics of the film alter remarkably; as Monika 'performs' womanliness, or female stardom, the background often fades to black, and she is lit intensely, creating an artificial and glamorised effect, reminiscent of the heavily contrived Hollywood movie seen earlier (a perfect example of this is the couple's first kiss, in which Monika even directly quotes the film). It is also in Monika's most fetishised moments that the film is more likely to employ fades and other devices that draw attention to the constructed nature of the otherwise fairly aesthetically realistic film. Expanding on Hubner's argument that the film

Sommaren med Monika (Summer with Monika), Ingmar Bergman, Sweden, 1953

aligns us with Monika's dreams of escape rather than Harry's, and remembering Monika's fascination with the escapism of cinema, in these scenes that seem deliberate nods to Hollywood, we are perhaps aesthetically entering Monika's fantasy, problematising Mulvey's paradigm of passive female object and male point of identification (Hubner 2007: p 42).

Mulvey's theory is further challenged by the fact that Monika can adopt the 'active' role. Mulvey argues that it is traditionally 'the man's role as the active one of advancing the story', but, despite Monika's exhibitionism and her aspirations to archetypal femininity, she often grows impatient of Harry's hesitancy (Mulvey 2009: 20). It is Monika who instigates the 'escape' from the city, ends the physical fight with Lelle, and breaks into the wealthy property to steal food whilst Harry lingers passively. Paradoxically, she is an active object.

Furthermore, Monika is far from the typical helpless object of the gaze. Male voyeurism often takes an aggressive turn – she is almost assaulted at work – but she proves herself able to overcome this, and thus capable of resisting the gaze (Hubner 2007: 33). In fact, she code-switches between male and female roles. This is even echoed in her appearance; when Monika is playing the passive 'female', she is well-dressed, well made-up, softly lit and glamorous, but when she becomes the active 'male', she appears quite differently: 'The unwashed hair, the mouth perpetually at work on gum, the proud, unboosted bosom: these built a new idiom into movie language' (Cowie 1992: 102). The enduring image of Monika is the heroine who undermined the 'strapped and laced eighteen or nineteen of the virgin woman in embryo we were all used to on the Big

Screen' (Bragg 2008: 17); she attracts not through submission to the gaze, but through toying with it.

Finally, Monika problematises the gender of looking *in* the film by the fact that she is herself a voyeur. She is fascinated by dreams of glamour and Hollywood, and as desperate to look as to perform. Her voyeurism also extends to her own image; mirrors in the film become identified with Monika, from the first shot in which she appears, continuing through numerous instances in the film. Even in moments of distress, whenever she sees a mirror, she will pause to arrange her clothes, hair and make-up. The gaze, then, becomes intriguingly self-reflexive; she is at once looking and looked at. Her exhibitionism is not exclusively for a male subject, but for herself. In the world of the gendered gaze, Monika is challengingly androgynous.

Monika's scopophilic appeal extends far beyond the diegetic frame. Film viewing is a reciprocal experience, creating an apparent subject-object hierarchy between the spectator and the screen. It is not only the onscreen bodies, but also the audience who are engaged in a voyeuristic dynamic with Monika. It is to this I refer when I use the term 'looking *at* the film'. According to Mulvey, this manifestation of the gaze is also gendered; the female body is to be looked at, the male to be identified with (Mulvey 2009: 20). She is the image, he the viewer's self-image. It is through cinema that the voyeuristic gaze is legitimised: 'what is necessary in this fiction for the establishment of potency and desire is presumed to be sufficiently guaranteed by the physical presence of the object: "Since it is there, it must like it"'. The on-screen look is self-consciously a surface on which the spectator can superimpose his own scopophilic fantasy in a manner unauthorised by ordinary life (Metz 1983: 62). This perspective coheres with *Sommaren med Monika*. Describing his experiences of the film, Bragg articulates the condition of most of its audience: it 'tapped itself into the real root of what I knew I had in some measure or would in some measure or wanted in some measure to experience. The bait was Harriet Andersson' (Bragg 2008: 17). He describes how Monika provided a bold counter-figure to traditional Hollywood heroines, who 'were not so much brought to us on the screen as separated from us by the screen' (Bragg 2008: 17). Expanding this idea, we could suggest that Monika managed to break through the 'separating' screen; her sensuality, more tangible than that of Hollywood, reached out almost physically to the audience, and they reached back.

According to Mulvey's theory, however, the primary point of identification for the viewer is the male protagonist. 'By means of identification with him [...] the spectator can indirectly possess her too' (Mulvey 2009: 22). This often obtains; even when he is the only figure in shot, we are rarely looking at Harry, but looking at him looking at Monika, and shots of her are frequently aligned with his legitimately voyeuristic gaze. He is allowed to possess her image within the narrative; therefore we (his anti-diegetic other by proxy of camera angle) are allowed to possess her too. Perhaps the most articulated example of this paradigm is the sequence in which the film shows Monika removing her clothes, cuts to Harry watching her (filmed from a low angle, to emphasise his privileged 'male' vantage point), and cuts back to Monika running naked across the rocks, from an angle that 'creat[es] a sense of voyeurism, closely aligned with Harry's gaze' (Hubner

2007: 31).This scene is returned to later in the film, as a memory, cross-cut with shots of his face in a mirror. The fact that the male is obviously filmed in the act of 'gazing' on both occasions 'foreground[s] the act of looking and male voyeurism, making clear links between Harry's gaze [...] and the spectator watching the film' (Hubner 2007: 31).

As previously mentioned, the lighting and composition of the shots indicate Monika as the object of the gaze. In her moments of exhibitionism, Harry is politely marginalised within the shot. As Monika lies decadently sprawled across the top of the boat, for example, in an intensely fetishised pose, she is clearly the visual draw, whilst Harry, facing away from the camera, is almost hidden by the boat as he literally 'drives' the action, but as a 'male figure [he] cannot bear the burden of sexual objectification' (Mulvey 2009: 20). Harry's physical presence is of no aesthetic interest; he is a euphemistic device moderating the pure, voyeuristic 'perversion' of unmediated looking (Metz 1983: 93).

However, we are not always reliant on the male protagonist to validate our gaze. The spectator is sometimes offered a privileged view of Monika, for example, in the sequence in which we watch her scurry about in her underwear before Harry wakes. Deprived of its diegetic mediator, however, the voyeuristic camera initially seems almost embarrassed; at first, we watch Monika from a distance, our view partially obscured by the long grass. Subsequently, the camera becomes increasingly confident, drawing closer to Monika with each shot, finally almost touching her as it follows her legs over the rocks. The view of the independent spectator becomes increasingly close and fetishised. Marks claims the spectator may 'touch' the film - and therefore the objects of desire – independently of the authorisation of onscreen bodies (Marks 2000: 162). Techniques such as 'a smoothly tracking camera movement [and] soft-focus cinematography, or an editing style dominated by lap dissolves', which Barker claims are used by the film to 'caress', are employed in conjunction with Monika (Barker 2009: 32). The 'tactility' and sensuality of *Sommaren med Monika* invites its spectators into an experience where 'the viewer's skin extends beyond his or her own body; it reaches toward the film as the film reaches toward it', long before Marks and Barker suggested their theories (Barker 2009: 33).

The gaze *at* the film is a powerful phenomenon in *Sommaren med Monika*. Monika's scopophilic pull is addressed not only to her diegetic spectators but also, constantly, to her 'real' audience; it is not only Harry's but everybody's summer with Monika.

Concerning the look *out of* the film, I refer mainly to perhaps the most discussed scene of *Sommaren med Monika*: the moment in which Harriet Andersson infamously shatters cinematic convention and stares directly down the lens. This shot is Monika's most definitive reaction to the scopophilic gaze. It is well-documented that such a mimesis-breaking action was 'forbidden' in cinema (Barthes 2000: 111); the film is 'not precisely something that hides, rather something that lets itself be seen without presenting itself to be seen, [...].This is the origin in particular of that 'recipe' of the classical cinema which said that the actor should never look directly at the audience (= the camera)' (Metz 1983: 63). Breaking this rule, then, Monika is 'presenting' herself, rather than 'letting' herself be seen. This makes her active; her stare back at the audience - out of the film - problematises the female as subject of the gaze, but also the film as subject of the gaze. It is an aggressive, meta-cinematic parody of the scopophilic impulse.

Bergman claims that this look was the first of its kind: 'here is suddenly established, for the first time in the history of film, shameless, direct contact with the viewer' (Bergman 1995: 296). This has since been contested, but it nonetheless made a powerful impression (Livingston 2009: 79). For Bragg, it was the most powerful and erotic image of the film: it 'made me hate her and lust after her in equal and unbearable conflict' (Bragg 2008: 17-18).This look is a popular source of critical debate. Many have interpreted it as a wanton stare, and the subsequent sequence of bright neon lights as indicative of Monika's doom; Cowie claims: 'this last passage suggests a return to the bleak, sordid life of the early Bergman films', whilst Wood is certain that 'we are in no doubts as to the life into which Monika is being sucked' (Cowie 1992: 104; Wood 1969: 41). This view seems suspiciously close to Mulvey's theory of the 'male' compulsion to subjugate the inherently 'guilty' female party (guilty as erotic object or perpetuator of 'castration anxiety') through either saving or punishing her (Mulvey 2009: 22). Certainly, the gaze of the object back at the subject, usurping its privilege, *is* threatening. It is hardly surprising that some viewers feel compelled to neutralise it through straightforward condemnation.

Hubner's interpretation is more convincing; she suggests this may be 'the moment when Monika becomes the movie star', reading the images that follow as indicative of Monika's achieved dreams of glamour (Hubner 2007: 45-46). This idea gains force considering the aesthetics of the shot; Monika is smoking, her hair and make-up near perfect, the lighting is striking and contrived, and the background effaced to black, all recalling the glamorous artificiality of Hollywood. Hubner's best point, however, is that the look is simply unreadable: a 'challenging, active and defiantly illegible gaze at the camera' (Hubner 2007: 46). Elements such as the *chiaroscuro* contribute to this ambivalence, but we might argue that the gaze *out of* the film is simply so challenging, so unsettling, and so unusual that the spectator cannot know what to make of it. It brings us to the surface of our own scopophilic impulse.

Monika's stare back at the camera is a perfect example of the threat that cinema can look back at us. We recall earlier instances in which Monika seems to place herself pleasurably before the camera – this 'defiant' stare shows that the scopophilic object is capable of change. It is a knowing, unsettling and aggressive stare. It reminds us of the multiplicity of film's touch; the image needn't be soft, pliant and pleasing (Barker 2009: 36). It can also pierce us. The film can invade our space, just as we can enter its space.

Sommaren med Monika both demonstrates and undermines the scopic drive in cinema. In *Persona*, that drive is brought absolutely to the centre; a 'film of a film from first image to last', it is a meta-cinematic exploration of its medium, foregrounding the gaze and the relationship between viewer and cinema (Vierling 1974: 49). Both are films in which the gaze is vital, almost agonisingly present, but the distinguishing element of *Persona* is that it no longer embeds these concerns in a coherent narrative. As Bergman himself writes: 'the gospel according to which one must be comprehensible at all costs [...] could finally go to hell' (Bergman 1995: 64-65).

The aim of traditional narrative cinema is to make its processes invisible; to 'eliminate intrusive camera presence and prevent a distancing awareness in the audience. Without these two absences [...] fictional drama cannot achieve reality, obviousness and truth' (Mulvey 2009: 26). The idea that this invisibility ensures 'reality' or 'truth' is absurd; what is truer than the fact that a film is a film? Conversely, *Persona* is profoundly aware of its own lie; by including shots of carbons, film stock, projectors, and even Bergman and Nykvist themselves (though all only as 'real-seeming artifice'), it draws attention to itself as constructed (Blackwell 1997: 136). Such process-exposing devices were hallmarks of the avant-garde, but Bergman differentiates himself by allowing *Persona* the vestiges of narrative convention (Mulvey 2006: 67). We can still conceivably speak of character, dialogue, development and occasional moments of narrative lucidity in the film, and its length, format and marketing are analogous to narrative cinema rather than avant-garde films. In its form, *Persona* often resembles traditional narrative, but in fact, any 'attempts to extract a coherent meaning from *Persona*' in a traditional sense are misguided (Hubner 2007: 76). *Persona* does not present us with a plot but a plot-shaped hole.

Persona exploits and subverts narrative convention in order to underscore the artifice of narrative itself. It uses several recognisable 'framing' devices; the flashback to Elisabet in costume at the start of her silence, Alma's monologue which directly addresses the camera, and Bergman's voiceover at the summerhouse. Repetition of such techniques would make them seamless, but as each is used only a single time (except the flashback, though it is repeated only once), they strike the viewer as unsettlingly incongruous, shattering any mimetic flow. In the opening scenes at the hospital, furthermore, the mis-en-scène is exaggeratedly minimal, recalling a theatre set more than a film, and certainly not suggesting any kind of 'reality'. These techniques are defamiliarising; by constantly reorganising the laws of its diegetic world, *Persona* prevents us from being convinced by its fiction, ensuring that we think of it as *film*.

Perhaps *Persona*'s most renowned 'defamiliarising' - and meta-cinematic - sequences are the beginning, ending, and 'breaking' of the film. These have been subject to extensive critical debate; Blackwell suggests that the images may be nods to Bergman's earlier films, whilst Vierling's view is that they exemplify how cinema can confront us on 'emotional' rather than 'intellective' level (Blackwell 1997: 137; Vierling 1974: 51). Expanding on this latter perspective, we can argue that the often 'haptic' images, and the range of sensory responses elicited, demonstrate cinema's heterogeneous 'touch'; by presenting us with a series of images that resist narrativization, but evoke a pre-intellectual reaction, the film forces us to recognise our own gaze (Marks 2000: 129).

These elements point to the fact that *Persona* is a film, but not a 'story'. By largely eschewing narrative, it makes us sensitive to the film-viewing experience and film-making processes, and the most important of these is the impulse to look. The presence of the scopophilic drive is felt overwhelmingly throughout; by acknowledging the impossibility of narrative truth, we are left with the only 'truth' cinema can plausibly lay claim to: the active/passive involvement of the viewer. And it is to this that any graspable 'narrative' of the film pertains. How do we describe what 'happens' in Persona? It is problematic to answer definitively, but we might simply suggest: 'two women meet. They look at one another.'

Insofar as there is any notion of narrative in Persona, it is the narrative of viewing a film. In a diegetic sense, we can read the relationship of the two women as an allegory of 'looking' in the cinema; their interactions reflect the various, complicated dynamics between spectator and 'spectrum' (Barthes 2000: 9). The allegory persists in plural manifestations.

In its most straightforward form, the dynamic of subject and object of the gaze is established in the roles of the two women. Elisabet is an actress, a 'sexual icon, a body on which male culture inscribes its narrative' and a patient, instantly the object of the gaze and authority of the nurse, Alma (Blackwell 1997: 144). In their early scenes together, Alma's role corresponds to a simplistic idea of the cinema viewer: whilst pleasurably in awe of her glamorous object, she is authoritative, and able to master the gaze. As actress and patient, Elisabet - subjugated, docile and pleasing – is literally there for Alma to observe. Her gentleness and silence initially connote her as incapable of intrusive or troubling response. In this manifestation, Alma represents the spectator's imagination of herself at a 'masterable' distance from the scopophilic object.

Pleasure derived from the privileged gaze is the basic manifestation of scopophilia. Mulvey has also highlighted the second nature of this drive, which 'comes from identification with the image seen' (Mulvey 2009: 18). Accordingly, in *Persona*, Alma views Elisabet not simply as image, but as self-image. She begins to dress, smoke, even move, like the actress; she even expresses the phenomenon directly, describing watching one of Elisabet's films, and thinking 'vi liknar' ('we are alike'). Initially, the act of self-recognition in the filmic other is a triumphant one: the spectator is impressed with her likeness. Alma enjoys looking at Elisabet, but does not immediately consider her position as unilaterally authoritative subject problematised; she considers herself the spectator.

The relationship of the two women represents that of spectator and on-screen body, but also that of spectator and film. It is pleasurable and dangerous; the cinema is 'one lawful activity [which provides] a *loophole* opening on to something slightly more crazy, slightly less approved than what one does the rest of the time'; a space for the 'projection of the [spectator's] repressed desire onto the performer' (Metz 1983: 66 original emphasis; Mulvey 2009: 17). Certainly, Alma's seemingly personal relationship with Elisabet introduces her to possibilities more bizarre, more carnal, and both more and less 'real' than those of her 'approved' life. Alma and Elisabet are filmed at an increasingly intimate proximity; Alma, as 'spectator', becomes increasingly, physically involved in Elisabet as 'film'. They caress and stroke one another; their relationship, as Barker says of that of film and view, is 'fundamentally erotic' (Barker 2009: 34).This is the authorised pleasure of the gaze. In allowing ourselves to gaze at the image, we 'come to the surface of ourselves' (Barker 2009: 35). This is part of Alma's experience; it is the 'slightly crazy' capacity of the scopophilic impulse that means that the process of looking gives license to her repressed side ('the *hurter* alongside the *healer*, the lesbian alongside the heterosexual'), allowing her to express her most 'unapproved' secrets (the orgy on the beach and her abortion, amongst others) (Vierling 1974: 50, original emphasis). In coming to her own 'surface', however, Alma's 'spectator' position as one of unambiguous mastery becomes problematic. She touches the image, but the image touches her back.

The notion that image and spectator 'create' one another is established; 'it animates me, and I animate it' (Barthes 2000: 20). This idea seems pertinent; the women *almost* 'become' one another. Bergman wanted to show two women who '*exchange personalities* [...one experiences] the condition of the other woman's soul' (Bergman 1995: 60). Cinema and spectator are incapable of such a literal 'mergence', but what occurs in *Persona* is a profound problematisation of the established hierarchy between the two (Blackwell 1997: 133). They do not 'merge', but the boundaries blur. Considering the idea that cinema resembles 'an erotic embrace, in which we sometimes cannot tell where one body ends and the other begins', the sequence in which Elisabet enters Alma's room becomes a visual metaphor for film-viewing (Marks in Barker 2009: 35). At first, they look at each other; then Elisabet sweeps back Alma's fringe, demonstrating their 'alike-ness', enacting 'scopophilia in its narcissistic aspect' (Mulvey 2009: 17). Finally, they intertwine, and the lighting fades, obscuring bodily boundaries. It is erotic and expository; they look, they resemble, they touch, they (almost) merge.

This is emblematic of *Persona*'s challenging of the spectator/subject and image/object. It is their closeness, and the 'notion of viewers' and films' bodies as surfaces in contact

[that] problematizes the strict division between subject and object in the cinematic experience, suggesting instead a more mutual experience of engagement' (Barker 2009: 34). The privileged gaze of the spectator is undermined consistently. Though Alma is initially suggested as bearer of the gaze, she is also the object of Elisabet's scopophilic impulse. As Alma recounts the orgy, for example, Elisabet becomes a voyeur; the scene 'foregrounds Elisabet's response' (Hubner 2007: 83). Some shots focus entirely on Elisabet; we recognise her gaze as voyeuristic and predatory. Bergman was fascinated by Liv Ullmann's face during this scene, claiming it actually 'swells' (Bergman in Blackwell 1997: 144). As Alma continues her story, she is filmed lying next to Elisabet, but her face is barely visible; Elisabet dominates the shot. The lighting is focussed on her, filmed in close-up, and we naturally concentrate on her intense *looking* at Alma. The scopophilic impulse, therefore, can go both ways. As Alma realises her lack of mastery, the nature of the gaze transforms. After discovering Elisabet's letter, she feels invaded; she has experienced the terrifying power of the object to become the subject.

Their relationship demonstrates the pluralistic ways in which film and spectator might 'touch' one another. As discussed by Marks, the bodies of film and viewer are capable of mutual, often tactile interaction (Marks 2000). However, this 'touch' is not always pleasant: 'films can pierce, pummel, push, palpate, and strike us; they also slide, puff, flutter, flay, and cascade along our skin' (Barker 2009: 36). Alma and Elisabet experience various 'touches', some comforting, some erotic, some violent. When her position as spectator was unchallenged, Alma's gaze was pleasurable; as she became aware of her own inadequate subjectivity, it became violent and critical (the gaze might '[examine] the film for weak sports, errors', as when Alma scrutinises the sleeping Elisabet, describing her flaws) (Barker 2009: 37). As Bergman explains, 'they insult, they torment, they hurt one another, they laugh and play' (Bergman 1995: 60-61). This may be a more literal 'touch' than implied by Marks and Barker, but their relationship demonstrates some of the tactile and emotional possibilities of film. That the experience is mutual shows how the traditional subject/object paradigm of cinema might be ambiguous.

However, though spectator and film may touch each other, affect each other, be both subject and object, they do not unite absolutely. There is ultimately an incommensurable distance between spectator and filmic other. The idea of 'mergence' between Alma and Elisabet is a fallacy; they blur, but do not 'become' one another. Alma finds this position deeply unsettling; 'flesh [of the viewer and film] resolutely refuses the possibility of either absolute distance or absolute proximity', and she does not know where to position herself between the two (Barker 2009: 27). At this point, all binaries are shattered; it is impossible to say definitively who is looking at whom, who is talking, and through whom, who is imagining and who is acting. Unable to perceive the film entirely at a mastering distance, or a comprehending closeness, the position of the spectator becomes troublingly ambiguous.

The symbolic relationship of Alma and Elisabet imitates the viewing experience. Through this, the 'de-narrativizing' of the film, and other techniques, however, we are also brought to the surface of ourselves, made uncomfortably aware of our voyeuristic tendencies. We find further expression of our scopophilic drive in Alma's recount of the orgy. Initially, this example recalls Mulvey's theory of male voyeur and female exhibitionist, but this is problematic. Firstly, as I have mentioned, Elisabet becomes a female voyeur, erotically involved in Alma's story; secondly, within the story, the gaze becomes reciprocal, and thirdly, we feel the women gain sexual pleasure from looking at each other. Several critics have tried to apply Mulvey's paradigm to Persona by calling *all* voyeurs 'male', and *all* scopophilic objects 'female' – Blackwell, for instance, attributes the 'male' gaze to Elisabet, sometimes simply because she is literally 'wearing the trousers' – but this is misguided; the near absence of men from *Persona* de-genders the gaze (Blackwell 1997: 81). 'The "orgy" of *Persona* is the orgy of merged spectatorship and participation'; it explores the complex gaze between subject and object, between film and self, but to make it about the gaze between men and women limits its meaning (Rugg 2004: 244).

In fact, Alma's story is significant because it imposes itself as a metaphor for *our* viewing experience; *our* gaze, and the gaze back. Throughout the majority of the shots in *Persona*, we are looking or looked at from one of the perspectives exemplified in the story. Often, we are looking from the viewpoint of the boys, either at uncomfortable, fascinated proximity, or abashed, voyeuristic distance. The use of close-ups and extreme close-ups are marked; we often view the actresses' faces at an unbearably intimate, almost intrusive closeness. Other times, we watch the characters at a distance, whilst the camera is obscured by objects; the scene, filmed at a distance, hidden amongst trees, in which Alma sits outside – even in swimsuit and straw hat – aligns us almost directly with the boys of the story. Elsewhere, we become the object, like the women at the beginning of the story; again there is an almost direct example, in which the camera sits on the beach, whilst we see Elisabet in a long shot, peering from the rocks. The look out of the film, so bold and shocking in *Sommaren med Monika*, is used profusely throughout *Persona*; at one point, Elisabet even appears 'from nowhere, seeming to take our picture', directly challenging our position as unambiguous spectator (Vierling 1974: 49). *Persona* is almost gratuitous in its audacious subjugating of the audience. We are not simply watching the possibility of heterogeneous subjectivity, we are actively involved. Most of the shots are uncomfortable and unnatural; the use of medium shots is notably limited, and we are most often either *too* close or *too* distant from the actresses, yet unable to achieve 'absolute distance or absolute proximity' (Barker 2009: 27). Aesthetically, the film delineates us as voyeurs, in a sense that is perhaps troubling, forcing us to examine our own scopophilic impulse; *how* do we look? *How* has it affected us? And, perhaps, *should* we look?

Persona is all about scopophilia. Bergman subverts the normal filmic laws of time, space and narrative to present us with a piece of cinema that can be about nothing but the film itself. We are gazing at the gaze; we watch two characters - perhaps two actresses - watch each other, and watch ourselves watching the film. Through a profound break with convention, and an aesthetic and psychological style that foregrounds our consciousness of our own voyeurism, the film forces us to explore its only valuable truth: our own relationship to it.

The scopophilic gaze is central to *Sommaren med Monika* and

Persona. Beginning with a simple, diegetic expression of looking, existing in both films, the idea develops into something such more sophisticated and self-reflexive, subtly and germinally in *Sommaren med Monika*, and reaching a point of vital and complex consideration in *Persona*. *Sommaren med Monika* explores the gaze particularly in its gendered aspect, centring on a figure clearly identified with the female scopophilic object, but also subverting this convention. It demonstrates traditional paradigms of the gaze only to question them. It exemplifies various, complicated forms of the gaze, from the diegetic, to the unsettlingly reflexive. In *Persona*, the scopophilic impulse is readdressed in extremely intricate and meta-cinematic terms. By largely effacing narrative realist convention, it exposes its own medium, foregrounding the nature of film itself, and the question of spectatorship. In interpreting the relationship of the protagonists as representing the ambivalent relationship between film and viewer, and recognising the film's address of our own viewing experience, we understand how the scopophilic impulse is at the heart of *Persona*. Both films successfully problematise any notion of a homogeneous, unilateral gaze in cinema. The scopophilic impulse of film is in fact complex, pluralistic, troubling, and ultimately unknowable; but it is far from straightforward.

Author's Comment

The essay featured here was a project for an undergraduate course in Nordic cinema, written in the final year of my BA in Italian and Norwegian. Since my introduction to Scandinavian film in an independent cinema in Cambridge during my time as a sixth-form student, I have been a great enthusiast of Nordic cinema, and particularly all things Bergman. I returned to film studies persistently throughout my degree, exploring various styles, genres and auteurs as part of my course and for personal interest, but Bergman always remained a strong favourite. Since first discovering *Det Sjunde Inseglet*, I have been fascinated by the distinct, haunting and meaningful aesthetics of Bergman's films, and therefore the subject of scopophilia and looking in his work interested me as a theme for an essay. I greatly enjoyed writing the project, and am generally pleased with the outcome. If I were to return to the essay, I should like to do so in a year or two, after the opportunity for further, more specialised study, and hopefully after having spent time broadening my knowledge of film studies, to see whether I might be able to use more theories and comparisons with other films for more expansive insight.

After finishing my undergraduate degree in the summer of 2012, I am returning in the autumn to begin an MA in European Culture, in which I hope, amongst various themes and courses, to continue exploring the world of European cinema.

References

Persona, Dir. Ingmar Bergman, AB Svensk Filmindustri (1966)

Sommaren med Monika, Dir. Ingmar Bergman, AB Svensk Filmindustri (1953)

Barker, Jennifer (2009). *The Tactile Eye*. Berkley; London: University of California Press.

Barthes, Roland (2000). *Camera Lucida*. London: Vintage.

Bazin, André (2009). 'The Ontology of the Photographic Image'. In André Bazin: *What is Cinema?* translated by Timothy Barnard. Montréal: Caboose.

Bergman, Ingmar (1995). *Images: My Life in Film*, translated by Marianne Ruuth. London: Faber and Faber Limited.

Blackwell, Marilyn Johns (1997). 'Persona: The Deconstruction of Binarism and the False Mergence of Spectator and Spectacle'. In Marilyn Johns Blackwell: *Gender and Representation in the Films of Ingmar Bergman*. Drawer, Camden House, Inc.

Bragg, Melvyn (2008). *The Seventh Seal (Det Sjunde Inseglet)*. London: Palgrave Macmillan.

Cowie, Peter (1992). *Ingmar Bergman: A Critical Biography*. London, André Deutsch.

Gunning, Tom (2004). '"Now you See It, Now You Don't": The Temporality of the Cinema of Attractions'. In Lee Grieveson and Peter Krämer (eds): *The Silent Cinema Reader*. London:

Routledge.

Hubner, Laura (2007). *The Films of Ingmar Bergman: Illusions of Light and Darkness*, Basingstoke: Palgrave Macmillan.

Livingston, Paisley (2009). *Cinema, Philosophy, Bergman: On Film as Philosophy*. Oxford: Oxford University Press.

Marks, Laura U. (2000). *The Skin of the Film: Intercultural Cinema, Embodiment, and the Senses*. Durham; London: Duke University Press.

Metz, Christian (1983). *Psychoanalysis and Cinema: The Imaginary Signifier*. London: The Macmillan Press Ltd.

Mulvey, Laura (2006). *Death 24x a Second*. London: Reaktion Books.

Mulvey, Laura (2009). 'Visual Pleasure and Narrative Cinema'. In Laura Mulvey: *Visual and Other Pleasures*. Basingstoke: Palgrave Macmillan.

Rugg, Linda Haverty (2004). 'A Camera as Close as Ingmar's: Sexuality and Direction in the Work of Ingmar Bergman and Liv Ullmann'. In Helena Forsås-Scott (ed.): *Gender, Power, Text: Nordic Culture in the Twentieth Century*. Norwich: Norvik Press.

Vierling, David L. (1974). 'Bergman's *Persona*: The Metaphysics of Meta-Cinema'. *Diacritics*, 4: 2, 48-51.

Wood, Robin (1969). *Ingmar Bergman*. London: Studio Vista.

Looking and Touching

Hands as Icon and Symbol of Touch

Lauren Godfrey

Hands are the part of a stranger that we shake when we meet them and the part of a lover we hold tightly; we entrust them to communicate our ideas in writing and to gesticulate as we speak; our hands can be enhanced with tools of creation or destruction, conversing with our brain to determine their course of action. The significance of hands in everyday life is often overlooked as they work so successfully in tandem with our progression. Hands are the symbol of man's evolution: Aristotle declared that 'Humans have hands because they are intelligent'. This statement could easily be reversed and read equally coherently. The relationship between the brain and the hand is interdependent; intelligence and progression depend on the conversation between the hand and the mind.

In cinema, hands are used as symbols, a part standing in for the whole, demonstrating the experience of a character through their most identifiable extremity. While the director is aware that s/he cannot truly make the viewer touch or feel something, s/he can attempt to make the 'dry words' - the two dimensional images on the screen - 'retain a trace of the wetness of the encounter' (Marks 2002: p.x intro.), that is, the physical experience of touching something. This visual-touch stimulation is referred to as the haptic, or 'fingery eyes' as simplified by Donna Haraway in *When Species Meet* (2008: 5). It allows the viewer to use his or imagination and association memory to elaborate on what the director offers. 'Riegel invents the term "haptic" to indicate that our eyes are able to

Looking and Touching

Images top row Left to Right:
Heftig og Begeistret (Cool and Crazy), Knut Erik Jensen, Norway, 2001
Ariel, Aki Kaurismäki, Finland, 1988
Höstsonaten (Autumn Sonata), Ingmar Bergman, Sweden, 1978

Images middle row Left to Right:
Persona, Ingmar Bergman, Sweden, 1966
Vredens Dag (Day of Wrath), Carl Theodor Dreyer, Denmark, 1943
Persona
Persona

Images bottom row Left to Right:
Idioterne (The Idiots), Lars von Trier, Denmark, 1998
Fanny och Alexander (Fanny and Alexander), Ingmar Bergman, Sweden, 1982
Mies Vailla Menneisyyttä (The Man Without a Past), Aki Kaurismäki, Finland, 2002

sense softness or hardness as well as contoured structure without touching the material by hand' (Thomsen 2006: 48). Previously, 'haptic' was used to describe the painterly surface of a picture and the lack of perspective in the Renaissance as a moment when optical perception was not the totality of the image. Nowadays it is used more to describe the conjuring up of a sensation when looking at something, particularly film. In this essay, I shall discuss the role of hands in Nordic cinema, regarding the physical significance of the hand on screen, haptic association and recognition and the importance of auteurship, the director's touch. I shall attempt, like Laura Marks, to 'show how and why cinema might express the inexpressible' (2000: 129) using 'hands' as my prop and Nordic Cinema as a case study. I shall explore the notions of hands as a representative of the whole, physically, emotionally and metaphorically; the potential for cinema to consciously distance the viewer and draw him or her in using haptic techniques; and the camera or prop as a corrupt extension of the hand, posing the director as a puppet master and an enculturating force upon the viewer.

> It was his hands that revealed him – as if his hand had betrayed him (Le Corbusier in Pallasmaa 2009)

Directors use the power and expression of hands to their advantage in cinema. To signal to the viewer that the character has hidden motives, the hands will play out their inner feelings. The part stands in for the whole as the camera frames the isolated hand. An archetypal example of this is demonstrated in Aki Kaurismäki's *Mies Vailla Menneisyyttä* (The Man without a Past, 2002). The protagonist, about whom we know little at this point, has been left for dead on a park bench. The film cuts to a station, the atmosphere is sinister and the few people present seem to veer away from the point of view of the camera, as if they are attempting to avoid our gaze. The shot cuts to focus on the hand, hanging limp and rich, red, bloody. We are aware it is not disembodied as the cuff of his coat peeps into shot and we can decipher the out-of-focus movement of his legs in the background. Our imagination can flesh out what the rest of his body may look like and we realise that the camera was showing us the view from his eyes as the people swerved away from his mauled figure. These signals combine to great effect; we do not need to see the whole body as we can imagine just from this graphic shot what it looks like. This gives poignancy to the scene and avoids a horror movie humour that could have dominated if Kaurismäki had shown us everything in explicit detail. The implicit part represents the severity of the whole.

This is contrasted in the art work *La Tache* (1985/6) by Jean François Guiton in which 'we see textures, skin and textile, brushing the screen' (http://www.guiton.de/Bandes/Tache/Tache.html). A blurred hand is manipulating fabric and wood; we know there is human interaction, but 'his presence is no longer bound up with figural representation' (Zech: 2000: 13). It is purely a hand we see, performing an action. In this case it is different from the narrative film because we do not desire to know why or to whom this hand belongs. It becomes almost erotic in its anonymity, representing the experience of touch without explicitly demonstrating the true mundanity of holding the fabric. This technique of hinting at the complete experience, using the hand as an icon, highlights the fundamentality of the hand as a key part of the anatomy, second only to the face.

In the silent film, *Körkarlen* (The Phantom Carriage, Victor Sjöström, 1921), the jealous Mrs Holm approaches the deathbed of Edit, led by her hands. Nobody else is present in the room and Edit's eyes are closed. She walks towards the bed, her hands wringing with destruction. In the absence of speech, she melodramatically demonstrates the anger and frustration she feels towards the seemingly innocent girl. As a viewer, we are captivated by the hands, despite the fact that the camera is not close, as in the case of *Mies vailla menneisyyttä*. Mrs Holm's hands dominate the screen in their intimacy and revealing role. We are aware at this moment of the power of the human hand and fear that she may put the pent-up energy and strength in her fingers to the task of strangling the already dying Edit. The soaring emotions in this scene forecast the progression of the film as a whole, providing a solid foundation for the narrative to unfold. This is the first time we meet Mrs Holm and we are comprehensively introduced to her role through this simple but potent movement.

In Bergman's *Persona* (1966), the hand physically experiences and represents the emotional trauma that Alma faces in the film. The famous opening sequence demonstrates all of the ideas and frustrations of the film, through a series of symbolic occurrences. The hand appears frequently throughout this introduction as a solo part. The child's hand grasping out in a fumble; the strong, manly hand controlling the sheep as it wriggles from his grasp and finally, the most poignant of all, the rusty, gnarled nail plummeting down into the hand. The clip is played three times at this point and then at regular intervals throughout the film to reaffirm its significance. The image lingers on the last time to show the fingers recovering from the crucifixion-like blow. The soft, vulnerable palm suffers the impact as the hand clamps in pain and the fingers curl up instinctively. This short and impactful shot pre-empts the progression of the film as a whole: 'the pierced palm anticipates Alma's turning of her hands which, in turn, suggests that the back and the flat of the hand have their counterparts in the left and right half of the human face, so spectacularly contrasted in the film' (Törnqvist 1995: 140). The idea of doubling and mimicry in the film is signalled early on, as well as betrayal and suffering. Through this ambiguous and disorientating series of images, Bergman encourages the viewers to fill in the gaps themselves; this lends itself well to the haptic potential of the film. 'The more open the symbols are to interpretation, the stronger is the stream of visual/sensuous thought which is triggered by what the viewer sees and also transcends it' (Zech 2000: 13). It is this transcendence, involving the memory or imagination of touch, that enriches the film as a whole. The almost pornographic detail of the nail-in-hand scene is incredibly sensuous and one can imagine and sympathise with the pain felt. The dilemma with this, however is that it is not a character that we are identifying with, but the experience: the separate and non-narrative nature of this sequence sets the tone for the reception of the rest of the film. It is not until the film progresses that we realise the significance of this moment and are able to empathise on a more personal level with Alma. At this point it is a purely indulgent, dramatic image, sensational for sense's sake.

As Christopher Hussey put it back in 1927, the force of the

picturesque was 'to enable the imagination to form the habit of feeling through the eye' (Bruno 2002: 202).

The indulgence of imagery on screen, allowing the viewer to identify with the experiences and to go beyond the objective association with the characters in a film, is used by directors to enrich the viewing experience. Harking back to the earliest days of cinema, when cinema-goers went purely for spectacle, the modern viewer is still hungry for enjoyment and satisfaction. The director has become aware of the presence of the viewer and the viewer herself is conscious of her own body in space before the cinema screen. As Giuliana Bruno romantically states: 'Seeing with one's own eyes involves a (dis)placement; becoming a direct observer, the tourist acknowledges her body in space' (Bruno: 2002: 191). This inclusion and consciousness on both the director and the viewer's part allows for a new level of understanding and identification as the film develops before the viewers' eyes. The film itself is completed through the viewing. This, of course, relies on a certain degree of awareness of the medium on the viewer's part. Although the all-encompassing sensory explosion on screen has some power to entice the viewer, the point is not to completely believe that one is feeling what the projected character on screen is touching. The artful use of haptics allows the viewer to be aware of the inability of the physical medium of cinema to fully conjure up these experiences. In the opening scene of Lars von Trier's *Antichrist* (2009), for example, the slow pace and sensuous description of the girl's experience as she walks towards 'Eden' lends itself to the haptic conjuring-up of senses. However, she appear to hover above the grass as she walks and ultimately lies down. Her physical body does not interact with the surface and so nor can ours. Trier is aware at this point that the actors on screen are fabricating an experience which we receive second hand. It is a series of imaginings of which we are presented with the most dilute version. There is a distance kept between us and the texture of the film, 'pointing to the limits of sensory knowledge' (Marks 2002: 20). This distance is not only physical. The intrinsic nature of film as a medium that can only record a visual souvenir of what took place before the camera distances us further. It represents a subjective filter through the eye of the director, who has chosen how we should experience this scene as observers.

The closest haptic relationship demonstrated in cinema is erotic. Film has its own language to illustrate the most sensory experience of all: sex. The hand is both the origin and the expression of pleasure, holding the ability to provide others with satisfaction whilst simultaneously experiencing it. 'We see something which is recognizable only in the traces of captured motion and transfer it in our imagination to something which has already happened or might possibly still happen' (Zech: 2000: 17). Our memory and personal sensory knowledge embellish the images we see, developing the visual experience into a relatable, physical one. Sexual encounters are difficult to recall visually, as sex is in its very nature about touch. Film directors take this into account and often zoom in on the surface of the skin, in order to stand in for human contact. Our eyes are so close to the skin, we are practically touching it. The physical parts become indecipherable and our eyes get lost in the vast landscape of flesh. In the controversial 'gang bang' scene in *Idioterne* (The Idiots, Lars von Trier, 1998), the camera is close to the writhing bodies. We see close ups of genitalia and skin as quickly as a slide show; it is mayhem on screen. The oblong of the film becomes a palate of beige, peach and brown. We can barely identify one body from another. The trauma in this scene lies in its explicit nature and its ability to involve the viewer in the action. The resulting experience forces us to look but denies us the clarity of recognition; we feel as though we are drowning in the images. Marks feels this lends itself to the very essence of the haptic. 'If you try to bring the images into focus, you get a headache. But if you allow these selectively bulging and blurring forms to do just what they do, a haptic universe unfolds in all directions' (Marks 2002: 70). On the other hand, the demonstration of touch with a caressing hand can be equally relatable. The viewer identifies with the physical representation of the hand performing the touching and can imagine using their own hand in the same way. Immediately after the explicit sex scene in Idioterne, the camera follows Jeppe upstairs where he finds Josephine, naked and vulnerable. Slowly, they touch each other sensuously and nervously. Their touch is tentative and the camera stays close to the hand, following its course around the body. They seem almost not to make contact, as though their hand is hovering above the other's skin, but it is incredibly delicate and we, as viewers complete the touch in our imagination. The contrast in pace to the previous scene adds to the sensitivity of this moment. It occurs almost in real time and we are given the chance to reflect on the intimacy of the touch. The hesitant hand appears extremely sensitive, so we can identify with the experience on a haptic level.

Hands are often used as a symbol of manipulation and control. Anne's powerful hand in *Vredens Dag* (Day of Wrath, Carl Th.

Dreyer, 1943) as she coaxes Martin is a prime example. At this point in the film, Anne has admitted her own fate. She realises that she is losing the support of those around her and decides to take control. Her movements are calculated and slow, the camera is close to Martin's back as she rubs it firmly with her articulated fingers to manipulate him. The movement could be received by Martin as caring and caressing but our close up point of view can detect the aggression behind the fingers and the deep pushing into his muscle. The technique of giving more to the viewer than the characters themselves is powerful. We feel privileged to understand the truth of the characters and are advantaged because of this. This is a filmic and narrative method that allows the story to unfold in a more complex way than in reality. While the character of Martin just sees Anne's smiling face, we get an insight into her true motives. The hand is an effective vehicle for communicating this. The touch of her hand fools Martin into complying with her, while the visual movement of the hand that we as viewers see speaks volumes of her intentions. Törnqvist writes of the power of a manipulative hand in the dream sequence in *Höstsonaten* (Autumn Sonata, Ingmar Bergman, 1978): 'Suddenly a woman's hand caressingly creeps into hers…The caressing hand remains unidentified, since figuratively speaking it is both Lena's and Eva's hand. The hand caresses Charlotte's cheek, then moves behind her head. Suddenly, it seems to tear at her hair' (Törnqvist 1995: 166). In this case, the hand acts as a symbol of desperation on the part of both Charlotte and her daughters. The unpredictability of the unknown hand is disorientating for the viewer and Charlotte respectively. The sensuous trust that the hand establishes though the preliminary caressing is betrayed as the dynamic changes, reflecting the plot in the betrayal of a mother's unconditional love. To pre-empt the dream, the camera shifts to Charlotte's own hand, limp on the bed, involving us directly in the guile of the dream. We are as shocked as Charlotte when the hand hastily changes course. Bergman uses the rectangular closeness of film, the intrinsic selection of our seemingly objective point of view, to draw us in, believing that what he is showing us is truth. He has not used the expected, recognised conventions of filmic dream-sequences where the shot becomes hazy or the image fades away and returns, showing a lapse in time or change of perspective. We are totally enticed by the seductive hand, experiencing the dream just as Charlotte does.

The ability of hands to master an art encompasses the world of performance and film. The quiet confidence of the pianists' hands in the opening sequence of *Kauas Pilvet Karkaavat* (Drifting Clouds, Aki Kaurismäki, 1996) and those of the accomplished concert pianist Charlotte in *Höstsonaten* hold a modesty that reminds us of the trust we can put in our hands. The muscle memory that hands possess is remarkable, proving particularly frustrating when they fail us. A melancholy moment in *Heftig og Begeistret* (Cool and Crazy, Knut Erik Jensen, 2001) takes place in the church belonging to the community. The organ player attempts to impress the camera with his playing but becomes increasingly frustrated as he cannot succeed. This moment works particularly well in Jensen's film because it is a documentary. We are aware that this is a real man who truly wants to be able to play the organ well at this special moment in time when he is being filmed. The truth of the situation gives the scene pathos. We join him in his irritation and genuinely feel for him as he cannot proceed. It is easy to relate to the feeling of being out of control of one's own hands but we identify with him, not on a sensory level, but an emotional one. The director has chosen to include this scene, rather than one where he plays immaculately, as it allows us to sympathise with the characters and develop a relationship with the lonely men.

In contrast to this, however, masterful hands are utilised in Bergman's *Fanny och Alexander* (Fanny and Alexander, 1982) to reference the very nature of film. The children perform a puppet theatre, an imaginary scaled-down world over which they have control. 'Behind the boards representing the world, there is a hidden manipulator who controls everything happening on these boards' Törnqvist (1995: 179) observes about the nature of the puppet theatre. Developing this notion into a broader spectrum, he adds, 'Also behind the world in which we live there is – perhaps – a hidden director' (179). This is also true of cinema itself. By using a puppet theatre Bergman not only suggests that the children are longing for more control, he signals the fact that we as viewers are being manipulated by a powerful figure: the director himself. The concept of the auteur in film is interesting to consider in terms of the hand of the director. The artistic vision and touch of the director is fundamental to the completion of the filmic experience. Often the prime impetus to watch a film depends on the reputation of the director. This is especially apparent in Nordic cinema where it seems that certain filmmakers become representative of their own Nordic country, gaining auteur or celebrity status because of their individuality. We are often aware of their presence whilst watching the film, armed with the knowledge and vocabulary of their previous films. Their name is spelt in capital letters at the start and the end of the feature, reminding us of their artistic expertise. In the 1990s, the Dogme 95 movement attempted to shatter this illusion by including in their 'Vow of Chastity' the commandment 'The director must not be credited'. This ironic claim is doomed to fail, as no matter how anonymous the director may attempt to be, they must sign the certificate that is projected at the start of the film with their own hand. There is no escaping the recognition they are entitled to. However, the statement that the Dogme 95 Brethren were making highlighted the intrinsic paradox that cinema faces. There is always an author. The artistic touch must be credited to somebody and, due to the hungry nature of the media and the star-studded realm in which they were working, there would always be a star behind the puppet theatre.

The physical movement of the camera itself could be interpreted as an artistic gesture. This is particularly prominent in the Dogme 95 Vow of Chastity in which it is declared: 'The camera must be hand held. Any movement or immobility attainable in the hand is permitted'. Here, the inadequacies of the hand as a firm tripod are celebrated or at least accepted. As viewers we are conscious of the physical interaction of director and camera and the aesthetic result is very recognisable. This does, however, contradict the rule I discussed previously of an uncredited director. We are constantly reminded of the presence of the director manipulating our view with his subjective selection of what we see. Employing the scene in *Idioterne* where Stoffer strips off his clothes and protests as an example, the aesthetic suggests a haphazard happening. The movements of the camera lend themselves to the panic that ensues, involving us in the drama. The handheld nature of the camera allows us to imagine that one of the 'idiots' is presenting the situation to us. The camera moves manically, reflecting the way that the 'idiots' act, providing the scene with another dimension of mayhem. It is this handheld quality that presents the camera as an extension of the hand and an expression of ideas, giving the film a similar status to drawing or writing. The unity of director and camera suggest a form of craftsmanship and expertise. There is a communication between the tool and the hand, a mutual reliance that implies that the 'tool is not innocent' (Pallasmaa 2009). The hand does not simply pick up the camera and manipulate it to its own delight. There are prerequisites that come with the camera; its weight and size in the hand; the balance it is provided with; the focus (whether the camera has an auto-focus function or manual); and the viewer (whether the eye must be put to the lens viewer or if there is a screen). Furthermore, the fact that the camera is handheld restricts the potential angles from which the camera can film. The camera can only go as high as the cameraman's arm can reach and only as fast as he can run. These factors give the film a physical, human element, prompting us to consider the tangible interactions that have taken place. The tool of the camera gives the director a certain power.

> The sense of touch fills nature with mysterious forces. (Focillon 1989: 28)

This potential, provided by a prop, is often interwoven into the narrative of a film. The possession of a tool or weapon in film is a signal that the character has a new capacity to destroy others. How they use this power, however, is very revealing. The tool of the dagger is introduced in *Det Sjunde Inseglet* (The Seventh Seal, Ingmar Bergman, 1957) early on, during the scene in the tavern as the squire protects Joseph by threatening Raval with his dagger. The squire's already large physique is made even more intimidating with the weapon he carries. Whilst it remains unused, it stands as a symbol for his potential as a character. The implement becomes an extension of his hand and hence his character as a menacing figure. Later in the film, Skat pretends to murder himself with a false dagger. He lies on the ground until the others have left and then climbs a tree to sleep. He is woken by Death sawing down the tree; his time has come. This charged symbol of a useless weapon that Skat thought he controlled backfires upon him and he is taken by death anyway. The matter is out of his hands and that which he held in his hand has betrayed him. This underlines the responsibility that accompanies the use of such a tool, and accentuates its lack of innocence. In Aki Kaurismäki's *Ariel* (1988), Mikkonen arms himself with an insufficient weapon. As he delivers the money to the men in return for passports, they fail to honour the deal of sharing the money. Mikkonen anticipates their attack by smashing a glass bottle against the wall. This makeshift weapon proves useless as he drops a wad of cash and reaches down for it. We see the man lunge towards him with a dagger at which point the camera cuts to Mikkonen's grasping hand near the floor. Reminiscent of the nail-in-hand scene in *Persona*, his hand becomes incapacitated and we visualise his pain through this one extremity. Mikkonen is let down by his inadequate tool and it is his empty hand that we witness suffering.

> The relationship between mind and hand are not, however, so simple as those between a chief accustomed to obedience and a docile slave. The mind rules over the hand; hand rules over mind. (Focillon 2007: 28)

As Focillon so aptly points out in his essay 'In Praise of Hands', not only does the hand touch and the brain identify, there is a conversation between the two parts. The brain can recognise something using the eyes, as in cinema, processing this through the brain and sending a message to the hands, which relates to the idea of touching something. As Mark Paterson puts it, 'this is an example of the multisensory nature of our perception. We never perceive by vision alone; in fact, percipere means "to grasp"' (Paterson 2009). We attempt to transform the visual nature of cinema through the entire sensory experience. This interdependent relationship can be likened to the conversation that takes place between cinema and culture. Cinema both embodies and enculturates us as viewers. We are represented in the sense that we can identify with the characters on screen; but we also use the film to enrich our existing lives and inform us on how to conduct them. Trends can be pioneered by cinema, for example. A particular brand of cigarettes can become fashionable, as in the case of *Ariel*, where the icon of the 'North State' cigarettes[1] persistently appears throughout the film. It is the pertinacious presentation of this image that enculturates the viewer as they watch. To develop the metaphor more concisely, it could be said that the cinema is the hand as it is the physical realisation of the conceptual idea; culture is the brain, the theorisation and development of the physical experience. 'We might expect the relationship between "viewer" and the more physical object of cinema to be more convincingly mimetic' (Marks 2000: 138), thinks Laura Marks, pondering the correlation between cinema and viewer in comparison to that of reader and written text. The reflection that film is more physical is interesting in view of the fact that one can hold a book in one's hands whereas film takes place beyond our physical reach. Film does, however, *show* the experience of being alive, whilst the book expects the reader to conjure up the images in their own, intangible imagination. It is this intimate closeness yet ungraspable distance that is so intrinsically characteristic of cinema.

'A hand is not simply part of the body, but the expression and continuation of a thought which must be captured and conveyed' (Balzac, quoted by Pallasmaa 2009). Cinema completes Balzac's desire, capturing and conveying the thought and physicalising it in the form of light on celluloid. To some extent, film makes solid the movements and intonations of the hand itself, preserving the muscle memory in a visual format. The image of a hand on screen is relatable and iconic, representing a tactile, haptic experience. However, Laura Marks argues that the image of hands is not fundamental to the reception of the haptic: 'Looking at hands would seem to evoke the sense of touch through identification, either with the person whose hands they are or with the hands themselves. The haptic bypasses such identification and the distance from the image it requires' (2002: 8). Although I appreciate Marks' point in relation to the entire vocabulary of the haptic in cinema, it has been worthwhile to discuss the specific notion of the haptic in terms of imagery and the significance of the hand, framed in the oblong of film. Through this investigation we have found that hands play many a part in the plot-thickening and metaphorical development of film, flirting with the surface of the film to enrich the viewer's haptic engagement despite the visual distance. At a further leap, we've identified that the hands behind the lens of the camera are also important, the visual record of the muscle memory of the camera operators' movements and the puppet-master nature of the director, pulling strings. It is clear that as a viewer one has a vivid and affective association with the representation of a hand in film and the experiences that it undergoes.

Author's Comment

I took the Nordic Cinema class as a subsidiary subject while in second year at the Slade School of Fine Art, studying sculpture. Inspired by my Northern heritage (my father was born and raised in the Shetland Islands) and after a recent trip to Shetland, I was drawn to the pensiveness of the culture and the dry humour. I had also been working on a documentary of my own, filmed in Shetland about a family friend and his remote, dilapidated house. The course complimented my work at the Slade in its sensitivity to the nuances of film and at the time I was nurturing an interest in the haptic touch in a sculptural sense as well as filmic. The two conversed nicely. Following the Nordic Cinema course I went on exchange for four months to Kuvataideakatemia, The Finnish Academy of Fine Arts in Helsinki. This was no doubt as a result of my enjoyment of the course and an expansion of my interest in Nordic cultures.

Looking back on the essay I feel that a discussion of the digital versus analogue film could be an interesting extension to the essay, though I am aware of the vastness of this topic. I still stand by this essay and I feel it sparked many related interests both in further pieces of writing and in artworks. I have since made work that confronts the relationship between the visual and the verbal when talking about art, including a personal audio guide to accompany an exhibition and a series of collaborative investigations into ekphrasis using radio and writing as formats. This seems to reflect the visual/touch relationship that I have explored in this essay.

1. An unreliable source on You Tube states that these cigarettes, that always appear in Kaurismaki films are called 'North State', known as 'Nortti', famous Finnish working class cigarettes. This was confirmed by www.cigarettespedia.com. Nevertheless, they are iconic.

References

Bruno, Giuliana (2002). *Atlas of Emotion*. New York: Verso.

Focillon, Henri (2007). 'In Praise of Hands' in *Poetics of the Handmade*. Los Angeles: The Museum of Contemporary Art.

Haraway, Donna (2008). *When Species Meet*. Minneapolis: University of Minnesota Press.

Marks, Laura U. (2000). *The Skin of the Film: Intercultural Cinema, Embodiment and the Senses*. Durham and London: Duke University Press.

Marks, Laura U. (2002). *Touch: Sensuous Theory and Multisensory Media*. Minneapolis: University of Minnesota Press.

Pallasmaa, Juhani (2009). Quotes from a lecture given in the Darwin Lecture Theatre, UCL, 25 November 2009.

Paterson, Mark (2009). Summary of forthcoming essay on haptic geographies. http://people.exeter.ac.uk/mwdp201/space.html viewed on 28/12/09 (no longer online).

Thomsen, Bodil Marie (2006). 'On the Transmigration of Images: Flesh, Spirit and Haptic Vision in Dreyer's *Jeanne d'Arc* and von Trier's Golden Heart Trilogy'. In C. Claire Thomson (ed.): *Northern Constellations: New Readings in Nordic Cinema*. Norwich: Norvik Press.

Törnqvist, Egil (1995). *Between Stage and Screen: Ingmar Bergman Directs*. Amsterdam: Amsterdam University Press.

Zech, Hanne (2000). *Body and Mind in the Painting: Sense and Sensuality*. Berlin: Neues Museum, VG Bild-Kunst.

Looking and Touching

INNI: Embodied Spectatorship

Rose-Anne Ross

> To touch is always already to reach out, to fondle, to heft, to tap, or to enfold, and always also to understand other people or natural forces as having effectually done so before oneself; if only in the making of the textured object. (Sedgwick 2003: 14)

I hear a low ring and hurry towards the figure silhouetted on the frosted glass; the lock clicks and with an effort I slide the front door open, take the square brown box and scribble my initials onto the electronic signature pad. Back in my room, I carefully unfold a side-flap and pull out a slate grey, shallow box, protected by a thin film of clear plastic, which I tear open with a fingernail; it is heavier than I imagined it would be, and smells like a new book. The words 'Sigur Rós' and 'INNI' are separated by the ghostly double moon image on the cover that I recognise from the concert poster. I lift off the cover, and run my fingers over the shadowy printed images on the inner side. Neatly arranged inside the box, the top paper sleeve holds a 7" vinyl single, and beneath that another cardboard case folds out to reveal four discs: a double CD live album recording of their show at London's Alexandra Palace in 2008, a DVD film of the show, and a short film, Klippa, *in which three dressmakers are shown cutting up the elaborate costumes the band wore into little squares. I remember gazing at the elaborate designs as they walked onto the stage to the sound of our cheers, which I hear once more when I play the first CD. In a small cardboard pocket is one of those squares of material, beneath an enamel pin badge and four photographic prints of the band in the same grainy pearlescent shades of the artwork that lines the box;*

they are stills from the film. I feel the rough square of cotton between my finger and thumb, and pull at a hanging thread loosened by the blades of the scissors. The last item is a shiny, black opaque envelope holding ten pieces of light-sensitive paper within it, with instructions on how to create images from shells, flora and other things that can be arranged on the surface of each sheet before it is left to develop in the sunlight. The contents of this square box are my multimedia, multisensory keepsakes - my experience of what was potentially the band's last show in the UK, materialised.

INNI is a limited-edition box set which was put together to celebrate the release of the film *INNI* (2011), directed by Vincent Morisset and featuring footage of Icelandic group Sigur Rós' two London performances of 2008, and the eponymous accompanying live audio recording of the full set. There has always been a certain textural feel to their music, faithfully translated into the audio, visual and tactile output of the band (artwork, films, clips, packaging, etched vinyl). Many of their songs feature a nonsensical language of sounds, and the rest of their lyrics are incomprehensible to the majority of their international fans who, like me, do not speak Icelandic: thus the human voice returns to sound without significance, contributing to the texture of the overall listening experience. As I researched the making of the film *INNI* and considered the impact of the other contents of the box set, I became increasingly confident that it could serve as a case study for the ongoing discussion around texture, tactility and embodied spectatorship in cinema and other media, with particular reference to the work of Laura U. Marks. Observing the visual style of *INNI*, and handling all the above-mentioned items

INNI: Embodied Spectatorship

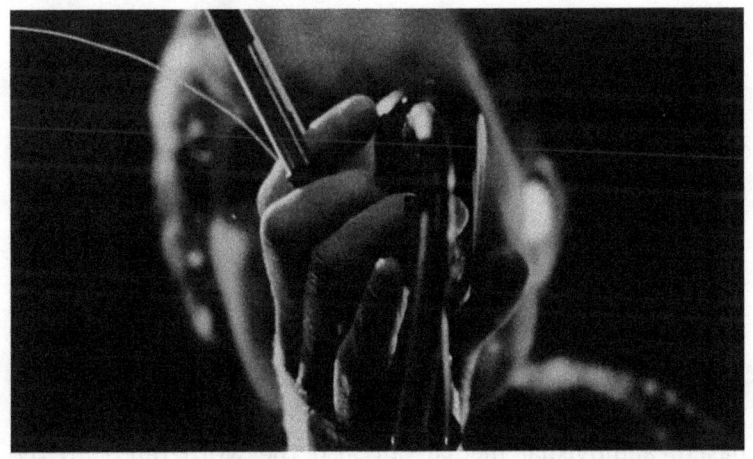

INNI, Vincent Morisset, 2011. Image courtesy of Sigur Rós

included in the box set, convinced me that Sigur Rós and the other artists involved in its production had documented the band's performance in a way that transcends the audiovisual media forms typically used in the music industry, to try to facilitate a more meaningful interaction between spectator and subject. Although I have no evidence that they were aware of the body of works I will be referring to, I do believe that my discussion of one will inform my understanding of and relationship to the other.

I am adhering to Marks' definition of cinematic works in my discussion of *INNI*. In her book *The Skin of the Film* (2000), Marks includes a number of 'marginal viewing situations' within the category of cinema, for 'not only are they all time-based, audiovisual media, but also the word refers to the experience of an audience gathered in a theatre' (Marks 2000: 6). At its simplest, this is precisely what characterises this film, which tries to recreate the experience of being in the audience of the actual live performance, and then gathered spectators again for screenings in cinemas worldwide before being released on DVD. Much of Marks' writing on touch and new media resonates with director Morisset's hopes for the general reception of *INNI*. Speaking to NPR Music about archiving these two shows, he states he wanted to 'focus on the details, give the time to the spectator to appreciate the virtuosity and the effort, understand the cause and effects, *feel* the unique energy of their performance' (Boilen, my emphasis). In Morisset's explanation there is more to the film than a visually pleasing spectacle, and something of its energy is transferred to the body of the viewer. The eye serves as the gateway to sensibility and emotion; in seeing the smaller details the mind understands the entirety of the performance, and the body *feels* an energy from the footage that traverses the screen. Morisset achieves this by bringing the spectator up close to the band – often so close that the frames communicate not a recognisable figure or instrument, but the minute textural details of the surfaces that come into contact with the eye of the lens. The original colours are drained away, leaving pearlescent greyscale tones that foreground shape and surface; then through various post-production procedures, the visually sharp and high definition images are rendered grainy and by turn dreamily indistinct, emphasising texture and suggestion over the usual clean precision of commercial cinema.

The importance of texture is explored more literally by Sigur Rós through the form and presentation of the INNI box set, with its layered contents inviting us to re-experience the live performance of the band through sight and sound, but also through touch, and even smell. The dissemination of pieces of their costumes is rather unusual; when read in the light of recent discussions of touch it appears to be an attempt at bridging the gap between spectator (and/or, in this case, the owner of INNI) and the live show, in a move that is not dissimilar to director Morisset's own experiments with the accompanying film. Constance Classen discusses the impact of this particular sensory encounter in her introduction to the anthology *The Book of Touch*. She affirms the value of touch, commenting that we now live 'in a society of the image,' and that 'the inability to touch the subject matter of the images that surround us […] produces a sense of alienation' (Classen 2005a: 2). In her article 'Touch in the Museum', she looks at the behaviour of visitors in the early museums, and evaluates the nature of touch as a uniting force:

> Sight requires distance in order to function properly, detaching the observer from the observed. Touch, by contrast, annihilates distance and physically unites the toucher and the touched. Handling museum artefacts gave visitors the satisfaction of an intimate encounter. (Classen 2005b: 277)

For Classen, touch facilitates a more meaningful interaction with an object than mere sight can offer. She uses the same vocabulary of closeness as Marks, who reminds us that cinema, asymptotically (Marks 2000: 192), may come ever closer to transcending its audio-visual medium, but (thus far) has never actually been able to let its spectators reach out and touch its filmic subjects. Nevertheless, as Marks argues, haptic or tactile cinema can still 'encourage a bodily relationship between the viewer and the image,' by forging a connection between the two in which a certain exchange of excess energy - although it cannot be seen - is certainly *felt* (Marks 2002: 2).

This idea of an excess of energy corresponds to Brian Massumi's useful designation of 'affect' as 'an ability to affect and be affected. It is a prepersonal intensity corresponding to the passage from one experiential state of the body to another [...] an encounter between the affected body and a second, affecting, body' (Massumi 2004: xvii). It is the energy that Morisset wants the spectators of *INNI* to experience. This definition will serve for all future references to affect, for it leaves enough space for conversation between other theorists and practitioners who play a part in this discussion. One of these former figures is Eve Kosofsky Sedgwick, who argues for the importance of our sense of touch, which mediates reality to us in ways that the other senses cannot. For Sedgwick, 'if texture and affect, touching and feeling seem to belong together,' it is because, '*at whatever scale they are attended to,* both are irreducibly phenomenological' (Sedgwick 2003: 21). Holding that roughly-cut square of costume, feeling the fibres of the material between my fingers, brings me straight back to the night of the live show; in fact, this artefact brings me closer than my memory of standing in the audience could ever do. I watch the film, and see the costumes worn by the band, then the accompanying short film *Klippa* shows them being cut into pieces by the dressmakers, and I experience the thrill of knowing that one of those squares in neat piles that I see on the screen has traversed time and space to be under my hands now. There is something irrefutable about the existence of a past event, and something affirmative of my connection with it, when I can physically hold and *feel* a piece of it in my hands. However, Marks asserts the multisensory nature of cinematic media, and it is in the light of her work that we may regard the entire box set as a vehicle for haptic perception, and Morisset's *INNI* in particular as an exploration of haptic visuality.

Both theorist and practitioner discuss their notion of a cinematic experience in which something beyond the audio-visual reaches out so that the body of the film is in contact with the body of the viewer. Marks calls this tactile experience *haptic*, and she explains her understanding of it in her volume of essays, *Touch: Sensuous Theory and Multisensory Media* (2002). In haptic visuality, 'the eyes themselves function like organs of touch [...] the viewer's body is more obviously involved in the process of seeing than is the case with optical visuality' (Marks 2002: 3). Haptic perception, then, is *embodied* perception – it is 'the way we experience touch both on the surface of and inside our bodies' (2). Her description traces a response to a contact with the skin which is also manifested within the body; Marks implies here that in haptic cinema the eyes are intimately related to the skin. However, if they are to function as organs of touch whatever is being perceived must have a certain discernible visual texture. In the process of seeing this texture the eye encounters something more - an engagement, an interaction – which is not isolated to the optic centre but takes place across and within the whole body. Furthermore, this embodied perception lends a symmetry between viewer and film, 'the [former] responding to the [latter] as to another body and to the screen as another skin' (4).

This inner response to outer stimuli, this inward-moving influence which works symmetrically on and in the two bodies, is a motif which appears in the work of other film theorists. Jennifer M. Barker's *The Tactile Eye: Touch and the Cinematic Experience* explores our relationship with cinema 'as a *close* connection', in which forms of tactility are expressed and shared by viewer and film, in 'a full-bodied engagement with the reality of the world' (Barker 2009: 2). Barker is more explicit about the inward reach of cinematic tactility, asserting that 'as a material mode of perception and expression, then, [it] occurs not only at the skin or the screen, but traverses all the organs of the spectator's body or the film's body' (Barker 2009: 2). On the official Sigur Rós website, Morisset explains that with INNI he wanted to give viewers the experience of 'going "inside" the music', using an expression that echoes the idea of *a move into another body*, one that the viewer is capable of just as much as the film ('About INNI'). Like Barker, he believes in the potential of cinema to profoundly affect the viewer in a specifically embodied way -

indeed, in an interview at the British Film Institute, he uses the insides of the human body to describe the impact of the film, through which he wants to transmit the 'visceral power' of the live shows, to get the audience 'in the guts' (BFI, n.d.). The title of the project means 'inside' in Icelandic, and neatly encapsulates the essence and reach of the film, as well as the organic, parallel affect that is felt within and moves between both bodies: from the viscera of one to the viscera of the other. Barker's book goes on to discuss the deeper significance of touch, which is 'not simply contact, but rather a profound manner of being, a mode through which the body – human or cinematic – presents and expresses itself to the world, and through which it perceives the world as sensible' (Barker 2009: 2). Morisset is clearly sensitive to the potential of a visual live music recording when it harnesses the power of tactile and visceral cinema.

Faced with the task of imbuing the recorded footage of a past performance with the spirit of a live show, the artists behind the INNI project have created a piece of cinema that resonates with both Marks' notion of haptic perception and visuality, and Barker's more explicitly organic conception of the embodied cinematic experience. Although it was initially filmed on HD digital, Morisset rejected the highly polished, visually perfect finish of this format, opting instead for effects that would breathe life into the images. In another interview he explains, 'in (gaining) details and (pristine) quality, you relate to it in the sense of how I view broadcast television – something really cold' (Blau, n.d.). Although there is a similar documentary aspect to recording a live performance, Morisset has gone for something more affective. He transferred the digitally edited footage onto 16mm, projected the analogue images in the studio and recaptured them onto digital, this time experimenting with the grading of the film, as well as moving his hands in front of the projector lens and placing glass prisms and other materials over it to impressionistic effect. During this exercise, he played Sigur Rós' music in the studio. For this final stage, he was 'inspired' by Neil Young's scoring method for *Dead Man*, who improvised on his guitar whilst watching the film for the first time, 'reacting to the images in an intuitive way' (Paste, n.d.). Morisset's use of, quite literally, *handmade* effects to manipulate these images is analogous to the embodied audience response he was aiming for; acting upon his natural, pre-subjective response to the footage and the music, using his hands – so strongly associated with touch and feeling – he translated his own response to the images and the music through his body, channelling the flow of affect between the film and the future spectator.

We do not have to look beyond the recent Nordic film context to find other cinematographers who have similarly transferred footage between different film formats to add texture to their images: Anthony Dod Mantle, filming *Festen* (dir. Thomas Vinterberg, Denmark, 1998) in adherence with the rules of the Dogme 95 movement, converted the digital video footage to very high-speed film stock for theatrical release, explaining that, 'that way, the digital noise starts to speak to the film grain. And I wanted this square, Academy, organic mass to bubble up on the screen' (Kelly 2000: 101-2). Like Morisset, he wanted to give the images life, an 'organic' quality, and to set them apart from the 'really cold' feel of so-called high quality film (Paste, n.d.). Lars von Trier has used inter-format transfer extensively in his work, as explored, for example, by Emma Bell in her article 'The Passions of Lars von

Trier: Madness, Femininity, Film'. When shooting his 1988 film for Danish television, *Medea*, von Trier, one of the founders of the Dogme 95 movement, used this technique and other additional effects 'to emphasise form as integral to content' (Bell 2006: 207). In this particular instance, the 'corrupted' footage is further enhanced 'with theatrical silhouettes, superimpositions and back-projections, creating a psycho-active mise-en-scène that reflects and intensifies Medea's emotional state' (207). Here, Bell posits the affective power of manipulating the surface of the film, demonstrating how complex visuality in film may communicate the emotions played out on the screen, as well as generating an emotional response in the viewer. However, she goes further in her analysis of this 'hyper-realism,' declaring that it has 'an ethical function: to disallow the passive spectatorship and emotional cliché of classical cinema, instead normalising drama by encouraging a sense of immediacy and witness' (209). Hyper-realism, with its demand for interaction between film and spectator, seems analogous to Marks' haptic images and Barker's notion of the 'engagement' facilitated by tactile cinema. Across the work of all these writers and cinematographers there is an emphasis on the importance of the textural qualities of the film's surface in establishing a meaningful and powerful connection between spectator and film.

Morisset uses a number of fixed and handheld cameras for the live show, so that the members of the band are captured up close and from many angles. The audience barely features at all, suggested only as a body of applause that has been edited and restrained so as not to impinge on the music. Even in the few long shots of the band, the stage takes up the entire frame;

Morisset's edit is all about what is happening on stage, taking the spectator right amongst the band and all their equipment for an intimate experience of their performance. The title of the film sums up the aim of everyone involved on-stage and behind the scenes of the project: according to their official site, the 'job' of *INNI* is to convey 'what it feels like to actually watch Sigur Rós play', Morisset employing post-production techniques 'to create an emotional understanding of being in the room with the band and going "inside" the music' ('About Inni', n.d.). Again, the verb *feel* is used; Morisset wants the experience of the film to go beyond mere aural or visual pleasure, to encourage an engagement with the subject matter on an emotional and affective level, and to experience appreciating the music as an inward movement that is more of an instinctive sensation than a physical possibility. His is an attempt to bring the viewer as close as possible to touching the performance, as though there is neither screen mediating nor any distancing lapse of time. Indeed, in an interview with AU Magazine he asserts, 'it will always be disappointing to try to do a photocopy of a live performance [...] Cinema is a medium where you can take the spectator by the hand and bring him to places that would be impossible otherwise' (Harrison 2011). This film is no exact, flat reproduction, but realises the full potential of cinema in opening up a world to be explored which is neither that of the viewer nor that of the film, but which is in some way liminal to both.

INNI's gaze and movement towards the 'inside' are approached through the way the performance is initially filmed. The cameras themselves do not move, only their subjects; there are no panning or zooming shots, nor any handheld shakiness, so that their mediating presence is easily forgotten, and the spectator's gaze may move over the images within the frame at will. This encourages 'haptic looking,' which is 'a labile, plastic sort of look, more inclined to move than to focus' (Marks 2002: 8). The chosen footage tends to favour an unusual perspective, so that our eyes are drawn to the overlooked or rarely seen details of a live performance; we are almost peering over drummer Orri's head and shoulders, which jerk from the impact of his drumsticks making the costume jewels on his hat sparkle; our eyes travel along the gleaming plastic-coated wires taped to the floor, and are dazzled by the trembling reflections on a metal cymbal; our gaze is directed at Kjartan's foot, in polka dot socks and shiny leather shoes, pressing down the pedals of the piano. Between songs, the handmade effects, which echo the stage effects and are inspired by the shape, movement and patterns of natural phenomena, pulsate and crackle across the screen like materialisations of the affect that traverses the screen between our bodies and that of the film.

According to Marks, haptic looking 'tends to rest on the surface of its object rather than to plunge into depth, not to distinguish form so much as to discern texture' (Marks 2002: 8). In Morisset's final cut, the cameras could have been following these remarks to the letter. They are consistently too close to their subjects for the eye to distinguish them in their entirety - yet this haptic looking is only fully facilitated by the post-production work. The grainy black and white footage bears a level of contrast that accentuates the texture of every surface that comes within the frame, be it skin, metal or fabric, smoke, shadow or light. This is particularly noticeable in the closest of the close ups; we glimpse the icy flashes of glitter particles on Jónsi's cheek; we discern the criss-crossing weave of a starched cotton shirt cuff and the grain of the wooden piano lid; we watch the ripple of tendons as Georg's hand works along the frets of his bass guitar. Sometimes the film's subjects are only just within the frame, the rest of the screen a shadowy blank space where the pulsing and unstable effects of Morisset's postproduction methods are much easier to discern. When the shot is far back enough to frame a recognisable figure silhouetted against the pale, flickering atmosphere, the blurred, smoky edges and the deeper shadows seep across the whole screen so that the figures, instruments and musical equipment no longer stand out from their background.

The style of the film '"horizontalizes" figure and ground', achieving a look which, like Barker, I would 'hesitate' to describe as flat, 'because of its richly textured surface' (Barker 2009: 42-3). Although she is discussing in particular how the cinematography of *Pather Panchali* (dir. Satyajit Ray, India, 1955) reflects the film's major theme of a family at one with its surroundings, her analysis resonates with the making of *INNI*, and more generally with Marks' discussion of haptics. Barker remarks that 'figure and ground mingle continuously in [*Panther Panchali*] with the help of cinematic effects that flatten the image into pure surface and texture' (Barker 2009: 42). The live footage of *INNI* has been manipulated in the same way; it now consists of images that Marks would call haptic. 'Haptic images invite the viewer to dissolve his or her subjectivity in the close and bodily contact with the image [...] The viewer is called on to fill in the gaps in the image, engage with the traces the image leaves. By interacting up close with an image, close enough that figure and ground commingle, the viewer gives up her own sense of separation from an image'

(Marks 2002: 13).

The band members are not foregrounded as four individuals, but are as much a part of the light, shadow and texture of each frame as their surroundings and the post-production techniques. And as Marks emphasises, the viewer, too, is moved to feel at one with the images, to be moved inwardly and let the images move inward. INNI, though, goes further in incorporating material and textural elements into its packaging. Just as the film visualises the affects it shares with the viewer, the multimedia package seduces the receiver into a multisensory relationship with the remnants and traces of the live show. If, as Marks puts it, the audiovisual text can only ever gesture to 'its own asymptotic, caressing relation to the real' (2000: 192), INNI materialises that caress in its provision of fabric from the show – fabric now touching, and touched by, the same hands that reach up, in the film, from the crowd towards the band.

Author's Comment

This was written for the final year/MA module 'STUFF: Media and Materiality in European Culture'; as a masters student, I had to write an essay on a topic of my own choice. Inspired by the contemporary media theory of Laura U. Marks, I decided to look at haptic cinema in more depth, and to bring my own experience into a dialogue with the texts I'd enjoyed reading. A recent release from an absolute favourite band was perfectly timed, and provided plenty of scope for discussion. As my graduate degree primarily involved studying literature and literary theory, exploring the history of the moving image and its potential for engaging with all the senses of the spectator was invigorating, and has changed the way I watch film. I am also grateful for being introduced to Nordic film, which has really whetted my appetite!

If I were to revisit this essay, I'd want to expand it and talk much more about the audio content - perhaps in an electronic piece of work, in the sprirt of Marks, in which I could employ audio/visual examples to illustrate the sort of experience I am discussing. It would also be interesting to compare other filmic recordings of musical performances to trace the development of the relationship between film, music and haptics.

This essay was previously published in *Scandinavica: An International Journal of Scandinavian Studies*, 51:1, 2012.

References

'About Inni'. http://www.sigur-ros.co.uk/band/disco/inni/. Accessed 17 April 2012.

Barker, Jennifer M. (2009). *The Tactile Eye: Touch and the Cinematic Experience*. Berkeley: University of California Press.

Bell, Emma (2006). 'The Passions of Lars von Trier: Madness, Femininity, Film.' In Thomson, C. Claire (ed.) *Northern Constellations: New Readings in Nordic Cinema*. Norwich: Norvik Press.

BFI: In Conversation. 'Sigur Rós: Inni'. http://www.bfi.org.uk/live/video/825. Accessed 19 April 2012.

Blau, Max. 'Vincent Morisset's Sigur Rós.' *Paste Magazine* 19. http://mplayer.pastemagazine.com/issues/week-19/articles#article=/issues/week-19/articles/inni-vincent-morissets-sigur-ros-doc. Accessed 17 April 2012.

Boilen, Bob (2011). 'Sigur Rós, Inni.' *NPR Magazine: All Songs Considered* http://www.npr.org/blogs/allsongs/2011/09/16/140471649/first-watch-sigur-r-s-inni. Accessed 17 April 2012.

Classen, Constance (2005a). 'Fingerprints: Writing About Touch.' In Classen, Constance (ed.) : *The Book of Touch*. Oxford: Berg.

Classen, Constance (2005b). 'Touch in the Museum.' In Classen, Constance (ed.) : *The Book of Touch*. Oxford: Berg.

Harrison, Daniel (2011). 'Shooting Sigur Rós.' *AU Magazine.* http://iheartau.com/2011/10/shooting-sigur-ros/. Accessed 17 April 2012.

INNI (Vincent Morisset 2011)

Kelly, Richard (2000). *The Name of this Book is Dogme95.* London: Faber and Faber.

Marks, Laura U. (2000). *The Skin of the Film: Intercultural Cinema, Embodiment, and the Senses.* Durham and London: Duke University Press.

Marks, Laura U. (2002). *Touch: Sensuous Theory and Multisensory Media.* Minneapolis: University of Minnesota Press.

Massumi, Brian (2004). 'Notes on the Translation and Acknowledgements.' In Deleuze, Gilles and Félix Guattari: *A Thousand Plateaus: Capitalism and Schizophrenia.* London: Continuum. Sedgwick,

Sedgwick, Eve Kosofsky (2003). *Touching Feeling: Affect, Pedagogy, Performativity.* Durham and London: Duke University Press.

Tancred Ibsen and the Norwegian Film Industry

Clare Glenister

This essay analyses Tancred Ibsen's film *Den hemmelighetsfulle leiligheten* (The Mysterious Apartment, 1948) with reference to the representation of secrets, lies and mystery. In addition, it places the life and work of Tancred Ibsen within the context of Norwegian film history up to and including 1948.

Of the cinematic output of the Nordic countries, it is perhaps that of Norway that is least known internationally. The towering figures of Ingmar Bergman, Aki Kaurismäki and Lars von Trier have placed Sweden, Finland and Denmark firmly on the cinematic world map, but Norway lacks such a figure. A front-running candidate for this position might be Tancred Ibsen, whose output of more than twenty films remains the largest of any feature film director in Norway. A reason for his relative obscurity might be the paucity of the availability of his work. Whereas the whole of Bergman's, Kaurismäki's and von Trier's output is available on comprehensibly subtitled DVDs, at the time of writing this is true of only a small fraction of Ibsen's oeuvre, namely *Fant* (Tramp, 1937), *Den hemmelighetsfulle leiligheten*, *To mistenkelige personer* (Two Suspects, 1950) and *Vildanden* (The Wild Duck, 1963). I do not recall ever having seen a Tancred Ibsen film shown on British television.

So who was Tancred Ibsen? The surname is, of course, famous in connection with Norwegian dramatic output in the second half of the nineteenth century. Tancred Ibsen (1893-1978) was the grandson not only of Henrik Ibsen but also of Bjørnsterne Bjørnson, and his father Sigurd, a diplomat, and mother Bergliot (neé Bjørnson) were both writers. As the 'double grandson' (doppeltbarnebarnet) of two literary geniuses and the son of a successful diplomat and author, it might have been expected of Tancred to follow his famous forebears into a literary career. At school, however, he was not an academic success. In his autobiography he writes in a light-hearted style of the difficulties he had in learning the alphabet and it has been suggested that he was dyslexic (Ibsen 1976: 12-14). Did these early problems with literacy nurture the development of a visual language? Not to be defeated, he resolved to take up a career which neither of his grandfathers could have done: he joined the military and became a pilot. His flying career was distinguished and in 1920 he founded A/S Aero, a commercial airline company (www.europeanairlines.no).

How did Tancred Ibsen evolve from pilot to film director? In 1923, he sold A/S Aero and accompanied his wife, the actress Lillebel Krohn, to New York, where she was to appear in the play *Peer Gynt* (Henrik Ibsen 1867). While Lillebel rehearsed, Tancred went to the movies, and on seeing D.W. Griffith's *Orphans of the Storm* (1921) decided that film could be 'art' and resolved to get involved in the moviemaking business. He gained practical experience by working as an electrician and handyman on King Vidor's *His Hour* (1924) and Victor Sjöström/Seastrom's *Tower of Lies* (1925). For a time he was a scriptwriter for MGM but none of his scripts was produced. He was determined, though, to apply his newly-gained experience to the making of Norwegian films, to 'Ibsenize' cinema. He and Lillebel moved back to Norway (Iversen 1993:

7-10).

What was the situation with Norwegian cinema at this time? By 1930, film production in Norway had had a somewhat chequered history and was emerging from a period of stagnation. The first public film screening of moving pictures in Norway, indeed in Scandinavia, had been in 1896. This new form of entertainment became hugely popular and by 1904 five cinemas had been established in Christiania (the capital city, now Oslo). In 1905, film played an important role in building up national identity after Norway's independence from the Union with Sweden, the footage of King Haakon's arrival in Christiania being a much quoted example (shot by Hugo Hermansen and currently available on the Norwegian Royal family's website). Fictional films, particularly the popular Danish erotic melodramas, were seen by some as being rather too much of a good thing, however. They came under the scrutiny of groups such as the Society for the Promotion of Morality (Foreningen til Sædelighetens Fremme) and in 1913, the Film Theatres Act (*kinoloven*) was passed. Under this Act, cinemas and film showings came under the control of the local municipalities (*kommuner*). They bought out the private owners and used the (often considerable) box office profits to finance projects for the public good. There was no obligation to plough revenue back into film production. Some enterprising individuals were willing and able to sponsor film production privately, but the results were usually 'one hit wonders' due to lack of sustained finance. In 1916, Peter Lykke-Seest established Christiania Film Compagni and directed six films (now lost) between 1917 and 1919. The earliest surviving Norwegian feature film is Halfdan Nobel Roede's *Under forvandlingens lov* (Under the Law of Change,

1911) (see Popplewell 1972, Cowie 1992, Iversen 1998).

In 1920, however, there was something of a breakthrough (*filmgjennombrudd*) when some privately-produced films were subsidised by the municipalities. Among these was *Fante-Anne* (Anne the Tramp, 1920), directed by Rasmus Breistein, the first Norwegian film to be adapted from literature. It set a trend for Norwegian film style, being shot on location in the countryside. Of the twenty-nine films produced in the 1920s, twenty-four had rural settings due, perhaps, to the paucity of studio facilities in Norway at that time. Notwithstanding, at a time of industrialisation, the new urban-dwelling audiences liked to see images of the countryside at the cinema. This success was not without a sting in the tail, however. Entertainment tax (*underholdingsskatt*) was introduced and production dropped (Iversen 1998).

When Tancred Ibsen arrived back in Norway he put his plan to 'Norwegianise' cinema into practice. In 1931 he secured the rights to Oskar Braathen's play *Den store barnedåpen* (The Big Christening, 1925) and produced it as the first Norwegian 'talkie', with leading actor Einar Sissener as co-director. It broke with the recently established tradition of rural settings, deploying instead working class characters within an urban industrial environment. 1932 saw another breakthrough for Norwegian cinema – the establishment of Norsk Film A/S with studio facilities at Jar, a suburb of Oslo. Ibsen's success with *Den store barnedåpen* led to five more films in Norway and seven in Sweden. These included *Synnøve Solbakken* (1934), based on Bjørnsen's 1857 novel, and starring Victor Sjöström. *To levende og en død* (Two Living and One Dead, 1937) and *Fant* (1937) for Norsk Film A/S returned to the rural settings of the

From Den *hemmelighetsfulle leiligheten* (The Mysterious Apartment, Tancred Ibsen, 1948)

films of the 1920s (Iversen 1993). In his autobiography, Ibsen writes about the location shooting in *Fant* as being a matter of expediency, because no back-projection nor other studio tricks were available (Ibsen 1976: 156-7). This gives the film an 'authentic' feel which it might not have had, had studio facilities been more readily available. (It can be noted at this stage that, apart from a few 'library' type establishing shots, *Den hemmelighetsfulle leiligheten* is shot entirely in the studio, back projections included). The 1930s have been labelled 'The Golden Age' (*gullalderen*) of Norwegian cinema when films such as Tancred Ibsen's *Gjest Baardsen* (1939) and Leif Sinding's *De vergeløse* (The Defenceless, 1939) could compete with American ones in the domestic market.

During the German occupation of Norway in World War II, the showing of American and British films was forbidden. The municipal cinemas showed German newsreels, alongside home grown comedies and other light-hearted features. Production continued at Norsk Film A/S (under German control) and Ibsen's *Tørres Snørtevold* (1940) and *Den farlige leken* (The Dangerous Game, 1942) were made there. However, in August 1943, due to his military background, Ibsen was arrested, transported out of Norway and imprisoned in Schildberg (Ostrzeszów) and Luckenwalde until the end of the war (Ibsen 1976: 203-228; oflag21c.ovh.org).

During the post-war recovery period, cinema attendance rose to a record 8 million in Oslo and 2 million in Trondheim (Iversen 1998: 121). Entertainment tax rose also but some of the revenue found its way into Norwegian film subsidy. As in other parts of the world, the experience of World War II contributed a wealth of new stories for feature films. In

Norway, the 'occupation drama' dominated for many years, such as Toralf Sandø's *Englandsfarene* (We Leave for England, 1946) and Titus Vibe-Müller and Jean Dréville's docu-drama *Kampen om tungtvannet* (The Battle for Heavy Water, 1948). Norsk Film A/S had produced no feature films since 1945 (due to lack of finance) but in 1948 it became a joint state and municipal concern and film production resumed. Its first production was Ibsen's *Den hemmelighetsfulle leiligheten* (Cowie 1992, Iversen 1998).

In this film, adapted from the novella by Kristian Elster junior, it was Ibsen's idea to let the audience into the thoughts of the characters. The use of voice-over monologues, he reasoned, would reveal more of their inner truth than by the use of spoken dialogue (Ibsen 1976: 238). According to Gunnar Iversen, the post-war period was one of restless experimentation for Ibsen. He was searching for a new style and wanted to try out modernistic forms. A similar (albeit later) experiment in modernism was Erik Løchen's *Jakten* (1959) (Iversen 1993: 23).

Den hemmelighetsfulle leiligheten has a complex temporal arrangement employing flash-backs and non-consecutive narrative, which had been a feature of film technique since the silent era. Indeed, Victor Sjöström's *Körkarlen* (The Phantom Carriage, 1921) had employed just such a technique. In *Den hemmelighetsfulle leiligheten*, the chronological order of the plot runs as follows (scenes labelled alphabetically):

(A) As a boy, Byråsjefen (The Office Boss) has found a secret compartment in his parents' bureau containing explicit love letters. He reads them and is shocked.

(B) At the theatre cloakroom where she works, Dora Danielsen (Dot) meets the former apartment owner and becomes his mistress. She spends evenings in the apartment.

(C) At the boarding house where he lives, Byråsjefen plays cards with his friends who persuade him to buy the apartment that has become available (complete with furnishings, maid and parrot) due to the previous owner's death from oyster poisoning.

(D) Byråsjefen views the apartment and decides to buy it due, partly, to his curiosity about the bureau and what it might contain.

(E) He has the apartment cleaned and tries to remove all traces of previous (deceased) owner.

(F) On the tram, Byråsjefen reminisces about recent events.

(G) He moves into the apartment and discovers explicit love letters hidden in the bureau. They are from a woman called Dot. He is disturbed by the parrot's mimicry of the previous owner.

(H) In the office, he considers what sort of woman Dot might be. He pays little attention to his client and leaves early.

(I) At night, Dot tries to get into the apartment to retrieve her letters. She has a key but there is a chain on the door.

(J) Next morning she visits to ask Byråsjefen to look for the letters. He pretends not to have found them but promises to contact her should he do so. She visualises her previous life in the apartment. She tells him she has come for the pills that the previous owner had given her. He was going to commit suicide and she was to follow but she forgot the pills. Byråsjefen tells her that he died of oyster poisoning in Paris. She educates him about the paintings. He takes away her key and promises to look for the letters.

(K) In her room, Dot talks to the photograph of her former lover.

(L) At the office, Byråsjefen starts to notice the secretary's attractiveness. The secretaries notice a change in his behaviour. He resolves to burn the letters and not see Dot again.

(M) On the tram, Byråsjefen decides to send Dot her letters.

(N) In the apartment at night, Byråsjefen starts to burn the letters, then writes that she must come and get them.

(O) In her room, Dot reads his letter.

(P) Dot comes to collect the letters but Byråsjefen gives her only some of them so that he can invite her back. She educates him about the music. She leaves when one of his friends telephones, inviting himself and the other friends to a party.

(Q) In her room, Dot reads his second letter. She is angry and wishes Byråsjefen dead.

(R) Byråsjefen goes shopping to buy things for her return visit.

(S) She visits and resolves to live there. He returns her key and clumsily suggests that she become his lover. She slaps him.

(T) Byråsjefen visits the theatre cloakroom and proposes marriage to Dot. They go to a café. She accepts in order to get back into the apartment.

(U) Byråsjefen throws a dinner party for his three friends. He educates them about the paintings and music. Dot charms them on her way out to the theatre. Byråsjefen tells the story of Dot's meeting with the deceased owner as if it were his own. He has taken on his persona.

(V) On the tram the secretaries gossip about Byråsjefen and he reminisces about the party.

(W) Byråsjefen (wearing the deceased lover's dressing gown) and Dot put the letters back into the bureau with the photograph of the previous owner. The parrot laughs...

The order in which the scenes appear in the film is, however:

(F), (C), (F), (D), (A), (D), (F), (E), (F), (G), (H), (I), (J), (B), (J), (K), (L), (M), (N), (O), (P), (B), (P), (Q), (R), (S) ,(T), (V), (U), (V), (W)

What is the point of this? Why not just enact the story? The use of flash-back, which in this case includes description by the characters in voice-over monologue, allows for personal elaboration by them. Indeed, there is no guarantee that they are telling the truth. They are acting as narrators and as such are not necessarily reliable. For example in (U), Byråsjefen repeats the story of Dot's meeting with her former lover as told by her in (P) as if it were his own story. On this occasion we know that he is lying, but how are we to know that her original story is true? Is it more likely to be true because it is 'enacted' as well as 'told'. Are 'actions' truer than 'words' according to the language of the film?

With regard to the so-called truth, from the outset the story is told through the eyes and in the mind of Byråsjefen. We accept him as the focalizer, as the controller of our reading of the events. This is because the use of voice-over takes us into his mind as was Ibsen's intention. It is as if we are reading a work of narrative fiction written in the first person. We hear him in the first person but see him, as it were, in the third person. We hear him on the inside and see and hear him from the outside. We know he is a liar because he tells Dot that he has not read the letters but we know that he has. Crucially, when Dot arrives, we read her as a character in his story but at some point doubt sets in and we begin to suspect that she might be the focalizer and controller of the story. So we might say that persuading us that we are watching Byråsjefen's story is a kind of lie too, because what we are actually seeing is Dot's story. When we hear her voice-over for the first time in (K) we hear a menacing tone. She cannot bear the thought of an 'art imbecile' living in the apartment. In (Q) we get the impression that she can be truly venomous, the reverse of the sweet exterior that Byråsjefen has fallen for.

> Byråsjefen (VO reading letter): If it is convenient, you can come around to pick up several letters. I found them in another drawer.[1]
>
> Dot (VO in a menacing tone): He has been going through his [2] drawers. He has found my letters! And probably other things too. Things of his!
>
> Dot (Speech): I wish he would die!

Another example of the use of use of voice-over is in the second part of (T), where the couple sit in 'silence' in the café. In the first part of (T), Byråsjefen has proposed marriage to Dot and is, presumably, awaiting an answer. We hear the thoughts of each of them in turn, an impossible situation in real life, but one which ought to fulfil Ibsen's intention of revealing the characters' inner truth:

> Byråsjefen (VO): I am sitting here...Quite relaxed. With a woman I have proposed to.
>
> Dot (VO): He wants to marry me! Even though I was his lady friend. Even though I hit him!
>
> Byråsjefen (VO): With her...I want to learn how to live, be like everyone else! She must forgive me!
>
> Dot (VO): I didn't hit him when he asked if I wanted a key. I knew he would never marry me.
>
> Byråsjefen (VO): She loved him! But he is dead...I will give her everything I am capable of.

> Dot (VO): If I marry him, it'll be my apartment. I can be there... among all the furniture, paintings and books. Everything he loved so dearly! He is quite handsome...I am sure he is kind. (Speech): Cheers!
>
> Byråsjefen (Speech): Cheers!

The paradox is, that by revealing the characters' 'inner truth', we are exposed to their lies. At times, this has a disturbing effect. A significant part of cinema-going experience is about identifying with the characters and in this case that identification can feel uncomfortably close to home. Nonetheless, by revealing the characters' lies, Ibsen is giving us dramatic truth. All this could be achieved without the use of voice-over, of course. Film is good at showing a character acting in one way in one scene and lying about it in another. With voice-over we can get 'truth' and 'lies' simultaneously.

Another kind of lying is hypocrisy. Byråsjefen's initial distaste for the apartment and its contents is reversed in the light of his growing attraction for Dot, and the possibility that he might come to possess her along with everything else. The paintings and music, for example, he comes to appreciate with her encouragement:

> Byråsjefen: Have you ever seen blue grass?
> Dot: Yes, but you have to be an artist or understand art to see it.
> ...
> Byråsjefen: Do you really like this music?
>
> Dot: Can't you hear how sophisticated it is? The voices countering each other? The solo in contrast to the orchestra?

Byråsjefen: Maybe so. Now you come to mention it.

He is happy to share this 'appreciation' with his friends and pass it off as genuine:

> (Looking at the painting of three nudes)
> Doctor: Have a look at this! How appalling! What an anatomy! That's not the anatomy I studied! [...]
> Lawyer: Have you ever seen such colours? [...]
> Byråsjefen: You are blind. You can't see.
> Friends: Are we blind?
> Byråsjefen: The grass isn't green. It is blue, gentlemen.

So much for secrets and lies. What about mystery? First, there is the mystery of the box of pills. This is found hidden in the bureau along with the letters. Dot says that she was unaware of the previous owner's death from oyster poisoning because she had been taken to hospital. Why? She believed that he had committed suicide and it was her intention to follow suit. For this purpose, he had given her a silver box of pills but she had left them behind. None of this is fully explained and after she has married Byråsjefen and got herself back into the apartment, one cannot help but feel concerned for his safety, especially as she has already pronounced that she wishes him dead and insists on displaying the photograph of her former lover in the bureau. I have suggested that the presentation of Byråsjefen as the main character is misleading, a 'lie'. On first viewing, we accept this presentation from the outset because we have no reason to think otherwise but after the appearance of Dot, and as the film draws to a close, some confusion sets in. On subsequent viewing it becomes clear that Dot is the controlling influence and Byråsjefen is the victim. Indeed, one could make a case for the story's primary influence being the deceased. After all, it is his taste that overwhelms the milieu of the film. In spite of Byråsjefen's efforts, he is still 'present' in the apartment through the paintings and the music and the smell of the cigarettes 'I was only allowed to smoke these' says Dot. This 'absent presence' brings to mind films such as *Rebecca* (Alfred Hitchcock, 1940) in which housekeeper Mrs Danvers keeps 'alive' her previous employer by the fetishistic preservation of her things. There is a touch of the 'Mrs Danvers' about the maid in *Den hemmelighetsfulle leiligheten* but she turns out to be a benign figure in comparison. Similarly, in plays such as Henrik Ibsen's *Hedda Gabler* (1891) and Anton Chekhov's *Three Sisters* (1901), deceased fathers (Generals Gabler and Prozorov) exert their influence from beyond the grave.

Another mystery concerns the film's genre. What is it? In some respects it is a comedy. There are some delightful moments not least involving the parrot which maintains the presence of the previous owner by imitating him. In fact, it is the parrot that has 'the last laugh'. The voice of the parrot is a living manifestation of him. The parrot can be read, though, as menacing, as a ghostly presence exacerbating the unease Byråsjefen feels about the apartment at first. He feels that he will never get rid of the smell and ambience of the deceased but when Dot turns up, Byråsjefen convinces himself that it is her ambience so he has to have her in order to complete the picture. So is it a romance? From his point of view it is. His fear of women, as pointed out by his Doctor friend in (C) (and likely to have been initiated by his boyhood reading of the erotic letters), is dispelled along with his other restrictive prejudices, such as his aversion to modern art and music. Here the film could be seen as a lesson in appreciation of culture. The mise-en-scène incorporates paintings by Norwegian expressionist Kai Fjell (1907-1989). There is a visual joke in (G) when Byråsjefen sits in a chair and unwittingly adopts a pose just like the one in the cubist portrait adjacent to it. The diegetic gramophone music, specially composed by Gunnar Sønstevold (1912-1991) in the style of Bartok or Stravinsky is similarly discussed. So have we entered the genre of art education?

So we have a romantic (black) comedy mystery with a bit of cultural education, possibly. The majority of Norwegian films of this period were concerned with the Occupation and *Den hemmelighetsfulle leiligheten* could be read politically as an allegory of collaboration. Dot's 'home' is under Occupation and she is prepared to compromise her integrity to get it back. This may not have been Ibsen's intention but it is not the intention that is significant, rather the reading. Perhaps this is stretching things a bit far.

1948 saw the release of more than 2000 films worldwide, including Ingmar Bergman's *Hamnstad* (Port of Call) and *Musik i mörker* (Music in Darkness), John Huston's *The Treasure of the Sierra Madre* and *Key Largo*, Michael Powell and Emeric Pressburger's *The Red Shoes*, Vittorio De Sica's *Ladri di biciclette* (Bicycle Thieves) and Laurence Olivier's *Hamlet*. In such company, it is not surprising that neither *Den hemmelighetsfulle leiligheten* nor the five other Norwegian films released that year received much attention at international level. At the time, Tancred Ibsen was perplexed that neither audiences nor critics were impressed with his idea of exposing the characters' inner thoughts. Meanwhile

David Lean's *Brief Encounter* (1945), with its extensive use of voice-over, had been hailed as an innovative masterpiece. Ibsen's film had some support, however. French director Georges Huisman said in an interview that it was 'a significant work' (Ibsen 1976: 238). A significant work, perhaps, that awaits the time for its secrets to be revealed and appreciated.

Den hemmelighetsfulle leiligheten is full of experimentation. The use of voiceover to show the inner life of the characters, the play with chronology and the departure from traditional location shooting all add up to a transition from the pictorial to the psychological in Norwegian filmmaking. Tancred Ibsen was active through some of the most important times in Norwegian film history, through its golden age and the journey to the modern era. In common with his distinguished grandfathers he was a fine storyteller, one whose chosen medium allowed for a kind of narrative sophistication those two gentlemen could scarcely have contemplated.

Author's Comment

I am a mature student who spent thirty years as a classical musician. I began a BA in Scandinavian Studies at UCL in 2009 and am due to graduate in 2013. I took Nordic Cinema as an option in the second year, as it suited my interest both in cinema and in all things Nordic. One of the films we studied was Knut Erik Jensen's documentary *Heftig og Begeistret* (Cool and Crazy, 2001) which is set in Berlevåg, Finnmark in the far north of Norway. In July 2012 I was able to visit this extraordinary place and hope to return before too long.

I first became aware of the work of Tancred Ibsen through his film version of Henrik Ibsen's *Vildanden* (The Wild Duck) and was intrigued to find out more. I was delighted to discover the high quality and level of innovation of his work.

Since writing this essay, I have read more on the history of Norwegian cinema, notably material in Norwegian, and have made some revisions which reflect this. I would love to gain access to the remainder of Tancred Ibsen's work, that which is not commercially available at present.

I have just returned from my year abroad, which I spent at Universitetet i Oslo, where I took courses in Norwegian language, Ibsen Studies and Film Studies. I visited and worked as a volunteer at film festivals in Oslo, Tromsø and Haugesund. It is encouraging to see the high level of input, both creative and financial, being invested in Norwegian cinema today.

1. Translation taken from film subtitles.
2. Italics refer to the deceased previous owner of the apartment, Dot's former lover.

References

Cowie, Peter (1992). *Scandinavian Cinema: A Survey of the Films and Film-makers of Denmark, Finland, Iceland, Norway and Sweden.* London: Tantivy Press.

Derry, T.K. (1973). *A History of Modern Norway 1814-1972.* London: Clarendon Press.

European Airlines (n.d.). 'Tancred Ibsen'. http://www.europeanairlines.no/tancred-ibsen-and-as-aero/ (Accessed 06/01/11)

Evensmo, Sigurd (1992). *Det Store Tivoli.* Oslo: Gyldendal Norsk Forlag.

Griffiths, Tony (2004). *Scandinavia: at War with Trolls.* New York: Palgrave Macmillan.

Grønlie, Tore (1995). 'The Years since 1945'. In Danielsen, R., Dyrvik, S., Grønlie, T., Helle, K., Hovland, E.: *Norway. A History from the Vikings to Our Own Times.* Translated by Michael Drake. Oslo: Scandinavian University Press.

Hayward, Susan (2007). *Cinema Studies. The Key Concepts.* London: Routledge.

Hölaas, Odd (1949). *The World of the Norsemen.* London: The Bond Publishing Company.

Ibsen, Tancred (1976): *Tro det eller ei.* Oslo: Gyldendal Norsk Forlag.

Iversen, Gunnar (1993). *Tancred Ibsen og den norske gullalderen.*

Oslo: Den norske filminstitutt.

Iversen, Gunnar (1998). 'Norway'. In Soila, Tytti, Astrid Söderbergh-Widding and Gunnar Iversen: *Nordic National Cinemas*. London: Routledge.

Kongehuset.no (Norwegian Royal Family online). Videoarkiv. *Kong Haakon VII ankommer Christiania* (King Haakon VII arrives in Christiania, Hugo Hermansen, 1905. Available at http://www.kongehuset.no/c74266/videoarkiv/vis.html?strukt_tid=74266. Accessed 11.9.2012.

Larsen, Karen (1948). *A History of Norway*. Princeton: University Press.

Monaco, James (2009). *How to Read a Film. Movies, Media and Beyond*. Oxford: Oxford University Press.

Nordstrom, Byron J. (2000). *Scandinavia since 1500*. Minneapolis: University of Minnesota Press.

Popplewell, Ronald G. (1972). *Norway*. London: Earnest Benn Ltd.

Store Norske Leksikon (1979). 'Tancred Ibsen'.

'Tancred Ibsen'. In Andersen, Alf G. (ed.): *500 som preget Norge. Norske kvinner og menn i det 20 århundre*. (1999) Oslo: N.W. Damm and Søn A/S.

Dreyer, Dogme and the Real

Martin Butcher

This essay explores film and the expression of reality. It offers a comparison and critique of the cinematic techniques of Carl Theodor Dreyer and the Dogme Brethren Lars von Trier and Thomas Vinterberg, with particular reference to the films *La Passion de Jeanne d'Arc* (The Passion of Joan of Arc, Dreyer, 1928), *Vredens dag* (Day of Wrath, Dreyer, 1943), *Ordet* (The Word, Dreyer, 1955), *Gertrud* (Dreyer, *1964*), *Festen* (The Celebration, Vinterberg, 1998) and *Idioterne* (The Idiots, von Trier, 1998).

> Everything depends on the 'right' balance between the realistic tendency and the formative tendency; and the two tendencies are well balanced if the latter does not try to overwhelm the former but eventually follows to lead. (Kracauer 1960: 39)

It is something of a cliché that all films are about the making of films. To make a film is to explore the ways in which cinematic techniques can be used to portray or express a narrative or subject. The film director has at his or her disposal a range of technical tools to assist in fashioning the end-product. The question arises whether these aids enhance or detract from the representation of the film's subject. At the most basic level all cinematic representation involves mediation between the subject and the viewer, because film cannot be made without a camera and it is through the camera's recording facility that the film is created in the first instance. (It is now possible to create a 'film' using only computer-generated imagery; for the purposes of this essay I am discounting that facility.) The 'raw material', as Dreyer called it, is captured by the camera and is mediated by its capabilities and its limitations. The film-maker may opt to employ every technical and other facility available; he or she may use only some of these aids; or he or she may be ascetic and interpose as few of them as possible between the raw material and the viewer, essentially aiming to reduce filming to a record made just by the camera.

The increasingly sophisticated cinematic technology of film raised much debate about the nature of film, what film should be, whether cinema is an art-form, and how it represents its subject-matter. Notable names in the field of film theory, such as Rudolf Arnheim (1957), André Bazin (1967) and Siegfried Kracauer (1960), argued their case for and against realism, expressionism and the purpose of film. Without producing manifestos or sets of rules, they preached what films ought to be and how they should be crafted. 'Art in the age of mechanical reproduction' (as Walter Benjamin called it, 1935) has diversified and proliferated so greatly, and the concept of art has become so multifarious, that the theorists' prescriptive attitudes can seem outdated and the issues merely academic. However, the superficial spectacle (modern-day cinema of attractions) producible by technology has provoked and kept ongoing debate about realism, illusion, methods of expression and art and non-art cinema very much alive. The Dogme 95 Brotherhood and their 1995 Manifesto and Vow of Chastity with their back-to-basics prescriptions are, in the context of Nordic cinema, the most celebrated protagonists on one side of the argument. In this essay I shall examine the film-making approaches of two Dogme Brothers, Lars von Trier and

Thomas Vinterberg (with particular reference to their films *Idioterne* and *Festen*), and of Carl Theodor Dreyer as an expressionist filmmaker (with reference in particular to his films *La Passion de Jeanne d'Arc*, *Vredens dag*, *Ordet* and *Gertrud*) with the aim of comparing and contrasting their cinematic methods and drawing some conclusions about filmic representation and film as an art.

In this analysis the role and attitude of the director are primary determinants. Although he acknowledged that film was a collective activity, Carl Dreyer was in no doubt about the director's role in making a film:

> within the collective, the director is and always will be – and has to be – the driving and inspiring force. He is the man behind the work . . . It is he who stamps the film with this inexplicable something that is called style. (Dreyer quoted in Skoller 1973: 178)

Such an approach marks him out as what would come to be known as an auteur, but apart from his determination to impose his own style on his work, the most significant feature is the commitment to control. Dreyer chose to work to texts by other authors, and in the cinematic representation of these texts he exercised absolute, even ruthless, control. This was for him essential to create the illusion which would convince the viewer of the truth of the representation. For Dreyer this striving after truthfulness was the only way to create film which is art. The director's role must be interpretative, and all the expressive elements of film must be used and refined to integrate form and meaning. The material of the mise-en-scène is raw material; it is not sufficient in itself to portray the essence of the text. Dreyer mediates the image of the subject-matter in form and in substance both in setting up the mise-en-scène and in the editing process. He adopts an expressive approach: every element in the frame must be made to contribute to the meaning of the narrative, whether literally or figuratively; he excludes all excess and superfluity, and reduces the mise-en-scène, the dialogue and the sound to the essential minimum. He would, for example, instruct his crew to build a set and furnish it; then he would strip it of everything he deemed inessential or non-contributory. He is said to have built rooms which were never actually used in shooting. This approach, which he called abstraction, is a set of self-imposed limitations, the constraints of form restricting the expression in order to create art by refinement. And Dreyer was in no doubt that in his films he was seeking to create works of art, and that it was through art that he could portray reality:

> The cinematic representation of reality should be true, but purged of trivial details. It should also be realistic, but transformed in the director's mind in such a way that it becomes poetry. It is not the things in reality that the director should be interested in, but rather the spirit in and behind the things. For realism in itself is not art. The realities must be forced into a form of simplification and abbreviation and in a purified state reappear in a kind of timeless psychological realism. (Dreyer quoted in Skoller 1973: 184)

The Dogme Brotherhood would have endorsed this aspiration to 'truth' in the cinematic representation of reality. They declare: 'My supreme goal is to force the truth out of my characters and settings', but they appear to have felt that art impeded realisation of this goal: 'I am no longer an artist. I swear to refrain from creating a "work", as I regard the instant as more important than the whole.' (The Dogme 95 Manifesto and VOW OF CHASTITY, 1995). Their purge involved the prohibition of all but the most basic technological tools rather than 'trivial details'. In this it could be argued that they confused artifice with art as the obstacles to truth. They too were interested in the inner reality of people and things, but their method was to prompt it to emerge by stripping away inhibition, superficiality, convention, hypocrisy, everything that covered the true self, or inner 'idiot'. The one approach might be likened to sophisticated portrait or domestic painting (the Dutch masters, Whistler and Hammershøi are referred to in connection with Dreyer's compositional art); the other might be compared to naïve painting. Whatever the differences, it is illuminating that Dreyer and the Dogme Brotherhood both use language with spiritual and religious connotations to describe how they will create their visions of reality. All three were engaged in a mission.

Much time could be spent, perhaps fruitlessly, assessing the seriousness with which the Dogme 95 Manifesto and the Vow of Chastity were intended, whether they were simply a clever publicity stunt, and how strictly Dogme directors adhered to the rules. A clutch of comments indicates the irony and self-deprecation which underlay this blast against convention and mainstream film. For example: 'Dogma is not about following the Brothers' Rules: it's simply abut setting some rules and some limitations . . . The idea is simply to gain creativity through self-imposition' (Lars Bredo Rahbek quoted in Kelly 2000: 80). 'I don't think it's necessarily crucial that the

Dogma rules be followed. I think the issue of whether you can gain something by throwing away total freedom in exchange for a set of rules is worth discussing" (Lars von Trier quoted in Hjort and MacKenzie 2003: 54). 'it is very solemn, and not rigid. On the other hand, it is a game, as it's defined in the manifesto, which is a bit arrogant, and, of course, ironic also' (Thomas Vinterberg quoted in Hjort and Mackenzie 2003: 54). The Manifesto and Vow may have been thumbing the Brothers' nose at big-budget, high-tech mainstream cinema, and the Manifesto may have been partly in jest; the Brothers were, however, committed to serious film-making. Before the camera started rolling they abstracted much of the normally accepted 'apparatus' of filming. The Brotherhood eschewed genre, style, much conventional technology (the fixed camera, non-diegetic lighting and sound, fabricated locations and sets) and the creation of illusion. Like Dreyer, they imposed a restricted form within which to operate and with a similar purpose – 'to force the truth' out of the characters and settings. Dreyer would not, however, have agreed with the sentence which followed this aspiration. 'I swear to do so by all means available and at the cost of any good taste and any aesthetic considerations' (The Dogme Manifesto, 1995).

The Dogme Brotherhood associated aesthetics with style and auteurism. The French New Wave had espoused these and 'it had proved to be a ripple that washed ashore and turned to muck' (The Dogme 95 Manifesto 1995). So, aesthetics and deliberate artistry were, purportedly, anathema. Directors were not to be credited; a controlling hand, even if active in the making of the film, was to be unacknowledged. This would appear to be diametrically opposed to Dreyer's attitude and methods. However, even if not credited as directors in the films, it is perfectly clear that Vinterberg in the case of *Festen* and von Trier in the case of *Idioterne* were very much in control of the manner in which the films were made. The manuscript for *Idioterne* apparently shows no significant improvisation or deviation from the script (Hjort and Mackenzie 2003: 71). Von Trier has said: 'My greatest problem in life is control versus chaos. I can get extremely afraid of not having control when I want it . . . All my worst anxieties are about losing control' (Schepelern 2005: 64).

The eye of the film is the camera, and how the director deploys his or her camera dictates how the viewer sees the film. Dreyer's use of the camera is fundamental to his technique and it was in some respects wholly innovative. He prepared meticulously: 'Everything must be prepared – if not you might suddenly find yourself lacking an elephant' (Kau 2010). The set having been created as in a painting, the camera was to be positioned and/or moved with unwavering precision: it was to capture a studied mise-en-scène. In *La Passion de Jeanne d'Arc* (1928) the greater part of the cinematography is a study in moving portraiture. The camera examines the human face and its expressions from every perspective: extreme frontal close-up, in profile, in one corner of the frame, from above, from below, motionless, animated, in various emotional states. When the face is not the focus of attention, shots are composed in highly artistic ways: passing laterally across the court-room and the torture chamber, movement interrupted by the verticals of people, columns and lances (a feature even more prominent in *Vredens dag*), the shadows of crosses cast on the floor, blood spurting from Joan's arm, aerial shots of crowds rushing to the execution. Dreyer's camera can sometimes be in the position of a theatre spectator looking in on scenes from a play, and this *Kammerspiel* mode is especially evident in *Gertrud* with its long static scenes. In all this the artistic potential of cinematography was exploited to create pictures, tableaux and compositions within which the characters were to express an inner reality. Film was mimetic in the same way as pictorial art:

> Dreyer ... does not even try to instil cinematic life into his film (*Day of Wrath*) ... perfectly illustrates the clash between the realistic and the formative techniques ... on the whole Dreyer fashions his imagery after paintings of the period ... It is as if old Dutch masters had come to life. (Kracauer 1960: 81)

This is especially true of *Ordet*. The narrative development is slow as the camera lingers in a succession of extraordinarily beautiful monochrome compositions.

Rule 9 of the Dogme 95 Vow of Chastity stipulates that 'the camera must be hand-held. Any movement or immobility attainable in the hand is permitted. The film must not take place where the camera is standing; shooting must take place where the film takes place'. By contrast with Dreyer's precisely planned shooting the Dogme camera appears to be just pointed at what is there, not mise-en-scène in the sense of what is put in front of it but rather what is found in front of it; that is, notionally at least, reality as it is rather than as it can be expressed. So, pictorially *Idioterne* and *Festen* have the appearance of home videos – uncomposed, poorly lit, jumpy, improvised, at times crude and clumsy (so much so that a cameraman and a sound boom are caught in shot in *Idioterne*. That said, in *Festen* in particular there is some deliberateness about the positioning of the hand-held camera: for the opening shot of Christian walking along the country road (a shot which figuratively represents his outsider status); cars arriving at the house are shot half-screen from low down behind a pillar; Lars, the butler, and Pia, the maid, are shot in baths from directly overhead. The 'getting warmer' game signs and the letter left by Linda, the sister who committed suicide, have to have been staged. Obviously the locations are not wholly fortuitous: the country house in *Festen*, the house, the restaurant, the swimming pool and the factory in *Idioterne* must be chosen, but thereafter relatively little is introduced to enhance the representation or expression of the narrative. The actors act in real environments, and the camera records what they do. The rules and the method are different, but the goal is the same: the portrayal of reality.

What were the subjects of the reality they aimed to portray, and what light do these shed on their approaches? Dreyer's main feature films were all based on literary texts, plays, short stories, a novel, the transcript of Joan of Arc's trial. Dreyer's construction of sets and use of internal locations, his camerawork and montage render the films analogous to stage plays with a sequence of consecutive internal scenes, interspersed with some external location scenes. There is a small cast of characters usually within a domestic situation. The dialogue is limited, even minimal, and concentrated on the psychological dramas being played out between the characters. Again, this is part of the process of abstraction and aesthetic refinement, the removal of the trivial and dramatically superfluous. Formal constraints are embraced in order to communicate a subtle, implicit, perhaps figurative truth.

The material for *Festen* and *Idioterne* is dramatic but with a far less structured development. Both scenarios are set in a communal environment, the one an assembly of friends and family in a country house to celebrate Helge Klingenfeldt-Hansen's sixtieth birthday, the other a rather randomly assembled group linked by their commitment to 'spassing', also living in one large house. *Festen* is said to have been based on a real-life incident; *Idioterne* was an original idea. Many of the events in the films appear to be improvised, both action and dialogue, and the camera records what transpired, but the narratives are not anarchic, not without order or unity; what was shot has been edited to create a dramatic sequence and chronology, indeed a beginning, a middle and an end.

The directors sought to extract truth and psychological realism from the characters and scenarios before the camera: how did they direct their actors to achieve this? Dreyer produced sets which were reduced to the absolute essentials for the drama. This meant the objects and architectures of the mise-en-scène – candles, crosses, walls, windows, pillars, doors, clocks, books, rooms – are as important for their aesthetic impact or figurative meaning as their physical reality (Monaco 1981: 44-45). Equally, he was insistent that his actors 'live' in the location, that it become their natural environment. He espoused a Stanislavskian attitude to the actors' performance: they were, as far as possible, to represent the inner lives of the characters and to feel what the characters feel. He is said to have pressed his actors, particularly Anna Svierkier as Herlofs Marte and Marie Falconetti as Joan, almost to the point of physical duress in order to obtain convincing performances.

Vinterberg and von Trier also strove for psychological realism and the revelation of inner truths. Given the prohibition on technical aids in the making of Dogme films, the performance of the actors becomes critical in conveying the drama. The actors improvised and the camera recorded what occurred spontaneously. Thus the actors were obliged to generate their emotions, responses and actions from within. For this to work it was probably essential that the main characters were a group who, for the duration of the filming, lived virtually as a commune:

> they all [the Dogme films] seem to be group portraits. They're all very melodramatic in a way; the emotional life is very explosive. And I think that's because you have nothing to tell the story with other than the actors; nothing else to use when you want to express feelings. (Thomas Vinterberg quoted in Kelly 2000: 114)

Naturalism was not confined to the main characters. Neither the extras at the dinner-party in *Festen* and the diners in the restaurant in *Idioterne* were told beforehand what was going to happen in Christian's speeches nor how the spassers would behave. The shattering of conventional propriety produces an excruciatingly uncomfortable non-reaction, especially in *Festen*; no one (not even the actors) knows how to behave in that situation. One guest claps, the grandfather gets up to tell his smutty joke; the instinct is almost to behave as if nothing had disturbed the civilised formalities. The result is a far more realistic portrayal than would have been achieved with rehearsal according to a learned script.

'While shooting one is already editing, one has already done the editing mentally' (Dreyer quoted in Nash 1977: 42). Montage can be argued to be the most fundamental part of both the material and artistic process of film-making: films are created in the cutting room (or perhaps nowadays by digital compilation and manipulation.) Editing turns the raw material of the shot film into the finished product and it is difficult to conceive of a film being made without this process. At one extreme Andy Warhol can shoot the Empire State Building from one point of view continuously over many hours and then simply show the resulting film; editing might do little other than reorder the timings or abbreviate the time-span. That kind of unmediated reality obviously has a different end from that of a narrative film. Most film-makers will exploit montage to dramatise the story, create attractions or sensations, or, as with Carl Dreyer, to produce expressive effects. For Dreyer the making of a film is an all-inclusive process, that is to say, having reduced the mise-en-scène and the dialogue to what he regarded as the essentials, he then set about creating his films in the most artistic way using every facility at his disposal. Edvin Kau (2010) calls this 'combinatory dynamics':

> Dreyer is in the process of formulating or exploring the abstract narrative potential of film language and its formal minimum elements through a highly refined technique of constructing moving images into narration, rather than settling for photographic recording.

Dreyer is celebrated for close-ups (of faces and objects), for lingering tracking and panning shots, and for the slow pace of his films created through the camerawork and the montage of scenes. In *La Passion de Jeanne d'Arc*, after the tour de force of the drama through the tableau of faces in the trial, the editing becomes uncharacteristically hectic and abrupt in the final scenes as Joan is burnt and the crowd riots: the juxtaposition of the suckling of a baby, the cutaways to the flight of doves, the soldiers' violence, the aerial shots of the crowds running. This camerawork suggests hysteria, heightening the gruesome tension of the event. In *Vredens dag* scenes are theatrically juxtaposed to create drama and figurative meaning: Herlof's Marte's cottage against Absolon's rectory, Laurentius's deathbed against Anne's seduction of Martin, then intercut with Absolon and his curate battling through the storm. In *Ordet* a slow succession of painterly scenes builds suspense to the climax of Inger's funeral. In *Gertrud* Dreyer edited in his most measured theatrical way with long takes showing minimal movement of the characters and extended scene following extended scene. Montage for Dreyer is another part of the compositional process with building or arranging the set, choosing the props, lighting the scenes and positioning the camera. These are the brushstrokes of his pictures.

In the Dogme Manifesto and Vow of Chastity von Trier and Vinterberg make no reference to montage: they vow to 'refrain from creating a work, as I regard the instant as more important than the whole.' Rule 3 stipulates 'The camera must be hand-held'. Rule 4 prohibits special lighting. Rule 7 forbids 'temporal and geographical alienation.' They eschewed both the artistic aim which Dreyer espoused and the technical features he used to accomplish it. The first two Dogme films are, however, manifestly dramatically coherent works which create suspense and engage the viewer's interest in more than 'the instant'. Notably, the Vow does not forbid editing to achieve dramatic coherence.

Festen and *Idioterne* are not without artistic quality or dramatic unity, different in kind from Dreyer's but equally powerful in their effects, and some of that impact is undoubtedly achieved through editing. Neither film is chronologically continuous or located in only one place: there are temporal lapses and changes of location. In *Festen* there are some notably meaningful juxtapositions created by editing: the maid Pia submerges herself in Christian's bath while Helene is searching for the letter from Linda who drowned herself in a bath; in the deserted dining-room after the dinner couples are dancing while Michael beats up his father; scenes of violent argument and sex, of revelation and confession in private rooms are interspersed with the formal calm of the dining-room. The drama in which abominable truths emerge has many moments of broad, even slapstick, comedy as well as very black humour: Michael is a clownishly incompetent figure, falling over in the shower, pulling the curtain rail down, running across the drive with his trousers falling down; Michelle pours water over him; some guests cannot distinguish whether the soup is lobster, salmon or tomato; Michael's racist reception of Gbatokai is embarrassingly funny. Indeed, the whole concept of a birthday celebration undermined by revelations of child abuse and sodomy is grimly comic in its illumination of the hypocrisy and superficiality of civilised propriety. In the narrative and the editing incongruous juxtaposition highlights the falsehood of what appears to be reality. This is montage 'to force the truth out of (the) characters and settings', and despite the Brothers' disavowals these are creatively artistic works. In *Idioterne* the locations are 'found', but they have been identified – a restaurant, a factory, a swimming pool, Karen's house – as places suitable for the impact of spassing. The shooting at these locations is completely devoid of any of the compositional applications of Dreyer and at times is almost slapdash. The camera is used to record authentically the life going on in front of it, but while there is virtually no attempt at artistic composition in the framing of the image because the image itself would then be a falsification, the apparently haphazard shooting has been edited to give a dramatic structure to the events. This is especially true of *Festen* in which there are many jump cuts, juxtapositions and short scenes interspersed with longer takes of, for example, the speeches. The truth is to be conveyed in the characters and their interactions alone; but purposeful editing enhances the dramatic impact.

The ascetic realism of the Brothers' anti-aesthetic mode is a little tainted by, for example, the interviews with the actors in *Idioterne*, who may or may not be speaking in character. This is temporal alienation and disturbs the viewer's suspension of disbelief. So, too, in *Festen* Linda, the sister who committed suicide, seems to appear in a vision or dream to Christian, a piece of artifice alien to the rest of the narrative.

Differences in the use of sound and the spoken word complement the cinematic approaches. Rule 2 of the Dogme Manifesto prohibits sound which is not produced at the time of shooting of the images. In *Festen* and *Idioterne* this rule appears to be adhered to, and the dialogue is as spoken at the time of filming. It is naturalistic, sometimes barely coherent, lacking in dramatic polish: it has the authenticity of ordinary speech. There is no non-diegetic music. Dreyer's films on the other hand have sound effects added which are essential to the plot development – in *Vredens dag* bells ringing, choirs singing, crowds baying, the sound of fire burning; in *Ordet* the ticking clock stops for the period of Inger's resurrection – and there is musical accompaniment to heighten the dramatic impact. The spoken words are like those of stage drama and are confined to what is necessary for the progress of the action. There is no improvisation or spontaneity here: as noted above, this is theatricalised film-making. For a Dreyer film the viewer must suspend his or her disbelief as he or she would do in a theatre and be moved by the power of the overall expressiveness of the imagery. The Dogme films, made in a home-video style, attempt to convince the viewer that the camera was simply present at what was happening: the viewer must believe it because it is real.

Real life occurs in colour: so the Dogme Brotherhood films had to be in colour (Rule 4). The Vow of Chastity allows no special effects, no special lighting, optical work or filters; there is no attempt to use colour or lighting for expressive purposes; there is no deliberate creation of a work. The light in *Idioterne* and *Festen* is natural, and as a consequence the picture on screen is sometimes shadowy, out of focus or obscure to the point of indistinguishability, notably, for example, in the external night scenes in *Festen*. There is no compromise with the principles in order to enable 'reality' to be seen clearly: no artifice is used apart from the camera. Dreyer, on the other hand, exploits the expressiveness of black and white and shades of grey to the full. Lines, shapes, shadows, contrasts, the irregularity of the human form and movement against geometrical patterns of furniture and architecture, grass or leaves or washing blowing in the wind against a grey sky – all such elements in the mise-en-scène are composed and lit with consummate artistry. With a monochrome palette he composes moving pictures.

Since the late nineteenth century virtually all established conventions and forms of art have been dismantled and all limits and constraints undone: art has become simply what it is, not what it has been or, by tradition or theorists' prescriptions, should be. Modern art in all media has exploded any idea that there can be prescribed ways of expressing truth or reality. Film as the most recent form of art could be said to be still exploring its form and developing its expressive capabilities. Relatively speaking, it is a young art form. How do Carl Dreyer, Thomas Vinterberg and Lars von Trier stand in this context? They strove in radically different ways to extract reality from the raw material in front of the camera and to convey it truthfully. Dreyer employed most of the artistic and technical facilities available to him to mediate between the material and the viewer; in that respect he was a conventional artist. Vinterberg and von Trier attempted to reduce the mediatory effects to a minimum; they worked against the received conventions. Dreyer chose to use established texts as his material and to express them in a highly controlled, pictorially artistic way: his films became animated tableaux with the depth of the masters of art. He produced masterpieces of complex and subtle film the meanings of which are to be interpreted slowly through contemplation. This is the realism of theatrical drama with the expressiveness of great art. By contrast the Dogme films of Vinterberg and von Trier have been likened to the *arte povera* movement in which natural and manufactured materials and found objects are presented as artworks in themselves, often with little composition or intervention by the artist. In these films the controlling hand of the director is obscured, and the viewer is presented with people and events that, apparently, just happened to be in front of the camera. The shaping of that raw material is reduced in the interests of authenticity. Vinterberg and von Trier created more spontaneous, crude everyday reality. Their films purport to be a slice-of life, and the viewer may make of it what he or she will because there is no overt artistic message. This is an attempt to capture reality as immediately as possible; the only abstraction is of technical facilities to reduce the mediation intervening between the subject and the viewer. The Dogme film-makers indulged in cinematic retardation: their film-making is spassing to provoke the audience out of complacency induced by the superficiality of conventional cinema. The material is deliberately provocative prompting the viewer into self-questioning.

Obviously there is some disjunction in comparing the film-making of these directors: they are from different eras (Dreyer made his first film in 1918, and his last in 1964, spanning the transition from silent to sound films and from black and white to colour; the first Dogme film was made in 1998); there have been step-changes in the technology within the last twenty years; their stated aims and aesthetic approaches are different to the point of being antipathetic. However, their common goal was to represent reality and truth as they conceived of it through film. They reacted against the artificiality and manufactured quality characteristic of much mainstream (often Hollywood) cinema. Commercial profit was not a primary aim; the authenticity of the vision of film was. Dreyer and the Brotherhood employed forms of refinement of the filming process – reductionism and abstraction in Dreyer's case, self-imposed technical asceticism on the part of von

Trier and Vinterberg – to express, in the sense of extracting, verisimilitude from their material. It could be argued that there is artificiality in both methods – the one through creative artistry, the other through a kind of Luddite self-denial. But their films succeed: they engage the viewer in the drama and convince him or her of their truth. At the same time they are provocative and stimulating because their films are self-reflexive: they are also works which are palpably exploring the art of film-making.

Author's Comment

I retired as a university administrator at UCL in 2005 and one of the activities I wanted to pursue in retirement was study of the Finnish language. I lived and taught English in Finland for three years from 1969 to 1972 and I am married to a Finn. After a few years of study as a Continuing Education student I was able to register as an undergraduate on the B.A. in Finnish and East European Studies at the School of Slavonic and East European Studies. I had taken the East European Cinema course as one of my optional courses before I took Nordic Cinema for which this essay was written. The course introduced me to the films of Carl Theodor Dreyer; Lars von Trier I knew only through *Breaking the Waves* (1996). The aesthetic approaches of Dreyer and the Dogme Brotherhood are apparently so different that the idea of comparing them seemed to offer fruitful ground for a discussion of film as a medium for representing reality and the techniques used for doing so.

References

Arnheim, Rudolf (1957). 'The Complete Film.' In Braudy, Leo and Cohen, Marshall (eds.) (1981): Bazin, André (1967). *Film Theory and Criticism*. New York and Oxford: Oxford University Press.

Bazin, Andre (1967). *What is Cinema?* Essays selected and translated by Hugh Gray. Berkeley: University of California Press.

Bell, Emma (2006). 'The Passion of Lars von Trier: Madness, Femininity, Film.' In Thomson, Claire (ed.) (2006): *Northern Constellations: New Readings in Nordic Cinema*. London and Norwich: Norvik Press.

Benjamin, Walter (1935). 'The Work of Art in the Age of Mechanical Reproduction.' In Braudy, Leo and Cohen, Marshall (eds.) (1981): *Film Theory and Criticism*. New York and Oxford: Oxford University Press.

Bondebjerg, Ib (2003). 'Chapter 4: Dogma 95 and the New Danish Cinema.' In Hjort, Mette and MacKenzie, Scott (eds.) (2003): *Purity and Provocation: Dogma 95*. London: BFI Publishing.

Bordwell, David (1981). *The Films of Carl Theodor Dreyer*. Berkeley: University of California Press.

Bordwell, David (1985). *Narration in Fiction Film*. Madison: University of Wisconsin Press.

Carney, Raymond (1989). *Speaking the Language of Desire: The Films of Carl Dreyer*. Cambridge: Cambridge University Press.

Drum, Jean and Drum, Dale D. (2000). *My Only Great Passion: The Life and Films of Carl Th. Dreyer*. Lanham, MD: The Scarecrow Press.

Elkington, Trevor G (2005). 'Costumes, Adolescence and Dogma: Nordic Film and American Distribution.' In Nestingen, Andrew and Elkington, Trevor G. (eds.) (2005). *Transnational Cinema in a Global North: Nordic Cinema in Transition* (2003).

Gaut, Berys (2003):'Naked Film: Dogma and its Limits.' In Hjort, Mette and MacKenzie, Scott (eds.) (2003). *Purity and Provocation: Dogma 95*. London: BFI Publishing.

Hjort, Mette and Mackenzie, Scott (2003). 'Introduction'. In Hjort, Mette and MacKenzie, Scott (eds.) (2003). *Purity and Provocation: Dogma 95*. London: BFI Publishing.

Hjort, Mette (2003). 'Dogma 95: A Small Nation's Response to Globalisation'. In Hjort, Mette and MacKenzie, Scott (eds.) (2003). *Purity and Provocation: Dogma 95*. London: BFI Publishing.

Kelly, Richard (2000). *The Name of this Book is Dogme 95*. London: Faber and Faber.

Kracauer, Siegfried (1960). *Theory of Film: The Redemption of Physical Reality*. Oxford: Oxford University Press.

MacKenzie, Scott (2003). 'Manifest Destinies: Dogma 95 and the Future of the Film Manifesto'. In Hjort, Mette and MacKenzie, Scott (eds.) (2003). *Purity and Provocation: Dogma 95*. London: BFI Publishing.

Milne, Tom (1971). The Cinema of Carl *Dreyer*. New York: A. S.

Barnes & Co.

Monaco, James (1981). *How to read a film*. New York and Oxford: Oxford University Press.

Sandberg, Mark (2006). 'Mastering the House: Performative Inhabitation in Carl Th. Dreyer's The Parson's Widow.' In Thomson, Claire (ed.) (2006). *Northern Constellations: New Readings in Nordic Cinema*. London and Norwich: Norvik Press.

Schepelern, Peter (2003). '"Kill Your Darlings": Lars von Trier and the Origin of Dogma 95'. In Hjort, Mette and MacKenzie, Scott (eds.) (2003). *Purity and Provocation: Dogma 95*. London: BFI Publishing.

Schepelern, Peter (2005). 'Film according to Dogma: Ground Rules, Obstacles and Liberation'. In Nestingen, Andrew and Elkington, Trevor G. (eds.) (2005). *Transnational Cinema in a Global North: Nordic Cinema in Transition*. Detroit: Wayne State University Press.

Skoller, Donald (ed.) (2004). *Dreyer in Double Reflection: Carl Th. Dreyer's Writings About Film*. New York: A. P. Dutton.

Smith, Murray (2003). 'Lars von Trier: Sentimental Surrealist'. In Hjort, Mette and MacKenzie, Scott (eds.) (2003). *Purity and Provocation: Dogma 95*. London: BFI Publishing.

Thomsen, Bodil Marie (2006). 'On the Transmigration of Images: Flesh, Spirit and Haptic Vison in Dreyer's Jeanne d'Arc and von Trier's Golden Heart Trilogy'. In Thomson, Claire (ed.) (2006). *Northern Constellations: New Readings in Nordic Cinema*. London and Norwich: Norvik Press.

Widding, Astrid Söderbergh (1998). 'Denmark'. In Soila, Tytti, Widding, Astrid Söderbergh and Iversen, Gunnar (1998). *Nordic National Cinema*. London: Routledge.

Wollen, Peter (1972). *Signs and Meaning in the Cinema*. Bloomington and Indianapolis: Indiana University Press.

Electronic sources

Christensen, Ove (2000). 'Spastic Aesthetics – The Idiots.' A Danish Journal of Film Studies, no. 10, December 2000. pov.imu.qu.dk/Issue_10/Section_2/artc3A.html. Accessed April 2010.

Conroch, Ian and Estella Tincknell: (2000). 'Film Purity, the neo-Bazanian Ideal, and Humanism in Dogma 95.' A Danish Journal of Film Studies, no. 10, December 2000 pov.imu.qu.dk/Issue_10/Section_4/artc7A.html. Accessed April 2010.

Doxtater, Amanda. 'Perilous Performance: Dreyer's Unity of Danger and Beauty.' Danish Film Institute website About Dreyer, english.carldreyer.dk/AboutDreyer/. Accessed April 2010.

Kau, Edvin. 'Camera and Space.' Danish Film Institute website About Dreyer, english.carldreyer.dk/AboutDr. Accessed April 2010.

Kau, Edvin Vestergaard Kau. 'Auteurs in Style: The Heresy or Indulgence of the Dogma Brothers'. A Danish Journal of Film Studies, no. 10, December 2000, pov.imu.qu.dk/Issue_10/Section_4/artc4A.html. Accessed

April 2010.

Laursen, Thomas Lind. 'The Agitated Camera: A Diagnosis of Anthony Dod Mantle's Camera Work in The Celebration'. A Danish Journal of Film Studies, no. 10, December 2000, pov.imu.qu.dk/Issue_10/Section_3/artc2A.html. Accessed April 2010.

Moor, Paul. 'The Tyrannical Dane.' Danish Film Institute website About Dreyer, english.carldreyer.dk/AboutDreyer/. Accessed April 2010.

Thomsen, Bodil Marie (2000). 'Idiocy, Foolishness and Spastic Jesting'. A Danish Journal of Film Studies, no. 10, December 2000 pov.imu.qu.dk/Issue_10/Section_2/artc4A.html. Accessed April 2010.

'It is Too Beautiful': Accidents and Auteurship in Lars von Trier's *Antichrist*

Pei Sze Chow

After a crippling illness that left him incapacitated for six months in 2007, Lars von Trier set about work on his latest project, a horror film. Premièring at the Cannes Film Festival in May 2009, *Antichrist* was screened to an audience that expressed outrage in very similar ways to the first audiences of von Trier's earlier films *Idioterne* (The Idiots, 1998) and *Dancer in the Dark* (2000) — with plenty of boos, hisses, people storming out of the auditorium, and a prolonged media furore. Despite the hailstorm of negative criticism surrounding *Antichrist*, Charlotte Gainsbourg left the festival with the *Prix d'interprétation féminine* (Prize for Best Actress) for her role in the film. This time around, there was no *Dogme 95*-esque manifesto, no 'Statement of Revitality' as issued in conjunction with *Direktøren for det hele* (The Boss of it All, 2006), nor any overt provocation of cinematic form. The only ruffle, as it were, came from the shock value of *Antichrist*'s objectionable content. Yet, despite being a horror film, it is not very far from the self-reflexive temper of von Trier's previous project, which was a comedy. Knud Romer (2009) notes that, like so many other remarkable auteurs, von Trier 'keeps making the same film over and over again in different, increasingly radical variations.' In acknowledgement of this pattern, von Trier remarks that the idea of the genre film is an inspiration and motivation for his desire for aesthetic innovation: 'I'll probably never really hit any genre straight on, because I think you should add something to them' (quoted in Romer 2009). On that account, the underlying connection between *Antichrist* and the other 'genre films' that von Trier has produced (*Dancer in the Dark* [2000] - a musical, *Breaking the Waves* [1996] - a melodrama), is that they are specimens by which he not only exhibits his mastery of storytelling, but also where he manipulates the aesthetic forms to explore metaphysical questions about truth and authentic expressions of emotion and spectatorship. The latter consideration is the 'something' that he adds to the horror genre which is of import to this analysis, especially since, in the context of his months-long depression and personal anxieties about control, von Trier has emphatically revealed to the press that *Antichrist* is a deeply personal film. Therefore, *Antichrist*'s innovative appeal is perhaps not as perspicuous and explicitly delimited as the experiments in form and technique that von Trier's earlier films boast. There is not as much direct rhetoric that surrounds the film as the manifestos and statements that came before, and no clear guiding aesthetic framework shapes the film. Instead, *Antichrist* is a rich visual text packed with symbolic imagery and a sophisticated style that seems to reflect von Trier's technical prowess with film. Significantly, the themes of control and authenticity as composed in this film have their genesis in a different circumstance that originated from von Trier's personal life at the time of the film's making.

A key line from the film signals this proposition: 'chaos reigns'. In this essay, the first argument occurs on the level of the narrative, where I argue that the idea of expressive authenticity is conveyed through the motif of chaos filling the gap created by a lack of control. The couple's conventional social roles as parents have disintegrated with their child's death. With their move into the woods, their chaotic and true natures are thereby coaxed to the fore to fill this gap in self-identity and meaning. The second argument posited here is that the incidental collaborative action from the near-absence of von Trier's artistic control results in a film that projects the authenticity of the creative dynamic between the various agents: actors, director of photography, and director. That is, in giving up a measure of his directorial control due to his illness, other creative agents have thus been allowed to fill that absence. I will first examine the film's treatment of chaos and control as a subject within the narrative, then explore how, despite von Trier's seemingly minimal involvement, this subject manifests itself in the production and performance of the film. Lastly, the collaborative nature of *Antichrist* calls to question the idea of the auteurist film as the artistic expression of a sole individual, where von Trier foregrounds the tension between performance and practice in the construction of his auteur identity. He does so through his publicity of the film as a carefully packaged product, and this will be evaluated alongside the implications of von Trier's gambit in releasing such a provocative film to public outcry.

Chaos Reigns

Antichrist tells the story of a couple — nameless except as 'He' (Willem Dafoe) and 'She' (Charlotte Gainsbourg) — who deal with the trauma from the accidental death of their infant son by retreating to a cabin in the woods, named Eden. He, a psychiatrist by profession, attempts to treat his wife by himself, hoping to cure her insuperable depression without the use of prescribed drugs but instead through rhetoric and cognitive therapy. His methods focus on taking her through visualisations of her fear, which reveal her perception that the woods and herself are evil personified. We learn that she had previously stayed in the same cabin with their son while working on her doctoral thesis about gynocide (femicide) in history, and there is the faint suggestion that she had attempted to harm the child then. Meanwhile, She struggles against her husband's rationalist attempts by interrupting their therapy sessions with sex, while He is confounded by the portentous signs that he stumbles upon in the cabin and in the woods. The difficult road to recovery turns to insanity and horror, resulting in graphic scenes of physical disfigurement and torture. Their move to Eden thus becomes a sharp descent into Hell, as She becomes even more convinced by the idea that women are evil, just as Nature is, and starts to embody this notion by committing a series of heinous acts that are focused on dismantling her husband's rational subjectivity. She physically attacks him in rages of fury, and goes as far as attempting near-castration, attaching a grindstone to a bolt drilled through his leg, and performing genital self-mutilation with a pair of rusty scissors. Von Trier spares not the viewer in this last section, depicting these scenes with significant visual detail, before ending the film with He strangling She and making his way out of the woods. The film is divided into four chapters sandwiched by a Prologue and Epilogue filmed in black and white. The chapters are respectively titled 'Grief', 'Pain (Chaos Reigns)', 'Despair (Gynocide)', and 'The Three Beggars'. The latter refers to the three animals that symbolise a trinity of death: a deer (Grief), fox (Pain), and crow (Despair), and, according to She, the simultaneous appearance of all three signals death. At various points, they individually appear before He, and are seen together only at the end of the film while he makes his escape.

'It is Too Beautiful'

Jan Simons tracks a pattern in characterisation evident in all of von Trier's films:

> The protagonist in each of his films enters a world in which he or she is a stranger and where he or she is confronted with the task of finding out what laws, rules, customs, and conventions govern the behaviour of its inhabitants. (2007: 188)

This trait is seen very clearly in the characters of Beth from *Breaking the Waves*, Karen from *Idioterne*, Selma from *Dancer in the Dark*, Grace from *Dogville* (2003), Kristoffer from *Direktøren for det hele*, and to an extent, Jørgen Leth in *De fem benspænd* (The Five Obstructions, 2003) as well. Already, it is unambiguous that such a set-up reflects that of a game, since, once the character learns and masters those rules and customs, he or she is able to manipulate and subvert them to his/her benefit to effect a release or catharsis of sorts. In *Antichrist*, this role of the protagonist is precariously split between the two characters, and the film is centred on the psychological struggle between them as they search for ways and means to resolve their emotional and psychological predicament. I suggest that the subject of control is analysed, subverted, and radically weakened with wild abandon — the film is in favour of the argument for the deficiencies of any kind of rationalist structure in our lived experience.

The terms of the struggle are clear, and the characters are unambiguously aligned to a specific dichotomy depicting control and chaos. He, representing the rational and the clinical, stubbornly insists that his scientific methods can cure his wife's trauma and depression, while She in this case might represent the irrational and emotional figure that resists being categorised or diagnosed. In a theological context, She is portrayed as the figure of Eve, who in the Christian tradition is represented as the personification of evil and bringer of death (Beattie 2009). Significantly, their move to the cabin in the forest, which She says is the place she fears the most, is charged through with symbolic references: as they make their way deeper into the primeval woods, they cross a bridge that symbolises the partition that separates culture and nature, reason and chaos, and sanity and madness (Beattie 2009). In a romantic sense, the forest also signifies illogic and the fear of the unknown, and von Trier highlights this emphatically with the expressionist visual design of the space. The psychiatrist, on the one hand, directs his wife through the ordeal of coming to terms with their son's death by his impersonal and dispassionate analyses, thereby asserting his power of reason and knowledge over her emotional and psychological infirmity. Yet, on the other hand, for all his rationalist scientific certainty, he is unable to identify the real source of her fear. Even though She arrives at the location not able to even walk on the grass due to her neurosis, she later tames her fear and embraces the primacy of the woods. At this point, her comment, 'Nature is Satan's church,' becomes much more resonant as She becomes the dominant figure in the later half of the film, rising to become the antichrist, as it were. Appropriately, the speaking fox also utters 'Chaos reigns' to the hapless psychiatrist in the woods. Even though He manages to kill her at the end, we are shown in the Epilogue an overwhelming mass of women coming out of the woods, engulfing him as he stares grimly into the sea of bodies.

Such a characterisation is an archetypal division of the sexes, indeed, where female sexuality is painted as dark and monstrous as the sprawling woods. Nature is portrayed as chaotic and abstruse in the film. Von Trier explains his choice of a forest setting:

> What characterises this virgin territory is maximal death: a great quantity of species fighting for life there, fighting for light, fighting for survival. Nature is filled with suffering and pain and death. ...
>
> Nature goes against everything religion talks about. Nature reminds us of inescapable death and does not offer any consolation about any possibility beyond. There is nothing godlike in nature. Nature seems more to be an idea of Satan. (quoted in Björkman 2009: 18)

As with von Trier's other films, such references are never unintentional, and they ultimately point to a larger discourse about the nature of good and evil which is pertinent to the theological framework that the characters fit into. While her qualities directly align her character with this conception of nature, evil, and chaos, Gainsbourg's character is not meant to be read as a target of misogyny, and von Trier takes care to subvert such a reading. Instead, the eventual triumph of the feminine figure, as signified by the mass of women at the end, is yoked to the dark fascination of fear and irrationality, which, to von Trier, is more compelling than the masculine perspective in the Christian discourse of salvation where female sacrifice is necessary to bring redemption to humanity. Von Trier notes also that it is the horror and fear of the feminine form that drives the film: 'I don't think women or their sexuality is evil, but it is frightening. ... Certain images and certain concepts are interesting to combine in different ways. They show pieces of the human soul and human actions. That's interesting' (quoted in Romer 2009). In other words, the focus of the narrative hinges on the argument that chaos does indeed reign in a world where secular power structures are unable to enforce their authority.

A short acknowledgement of the notion of abjection might further illuminate the imbalance in power between chaos and reason, and further link chaos to von Trier's articulation of authenticity. Aristotelian tragedy has been formulated as a form of contamination (*miasma*), which is balanced in the end through ritual cleansing (*catharsis*). In this formulation, contamination leads to imbalance and chaos, which is then cleansed and purified in order to restore a certain balance and order to the social world (Sjöholm 2005: 96). In *Antichrist*, however, there is neither cleansing nor purification to speak of, since She is contaminated by the ontological evil of her womanhood, and She in turn contaminates Nature. Eden and its environs, including He in it, become the totality of the abject. Sjöholm (2005: 97) notes that Julia Kristeva describes abjection as a state of being cast outside of the symbolic order of reason and society, of which it was once a subject, and argues further that the presence of the abject is 'a confirmation of the fact that the subject can only be conceived of as a heterogeneous construction that is always already contaminated.' In such terms, She embodies the full ambiguity of evil, and since abjection is the 'in-between, not respecting borders, positions and rules,' this also explains the inability of both He and She to identify and categorise her fear and psychosis (Sjöholm 2005: 97). Throughout the film, She is projected as the embodiment of the abject that is violently positioned outside of the cultural world without a clear sense

'It is Too Beautiful'

of selfhood, and it is significant that the film's grim ending sees a symbolic eclipse of women forcing her husband out of the woods. This particular moment's significance lies in the fact that it is a reversal of the idea of expulsion: it is the expulsion of not the abject, but rather, the subject who had tried to purge the contamination within the abject. It is interesting, therefore, that von Trier's perversion of Aristotelian catharsis *does* come to an uneasy balance and order, but only with chaos and the uncanny with the upper hand. Furthermore, if the abject represents the inherent, authentic nature of humans previously subdued or masked by rational convention, then the image of a mass of women emerging from the woods and engulfing He might similarly symbolise a reemergence of the authentic.

In a more personal context for von Trier, the formulation of chaos here is perhaps an expression of his partiality to what one might conceive as the authentic and 'human' aspect of art-making, echoed from *De fem benspænd* and the romanticised notion of 'spassing' from *Idioterne*.[1] That is to say, the imperfect artist, unrestrained and working against convention and habit, has the advantage of being able to make meaningful and genuine discoveries, either by accident, instinct, or through experimentation. The 'accident' is a key term here that characterises the relationship that chaos has with the text. The motif is manifested in two further ways: first, through von Trier's methodology, and second, through the actors and their performance of the text. Instead of following his regular method of handling the camera, controlling the images while at the same time being close to the actors during the filming (as he was wont to do before), he now has to physically stand back and direct from a very different perspective.

The first expression of the motif lies in von Trier's experience in the production of the film. He had wanted to make a horror film in 2007 after the completion of *Direktøren for det hele*, but could not do so due to his illness. He discloses that taking on the project was a kind of therapy for him to counter his severe depression, and that it was critical for him to 'do something straight away and something hard'. He explains further:

> My experience with anxiety and therapy was unfortunately quite big, so that became very quickly the theme. The good thing about this whole process was that I was not really feeling very well, so I wasn't rewriting a lot of the time, and things were done more instinctively. I just wrote it through once, and I didn't analyse it. (quoted in Kehr 2009)

There is a dominant sense here that von Trier has embraced a form of easing his control over the film that is much less conceptual and abstract than his previous films. Perhaps the key to understanding the aesthetic of the film is as von Trier says — that *Antichrist* is 'a film where I had to throw reason overboard a little bit' (qtd. in Romer 2009). In another interview he says that he used to be much more "clear and mathematical" about his earlier films, but instead, *Antichrist* felt 'more like a dream' (quoted in Bourgeois 2009). Here, he has chosen to work with a degree of primal instinct and a more organic process that produces a certain freedom for the development of the film. Björkman (2009: 19) rules that the film works more like a stream of consciousness, a far cry from the predominance of overt rules in von Trier's earlier projects, and the latter agrees that there is 'a feeling that the film has a more *accidental* character. That's what I tried to attain. I felt so miserable when making the film, I just had the strength to take one scene at a time and hope for a more haphazard result'. What he means by 'accidental' might be better understood as 'instinctual' — that is, where his previous involvement in his films were more intellectual and abstract, his approach to creative action in *Antichrist* was based on instinct instead. The 'accidents' or incidental creative moments that arise from the filming are due to this unintentional obstruction to von Trier's involvement in the film; he says in the same interview that he felt like 'a runner who was suddenly put in a wheelchair'.

Here, the motif of a relaxed direction that engenders creative imagination is made manifest. Visually, and aside from the grislier scenes, the film stands out particularly with its painterly mise-en-scène and exceptionally long takes reminiscent of the films of Andrei Tarkovsky, to whom von Trier dedicates *Antichrist*. Tarkovsky's work favoured overt spiritual interpretations and possessed an emotional and aesthetic reliance on nature — both traits are indeed mirrored in *Antichrist*. Perhaps the more illuminating note about Tarkovsky's philosophy of cinema is that in the later part of his life, he came to realise that overindulgent control over a film's genesis restricts the imagination (Totaro 2000). Like Tarkovsky, then, von Trier's temporary physical and psychological affliction has led him to turn to a 'freer' mode of working. He says that 'it was also a choice of [his] not to make the film too logical' (Schepelern 2009). For example, several scenes within the film deviate from the narrative in an elliptical manner. While explicitly positioning *Antichrist* in the horror genre, the protracted shot in extreme slow-motion of

She walking through the woods, or He standing outdoors in the midst of a shower of acorns in extreme slow-motion evokes a distinct aura that is incongruent with the flow of the narrative. The latter example is particularly striking as the image breaks the fourth wall by featuring He staring directly into the camera. Similarly, the lengthy academic discussions that He and She have transform the diegesis, acting as a kind of break from the action and intense visuality of the woods, drawing the film away from the more visceral elements of horror. In this sense, one might say that the film does not conform to conventional rules of horror and narrative cinema. As a result of this diminished desire to craft a meticulously planned film, it seems as though von Trier has approached his own earlier calls for an ascetic methodology now in a different mode from the apparent self-ironic simplicity of *Direktøren for det hele*. Instead, the style is less determined, abstract, and rational, but now more instinctual and borne of the psychological drama from within the narrative. Therefore, one might characterise *Antichrist* as a film that expresses an expansive visual style as well as a plot that draws heavy influence from August Strindberg's discussion of the psychological relationships between men and women in his plays. He remarks that he 'let this film flow to me instead of thinking [it] up' and this is shown in the diverse, if sometimes labyrinthine mythical imagery that is expressed in the film (Corliss and Corliss 2009). In other words, the images of the woods painted in a muted palette of grey and near-colourless green express not only the fear of darkness, but perhaps also suggests the internal chaos and uncertainty from which an instinctual and evocative artistry emerges.

He continues to declare that he is immensely pleased with the film's visual style: 'They come out of an inspiration that's real to me. I've shown honesty in this project' (quoted in Romer 2009). Where 'honesty' is concerned, the idea is better understood through the near-total relinquishing of control over the film's aesthetic design. *De fem benspænd* boasted a strict framework, while the only restriction in *Direktøren for det hele* was the framing of the Automavision. In both cases, von Trier asserted his aesthetic authority in explicit ways. Here, he compares *Antichrist* with his earlier films as having almost no rules: 'It was also a choice of mine not to make the film too logical'. By not insisting on or adhering to his tendency to effect austere aesthetic rules and instead, relying on a completely spontaneous mode of filmmaking, von Trier is indeed working from inspiration — as shown in his undisguised references to other auteurs' works and the looser narrative flow. As he remarks, he gave more control away in the sense that he 'did not want it to be too constructed' and 'allowed pictures to come in that was strange [sic] and not kind of in the right mathematical place' (Schepelern 2009). A few examples illustrate this point: He and She's discussions about Nature and Evil meander considerably throughout the film, and their speech is frequently elliptical, with large gaps left unexplored. The same elliptical quality is seen in the editing of the narrative scenes, where abrupt jump cuts interrupt what would otherwise be a single shot. Furthermore, the stylised, steadier slow-motion shots that punctuate the story appear in an arbitrary manner, as are the overt and poetic references to other artists, such as the burning cabin at the end of the film as a nod to Tarkovsky, the thematic link between women and nature characteristic of August Strindberg, and the scene with the windswept birch trees from

Ingmar Bergman's *Jungfrukällan* (The Virgin Spring, 1960). Where the von Trier of old would not have admitted readily to such borrowing of themes and images from other auteurs, here he readily conveys his inspirations overtly and plainly.

Alongside this instinctive and honest filmmaking, a level of authenticity, albeit subjective, manifested itself especially in his direction of the actors. Addressing the second point regarding the actors' performances, Gainsbourg speaks about her experience working on the set with von Trier:

> At the start of the day Lars would just say, 'Go on, do it,' with no indications, nothing. Nobody knew what we were really supposed to do, so the first take was often quite bad, and he would say so. It was a first step, and then he would give a lot of directions and a lot of ideas. I got the impression that he was just interested in *the truth*, in *true accidents*, and just working in all sorts of directions. (my emphasis, quoted in Kehr 2009)

Partly motivated by his weaker constitution during the filming, this working relationship on the set of *Antichrist* distinctly embraces the value of relinquishing control as an essential measure to allow the expression of the 'true accident' and 'human' to surface. That is, the actors respond instinctually to the demands of the script in their performance. Dafoe is of the same opinion about von Trier's methodology: 'He feels there's more truth in accident and more truth when the actors aren't controlling what they're doing, and they're either scared or confused or struggling' (quoted in Kehr 2009). Dafoe continues in his favourable assessment that without pre-shoot rehearsals or preparation, one starts to 'get very flexible and open with impulses' (quoted in Bourgeois 2009). The utterly convincing and evocative performances the two actors turn in indeed earned them critical praise, perhaps also with some thanks due to their unbounded willingness to perform outrageous and to most, abhorrent scenes. According to von Trier, the filming was a significant challenge to Gainsbourg, but a liberating one: 'She claimed she had a lot of hang-ups as an actress. "I cannot cry on film," she said. Which isn't true, as you can see in the film' (quoted in Björkman 2009: 19). The unique liberty that Gainsbourg and Dafoe had in von Trier's absence allowed them to explore their characters until an authentic expression was achieved. Despite the difficulties within the chaos of uncertainty and the lack of power and constraint, von Trier seems to be making the argument that those are precisely the conditions that engender a verity in performative expression. An outstanding example is the scene where She aggressively knocks He out with a violent blow to his genitals, then proceeds on to her attempt to disfigure her own in painful, visceral detail. The strength of Gainsbourg's interpretation is manifested in the sense of complete discomfort that the viewer experiences while watching the thoroughly violent and tense scene with explicit sexual acts that stretches on for about twenty minutes. Similarly, the choking scene is just as discomforting to watch, as its length and extreme close-up gives it verisimilitude. The sustained presentation on Gainsbourg's part in these scenes, perhaps the most unsavoury parts in the film, is for the viewer her most striking performance that blurs the line between acting and instinctually manifesting the character, in support of the thesis of authenticity in the actors' performative expressions.

Von Trier, the Antichrist Auteur

Lastly, the express absence of an aesthetic schema in *Antichrist* has resulted in a text that opens itself up to a multitude of interpretations due to the unbridled use of symbolism and von Trier's heavy hand (through his Director of Photography) in asserting visual elegance. This latter point must be acknowledged because, despite the seeming distance von Trier puts between himself and the film by highlighting his depression in various press conferences and interviews, there is always the notion that the director is consciously defending his artistic presence in the art cinema milieu. Hence, one must interpret his exceptionally public defence of the film in a more critical light, especially when his penchant for provocation is articulated emphatically in this instance.

In this film, he deviated from the hand-held film technique that dominated his more recent projects and even turned the photography of the film over to Anthony Dod Mantle, his long-time Director of Photography, because he was in no physical shape to operate the camera. Mantle says that it is nonetheless significant that despite this limitation that von Trier faced, the latter still managed to make it one of the most technically demanding films yet, in terms of visual design. For example, it was upon von Trier's insistence that the black and white prologue was shot with a super-high-speed camera and then slowed down tremendously:

> It was Lars's intention to make that contrast between the roving physicality of the rest of the film and the amazing stillness you get when you use a high speed. What you're seeing is slowed down so much that for the first time in the cinema I

had the sense of watching a film in the way that I look at a painting. (quoted in Johnston 2009)

This must not be mistaken as an abandonment of two of the main traits that define von Trier's artistic identity — control and innovation. Contrary to that perspective, *Antichrist* is simply von Trier's complex variation of relinquishing control to showcase and parade his artistic ego. Mantle's comment compares the visual design of the film to that of a painting, and as mentioned earlier, the references are not without purpose — that is, to align his work with those of noted European auteurs and thus situate his work within that milieu. In slowing down the shot and not ascribing further action to it, the viewer's gaze is simultaneously and deliberately focused on the image to a minute degree. This not only calls attention to the technique and artistry of the camerawork, but also suggests an insistence on acknowledging this stillness as a dissolution of the boundaries between cinema and painting. Such a shot thus interrogates the nature of cinema from an ontological perspective: as still pictures in motion. In this sense, von Trier is indeed presenting the possibilities of cinema by foregrounding what Heidegger (2000: 94) would term the 'thingness' and truth of film. According to Heidegger, the authentic is that which possesses 'unconcealedness' in the work — so too does *Antichrist* feature this 'unconcealedness' especially in the shots in extreme slow-motion described earlier. Hence, it is not that von Trier has completely surrendered artistic control over the film completely, but that, in a manner that typifies his ironist trait, he still unequivocally performs his formal mastery of cinema in spite of his frequent laments that he is physically and mentally only 'functioning at sixty percent' (Kehr 2009).

As Schepelern (2005, 'The King of Dogme': 11) writes, his public image is a combination of 'detached, complex artist and challenging media personality'. As is his wont, von Trier is oxymoronically a shy exhibitionist. What his highly publicised depression and the theatrics in press conferences have done really is to draw even more attention to not only *Antichrist* but also himself and his *oeuvre*. When pressed by an indignant journalist to explain why he made the film, he said, 'I never have a choice. It's the hand of God. And I am the best film director in the world' (quoted in Bourgeois 2009). The provocative retort manages to side-step a logical explanation of the film, since he has none, while at the same time drawing the attention closer to his personality. An auteur defines his signature mark by way of the strength and originality of his work, and in von Trier's case, by his personality and the construction of his artistic ego. Such an initiative of his highlights not only the ingenuity and coherence of his *oeuvre*, but also his principal trademarks, irony and provocation. As von Trier once noted early in his career, 'a film should be like a pebble in your shoe' with the intention to unsettle, and in the case of *Antichrist*, repulse with its provocative subject matter (quoted in Schepelern 2005: 116).

Moreover, von Trier's exaggerated and tongue-in-cheek utterance at the press conference underlines another key point regarding the visual design of *Antichrist*. It is striking that von Trier's self-conscious proclamation positions himself in the pantheon of great directors and his frequent references in his interviews to renowned artists in film, theatre, and painting also serve the same function of reaffirming his auteurship. Consequently, *Antichrist* is redolent of von Trier's reverence for those great artists, and the film consciously acts as a collection of visual quotations, as if to declare his affiliation to the coterie of auteurs. The visual and technical motifs that echo Tarkovsky and artists such as Hieronymus Bosch and Henri Rousseau are evident especially in the painterly, meticulously shot scenes that utilise extreme slow-motion to the point that the shots look like still pictures, as discussed earlier. The camera lingers on each of these visual references – the burning before the cabin borrowed from Tarkovsky and the intricate tangle of the trees in the woods that reference Rousseau's paintings are examples – and thus creates a tension between the autonomy of the image and its place in the overall narrative. Hence, one might argue that von Trier is lacking control over the images, in the sense that such images are allowed to exist on their own, almost divorced from the logic of the plot. That von Trier has borrowed heavily from influential artists is not an unintentional laxity, even when he complains that the film is 'too beautiful overall,' and again, blames it on his poor health at that time (quoted in Björkman 2009: 19). The complaint is certainly a self-compliment in the same instance. This comment nevertheless reflects the pattern that von Trier has experienced a mode of liberation through an obstruction of sorts: in having to renounce his proclivity for abstracted aesthetic frameworks, he has returned to a stylistically conventional mode of filmmaking that now allows him to indulge in adornments and even overt narcissism with regard to his formal mastery. In all, von Trier's citations in and outside of the film are self-consciously and carefully placed in order to evoke an alignment to the auteurist stance.

To conclude this argument, an alternative perspective might colour this egocentricity as an anxiety. Coincidentally, two directors whom he greatly revered passed away on the same day in 2007: Michelangelo Antonioni and Ingmar Bergman. The passing of the latter was particularly hard on von Trier as a fellow Scandinavian, and it has been suggested that *Antichrist* is von Trier's oblique response to his anxiety about the economic and cultural viability of an auteur in the context of Hollywood genre domination (Gross 2009: 40). The choice of genre might then be seen as an interesting engagement with the idea of an auteur defending his artistic individuality against the Hollywood machine. The combination of horror and, to an extent, pornography articulates not only the presence of a great deal of self-reflexive gestures (through the customary 'horror' soundtrack, tone, and subject matter), but also von Trier's alterations of the genre. The traits of horror and pornography are taken to extremities far beyond what the placid and tamer mainstream variants offer, and this is precisely what he meant about reworking genres to 'add something to them' (quoted in Romer 2009). Thus, by re-examining the elements of the horror genre, he is putting into play its conventional expressions by turning them completely around, or in other scenes, amplifying them beyond orthodox boundaries of taste. In doing so, he has added his artistic mark on the film and the genre at the same time, and again, such a gesture affirms his position as an auteur in the art film canon. Furthermore, the most striking impression about *Antichrist* is the looseness in the coherence of its plot and the overwhelming intensity of its visual imagery. Thus, in letting go of the impulse to create a structured and logical film, and in his instinctual and impressionistic approach to the visual design, von Trier has achieved an expressive authenticity of examining the relationship of the art cinema to its ontological root, the image.

While the film has invited much negative criticism due to its offensive subject matter, critics still interpret the film as a remarkable piece that has managed to provoke and perturb even the most inured of spectators. This horror film is as cerebral as it is visceral, and that in itself is an outstanding quality that mainstream films lack — a quality that only an transgressive auteur such as von Trier might achieve (Ebert 2009).

Author's Comment

This essay is adapted from a chapter of my MA dissertation entitled *Losing Control: Lars von Trier and the Production of Authenticity and the Auteur*, completed in 2010 at the National University of Singapore. The dissertation sought to examine von Trier's three latest film projects and read them as variations on a theme of control that is present throughout his *oeuvre*. I began writing this chapter shortly after the film was first screened in 2009, right in that exciting space of time between a film's release and the initial publication of scholarly articles on it. When I say 'exciting', I also mean 'daunting' because, as a student, treading new ground without having the comfort of more established scholars interpret the film before you can be perplexing: 'Does my analysis hold water? Have I overlooked some obvious and significant angle? Should I throw some Deleuze in there?' Nevertheless, this anxiety is precisely what makes research an invigorating exercise in overcoming self-doubt, and such an endeavour becomes a genuine delight when you realise you are contributing your own voice, and not rehashing someone else's.

While my academic background was in English Literature, I have always had an affinity for film and visual studies, particularly aesthetic experimentation in cinema. An earlier encounter with von Trier's *Dancer in the Dark* distressed me so much that writing both my BA and MA theses about the director's work was my only (productive) means of catharsis. I continue to be harrowed by von Trier's work, even though my interests have shifted to slightly different themes and aspects of film analysis.

Since 2011, I have been a PhD candidate in the School of European Languages, Culture and Society at UCL. My doctoral project focuses on cinematic representations of transnational space and architecture, analysing film essays from the Øresund region and Berlin.

1. The lead character, Stoffer (Jens Albinus), championed the thesis that 'spassing' (behaving like an idiot, or pretending to be mentally retarded) not only challenges and confronts convention and conformity, but also offers the space and means for authentic, unrepressed emotion to be expressed. Read in the context of the Dogme framework, *Idioterne* argued for the foregrounding of imperfections in everyday experience as a kind of freedom to allow one's 'inner idiot' to be exposed, leaving room for emotion and psychological truth to germinate.

References

Beattie, Tina (2009). '*Antichrist*: The Visual Theology of Lars Von Trier.' *openDemocracy* http://www.opendemocracy.net/article/antichrist-the-visual-theology-of-lars-von-trier. Accessed 13 August 2009.

Björkman, Stig (2009). 'Making The Waves'. *Sight & Sound* August, 16-19.

Bourgeois, David (2009). 'Lars Von Trier, "Best Film Director in the World," Holds Press Conference.' *Movie|Line* http://www.movieline.com/2009/05/lars-von-trier-best-film-director-in-the-world-holds-press-conference.php. Accessed 30 December 2009.

Corliss, Richard and Mary Corliss (2009). '*Antichrist*: Von Trier's Porno Horror Rhapsody.' *TIME Magazine* http://www.time.com/time/arts/article/0,8599,1899134,00.html. Accessed 24 July 2012.

Ebert, Roger (2009). 'Cannes #6: A Devil's Advocate for *Antichrist*.' *Roger Ebert's Journal* http://blogs.suntimes.com/ebert/2009/05/a_devils_advocate_for_antichri.html. Accessed 30 December 2009.

Gross, Larry (2009). 'The Six Commandments of the Church of the Antichrist.' *Film Comment* 45:5, 38-46.

Heidegger, Martin (2000). 'The Origin of the Work of Art.' In Cazeaux, Clive (ed.): *The Continental Aesthetics Reader*. London: Routledge.

Johnston, Trevor (2009). '*Antichrist* Cinematographer Anthony

Dod Mantle: Interview.' *Time Out London* http://www.timeout.com/film/features/show-feature/8257/antichrist-cinematographer-anthony-dod-mantle-interview.html. Accessed 31 December 2009.

Kehr, Dave (2009). 'Away from It All, in Satan's Church.' *The New York Times* http://www.nytimes.com/2009/09/13/movies/13kehr.html. Accessed 13 September 2009.

Romer, Knud (2009). 'A Hearse Heading Home.' *FILM #66* http://www.dfi.dk/Nyheder/Tidsskriftet-FILM/Artikler-fra-tidsskriftet-FILM/66/A-Hearse-Heading-Home.aspx. Accessed 9 September 2009.

Simons, Jan (2007). *Playing the Waves: Lars Von Trier's Game Cinema*. Amsterdam: Amsterdam University Press.

Sjöholm, Cecilia (2005). *Kristeva & the Political*. London: Routledge.

Totaro, Donato (2000). 'Art for All "Time".' *Film-Philosophy* 4:4. http://www.film-philosophy.com/vol4-2000/n4totaro. Accessed 30 December 2009.

Schepelern, Peter (2005). 'The King of Dogme.' *FILM #Special Issue/Dogme* Spring: 8-10.

Schepelern, Peter (2005). 'The Making of an Auteur.' In Grodal, Torben, Bente Larsen, and Iben Thorving Laursen (eds.): *Visual Authorship: Creativity and Intentionality in Media*. Copenhagen: Museum Tusculanum Press, University of Copenhagen.

Schepelern, Peter (2009). 'Interview with Lars Von Trier.' *Antichrist* http://www.antichristthemovie.com/?p=252&language=en. Accessed 19 December 2009.

Auteur and Style

Alternative Endings in Early Danish and Russian Cinema

Anna V. Strauss

Introduction

Towards the beginning of the last century film companies began producing and exporting alternative endings for different national markets, drawing on stereotypes to create a film narrative that would satisfy the imagined foreign audience. At the centre of this study are two countries, Denmark and Russia, who were to exchange specially adapted endings in the 1910s until the Russian Revolution in 1917 was severely to restrict trade. In both cases, the endings consist of a final scene in which the fate of the characters is altered. This meant that Danish actors would come to a tragic (often fatal) end on the Russian screen when they would enjoy a happy resolution in other markets, such as the UK, US, Denmark and Sweden. Meanwhile Russian film companies would retain the 'inevitable' end for the domestic audience and produce an alternative 'happy' ending for Western spectators of the same film across the border.

Any previous scholarly reference to these endings has been restricted to a national context. The unhappy Russian endings produced by the Danish film company Nordisk Films Kompagni have been viewed as a quirk of general director Ole Olsen's production policy and international ambitions. In an article by Casper Tybjerg in *Kosmorama* the tragic Russian endings produced by Nordisk were cited as evidence for the importance of Russia as an export market, whilst they were considered by Paul Malmkjaer to be the beginnings of a production culture centred on satisfying foreign demand (Tybjerg 1997: 19; Malmkjaer 1997: 163). The endings produced in Russia, meanwhile, have been considered against the background of a struggling cultural identity. Here the opposition of the happy and unhappy endings has been seen as evidence of the opposition of Russia to America in a process of Russian self-definition (Tsivian 1989: 24). Whilst academics in both cases acknowledge the existence of alternative endings in the other's country, neither has ventured outside of their national framework to seek explanation for the emergence of the phenomenon (Thorsen 2009: 139; Tsivian 2004: 341; Nielsen 1999: 6).

This study will focus on two factors that informed the practice of producing alternative endings. The first concerns developments within the film industry at large. Changes in film length, narrative structure and the characterization of national film styles raised the question of how to end a film. The second factor is commercial production policy. The motivation to sell more films on a more diverse distribution network encouraged the development of alternative endings as part of a production policy aimed at appealing to wider markets. Cultural perception is closely tied with production policy and constitutes a third factor not addressed in this essay due to its limited scope.

Two academics have been responsible for the exploration of alternative endings in Denmark and Russia thus far. Both use a national framework to explain alternative endings. Isak Thorsen has written on the alternative endings produced by

Nordisk Films Kompagni. The endings formed part of his work on the development and significance of Nordisk in the international market from its conception in 1906 to its liquidation in 1928 (Thorsen 2009:139; n.d.: 2). According to his research, the unhappy endings filmed for Russia can be explained within the framework of Nordisk's own development and history. Thorsen groups the endings together with 'self-regulation' and adherence to censorship laws as features of a production policy centred on international export (Thorsen 2009: 126, n.d.: 2). General Director Ole Olsen's grand plans for expansion and participation in the international market are considered fundamental to the emergence of these practices (Thorsen 2010a: 2). For Thorsen, the endings present another example of Nordisk's process of 'tailoring' a film to its (various) audiences, a process which was to become part of long-term production policy and for which the company became renowned (Thorsen 2010a: 2; Malmkjaer 1997: 163). The production of the unhappy Russian ending is seen directly to correspond with the project to expand into Russia in the 1910s (Thorsen 2009: 69, 139, 203). As such, the endings can be fully explained by the commercial strategy of Nordisk.

Yurii Tsivian refers to the alternative endings in several of his works on pre-Revolutionary and early Soviet silent film (Tsivian 1989, 1991, 1994, 2004, 2008). Although Tsivian comes to differing conclusions in his various essays as to the reasons behind the practice, the basis for his understanding of the 'Russian' and 'Western' endings varies very little across his papers. For Tsivian, the endings are linked to expressions of national culture. He understands alternative endings as part of a process of cultural definition in Russia (Tsivian 1989, 1991,

2004). His latest reflections link the endings with other features of the 'national' cinema style that Russian filmmakers were attempting to define and to export (Tsivian 2004: 339). The acting style and the pace of the action, in his view, combine with the Russian ending to constitute a 'national' film style, aimed to differentiate Russian cinema from both its American and European counterparts (Tsivian 2004: 342, 345). According to his arguments, the endings are inextricably linked with an emerging national(istic) sentiment (Tsivian 1989, 1991, 2004. See also Hutchings 2008:9).

This study cross-references the work of Thorsen and Tsivian, developing a new international perspective on the alternative endings. Taking the focus on industry prevalent in Thorsen's work and considering it alongside the cultural explanations offered by Tsivian, this study aims at a more comprehensive understanding of the factors that influenced the emergence of the phenomenon. Whilst recognising that the film industries in Denmark and Russia have different histories, both were engaged in trading their films on an international market. Indeed, the production of alternative endings evinces the importance of foreign markets in both cases. International contexts must, therefore, be central to any explanation of this practice.

Research into this era of film is constrained by the loss or disintegration of the majority of films, and must rely on fragmented written accounts to piece together cinematic moments otherwise lost to posterity. Given these practical limitations, this study will understand films as the product of an industry in order to piece these fragments together. Cultural audience design is part of this theoretical framework, but this must be differentiated from attempts to define a national psyche.

Films of the silent era, as Bo Berglund reminds us, 'die in their cans every day' (Berglund 1999: 63). Of the endings that are the subject of this study, only five are known to survive. They are all of Danish origin.[1] While extensive resources in the various Nordic Film Institutes allow for a reasonably detailed understanding of the situation in Denmark, the same cannot be said for Russian film. Thus far, no alternative endings for Russian-made films have been discovered by any academics working in the field of silent film. Knowledge of films with alternative endings is tied to scripts, correspondence, synopses and memoirs. Ground-breaking work has been done by Jay Leyda and Yurii Tsivian in this area but there is still much that remains unpublished or unknown in relation to this period of Russian film history (Taylor and Christie 1994: 1; Tsivian, 1989: 1). As a result this essay relies heavily upon those studies done by other academics, films re-released on DVD, journals and resources available online for its evidence.

In addition, the endings that have survived constitute only a small percentage of the overall number of films that have survived from the period, and an even smaller percentage of all films that were produced at the time. The number of films from which I am working is necessarily a tiny fraction of the total and this must be remembered when making generalising observations.

This study will adhere to an understanding of cinema 'not merely as an aesthetic phenomenon, an art form, but as an administrative and industrial complex, with all the additional perspectives that this implies' (Taylor and Christie 1994: 2). As such, films are not to be analysed purely for their aesthetic and narrative qualities, but as products of an industry. Consequently, the films and their various endings must be considered the result of a production process.

It is also important to establish the limitations of cultural analysis. This study follows Tsivian in stating that 'culture is useful insofar as it helps us to understand films, not the other way round' (Tsivian 2004: 347). The films will not be used as a means for understanding the culture or psyche of Russia or Denmark. The unhappy endings for the Russian market, for example, will not be taken to reveal something of the 'terrific Slavic emotions' (cited in Tsivian 2004: 341). Investigation into the origins of the 'Russian ending' would prove complimentary to this study but the films under examination here have been produced with an assumption about these 'Slavic emotions' in mind. They serve only to demonstrate the existence of such a perception amongst film-makers and traders at the time. These perceptions and their realisation in films, though, aid us in our attempts to understand how stereotypes are constructed, re-negotiated and disseminated.

As such, Kazimierz Musiał's concepts of stereotyping add a new perspective to this study. Although championed in his work in the field of politics and the Scandinavian model of progressiveness, auto- and xeno-stereotypes, applied to the object of this study, provide an important theoretical framework. Musiał, in his article *Tracing the Roots of the Scandinavian Model* argues that 'the image of a progressive Scandinavia has been shaped and enhanced by two dimensions which in the course of its development remained in constant interaction: an external, foreign dimension and an internal, native one' (Musiał 2002). In this case, he suggests, the xeno-stereotype of Scandinavia as 'progressive' then influenced 'the constitution of what the Scandinavians thought of themselves' (Musiał 2002). Returning to silent film with this in mind, the alternative endings filmed for different national markets serve as products of the processes of internal and external identity-construction that Musiał describes. As cultural products circulated in a multi-national industry, however, the exportation of alternative film endings is also implicated in the manufacture and perpetuation of such images. Moreover, they translated stereotypes into a new visual medium.

Developments within the film industry

Developments in the international market in the period in question, including the move from shorts to features, a boom in the number of cinemas and film companies, and an increasingly dominant role played by the US industry, impacted upon the policies and production of global competitors. Fears of cultural insignificance and financial loss led European film companies to seek distinction and definition in the face of the seemingly homogenous and threatening American film industry. The threat of American dominance was real enough for Olsen to play to it in an interview when justifying an expansion of share capital in 1915:

> 'America possesses a large quantity of finished negative, and at the first opportunity will throw these out on the European market at prices that will exclude all European competition. This will mean the death of the European film industry, which

is what we're trying to prevent by taking these actions' (cited in Thorsen 2010b: 471).

The promotion of a Hollywood style served as a model for the 'happy' endings deemed necessary for the sale of film to the US, and, Tsivian argues, a negative model for the film endings that Russia wished to promote amongst its own audience. I propose, however, that the sad endings circulated in the Russian domestic market were less a product of national definition and more of a production policy, which aimed at success in the West.

Narrative and American Endings

The move towards feature-length films raised new issues and opportunities for film-makers. Amongst these was how to end a film. According to Noël Burch:

> It was more than ten years before film-makers knew how to end their films in a way allowing the spectator to withdraw 'gently' from the diegetic experience, convinced that he or she had no more business in it and not feeling that the dream had been interrupted by a beating or by being kicked out of it. (Burch 1990: 222)

The alternative endings are evidence of this process. The Russian ending for *Evangeliemandens Liv* (1915) and *Atlantis* (1913) from Nordisk and *Rukoj Materi* (1913), *Drama po Telefonu* (1914) and *Nevesta Ognya* (1911) from Russian companies all demonstrate a 'punitive' ending (see Tsivian 1989: 24). This type of ending is characterised as abrupt and featuring the punishment of one or all of the main characters. In each of the examples above, the Russian ending features the death of at least one central character. In comparison with their counterpart endings the Russian endings are left 'open'. 'Non-closure' is a quality that Burch attributes to a 'primitive mode of representation' and thus identifies these films with early cinema, and a period of film production prior to the 'institutionalised mode of representation' later to be associated with classical Hollywood style films (Burch 1990: 220). The different film endings 'draw attention to the process by which the "satisfactory" endings of the institutions were constructed' (Burch 1990: 222). The production of happy endings as alternative, then, reveals an awareness of the emergence of Hollywood style and recognition of its increasing authority within the international film industry.

Development and promotion of the 'classic Hollywood cinema style', which according to David Bordwell et al. was already in place by 1917, brought with it new pressures and models for other global firms (Thompson 1985: 157). Significant for this study is the development of the 'Hollywood' or 'American' ending. The happy ending was a part of the construction of the Hollywood style and 'mode of production', which 'began to crystallize around 1908' and aimed to (re)claim the American domestic market from Pathé Frères (Tsivian 2004: 342). As early as 1909 the American trade journal *Moving Picture World* urged exhibitors to 'Give the public good cheer and watch the increased stream of dimes and nickels which will flow into your coffers' (cited in Trumpbour 2002: 19). This is the type of ending that the Russian market felt compelled to produce and export in order to make sales of its films abroad a possibility in the 1910s. Similarly, within Nordisk, Blom was to write to director Hjalmar Davidsen: 'I will kindly remind the directors about the rule that for every film with a sad ending, even if it seems misleading, must always be supplied with an extra ending scene...' (Thorsen 2009: 141) Most often these endings twisted the plot so as to end the film with the happy union of a couple, the recovery of a dying character or the successful rescue of a character in danger.[2] Previous to this, the endings that we now recognise in the negative as *un*happy were the norm (Tsivian 2004: 342). The increasingly dominant 'closed' endings within the Hollywood style became a model for Russian and Danish filmmakers with an eye to the 'West'.

The production of both open and closed endings identifies this period as an experimental one, in which alternative endings could be marketed and produced. At this time, styles, genres, and narrative structures were in a stage of development rather than having been standardised and institutionalised. The 'predominance of narrative structure' was not yet in place and as such there was opportunity to experiment with features such as endings, the style and structure of which would soon become set in stone (Thompson 1985: 157). It cannot be assumed that the happy ending was inherent to cinematic narrative. In fact, there was a tendency towards 'punitive' endings, which as Burch claims, were adopted from the circus (Burch 1990: 222; Tsivian 2004: 342). Although to the modern-day viewer it seems that the *un*happy endings exported to Russia need more explaining than those *happy* endings exported from Russia at this time, in fact, the definition of any particular type of film ending in this period requires critical consideration. The uncertainty surrounding the issue of ending a film made the production of alternative endings feasible and, as such, the endings must be understood in this international context of formal experimentation. The move to feature-length films and the rising authority of Hollywood film style with its happy endings gave rise to an atmosphere conducive to the production of alternative endings in Denmark and Russia.

Narrative and the medium of film

The alternative endings that were developed were only a fraction of the whole product being exported. Other features of experimentation by film-makers suggest that film in this period was a site of negotiation between narratives, their visual realisation and spectacle (Gunning 2004: 41). This negotiation allowed for the flexibility that enabled the production of alternative endings to become so widespread a practice. Narrative works by 'posing an enigma...[and] delaying the resolution of that enigma' (Gunning 2004: 43). As is shown by the production of alternative endings, the nature of that resolution was not considered as important as the process of leading to a resolution. Instead, features of both Russian and Danish cinema in this period highlight a 'dynamic relation to nonnarrative material' (Gunning 2004: 43). Russia, for example, developed a slow pace of action and a 'psychological' acting style, which brought to the fore the image of the film star (Tsivian 2004: 342). Denmark became renowned for its settings, film stars and erotic spectacle (Engberg 1993: 441; Sandberg 2001: 6). These features are less to do with the plot and more to do with the image projected on screen. In addition, criticism in journals often focuses upon the technical or aesthetic aspects of films, whilst details of the plot are reserved for programmes and synopses. The plot and the film, although reliant upon one another, are dealt with separately. Altering the ending to the plot was therefore not considered as significant as it would be today.

According to correspondence that Tsivian has come across in his research of early Soviet cinema, directors at that time did occasionally attempt to resist the changes prescribed by the Export-Import Division regarding the endings of films (Tsivian 2008: 24). Similarly, re-editing done within the Soviet Union was not well-received by Western film companies, who in some cases had already made alterations for their export to the Union (Tsivian 2008: 33, 26). The absence of any such resistance by pre-Revolutionary directors when the policy of making alternative endings was originally implemented implies that a change had occurred that made such alterations to the plot and narrative less acceptable to film-makers in the 1920s than it had been in the 1910s. Aside from the political developments that led to a definite opposition of post-Revolutionary Russia to the West, ideas of narrative had changed. For Soviet editors, the 'man in the shot' was 'raw material' to be manipulated and plots increasingly became dictated by political propaganda (Tsivian 2008: 40). In post-war Europe, however, the dominance of American film became fact rather than simple prediction and as a result character and plot emerged as central to any film in accordance with the classical Hollywood style (Staiger 1985: 109; Thorsen 2009: 143). The practice of producing alternative endings arose before these changes came into play. The dynamic changes and developments to the film industry and attitudes of film-makers in the 1910s meant film endings at this time could be manipulated for marketing purposes.

National endings in a global cinema

Tom Gunning has argued that 'in its first decades... a primary way that film understood itself was as a medium that could express a new sense of global identity' (Gunning 2008: 11). Olsen recalls this 'new consciousness of the global' in his memoirs when he writes: 'we had to be careful and make the films in such a way that they could be understood everywhere' (Gunning 2008: 13; Thorsen 2010a: 2). It seems that Olsen's belief that Nordisk films could be made wholly exportable and translatable was founded in his understanding of the film market and the film medium as international. However, it also highlights national difference implying that films had to be made in a particular way to be universally understood.

At Nordisk, writers were instructed to compose 'simple stories, which were easily understood not only in Denmark, but everywhere', 'to use as few intertitles as possible', instead telling the story 'by means of the pictures shown' (Engberg 1993: 63). Olsen's international ambitions, thus, impacted upon the style, genre and content of his company's films. To some extent the trade that went on between Russia and Denmark, best documented in the archives of the DFI, is demonstrative of this idea and encourages belief in the 'internationality' of early silent film that Gunning describes (Gunning 2008: 11). Indeed, it has been observed that 'neither the exhibitors, nor the public seemed to restrict their film interests by country of origin' (Leyda 1983). This suggests that the belief Olsen held in the quality of the picture and comprehension of the plot being that which would sell a picture was a well-founded one. Judging by those I have been able successfully to research, the alternative endings consist of a final scene or two, without intertitles. The endings are self-explanatory. These endings would have been comprehensible to any audience, regardless of cultural background. The wish to appeal to an international audience, therefore, dictated the nature of the endings and encouraged a tendency to extremes i.e. either death or the happy union of the main characters. The understanding of film as a universally comprehensible medium led to the belief that companies could make films that appealed to all different national markets. This encouraged ambitious businessmen like Olsen to look beyond the borders of their own small nations convinced that with particular films they could tap into the rich international market.

The different endings were clearly defined and aimed at national audiences, however. (There would be no mistaking a happy American ending for a sad Russian one, for example). The need or desire to appeal to individual markets through adaption of the films in a supposedly global industry requires explanation.

Alternative endings arose at the coincidence of a global film industry and fierce nationalism exaggerated by war. Increasing national consciousness amongst film-makers in part explains the timing for the development of alternative endings. America and Hollywood were not the only film industries to be developing a distinctive national style. Several scholars have noted the emergence of 'national traits' or 'characteristics' within Europe in this period (Low 1949: 206; Neergaard 1960: 39; Engberg 1977: 441, 1993: 441; Abel 1994: 299; Lebedev 1965). Danish film was associated with 'social drama' and 'erotic melodrama' (Neergaard and Engberg cited in Thorsen 2010a: 9). Russian film-makers initially focussed on 'Russian' subjects such as its 'glorious past' or folklore (Leyda 1983: 38). Evidence for this juxtaposition of the global and the national can be found in the Russian press of the time. Russian trade journals include on their pages an increasing awareness of the domestic industry and its responsibility to promote a national product, along with articles written to report on the success of Russian films abroad and comparisons of the Russian product with that of the States and Europe. The development of a self-consciously national industry defined by its place in the international market demanded recognition of the difference between domestic and foreign markets in a way not so apparent before. In this atmosphere, established stereotypes could be appealed to by the film industry in attempts to sell to a given national market. The endings were imagined in an atmosphere where national traits and national industries were developing; constructing national borders within what was a global industry.

The production of national identity in film endings must be understood in a global commercial context. Investigation of the developments within the international market reveals traces of these developments in the films and the endings themselves. The prevalence of film as a new visual medium, increasingly aggressive nationalism and the question of how to end a film in the new era of multi-reels made the widespread production of alternative endings possible. In these ways the multi-national film industry shaped the forms of nationalism in film and dictated the framework within which national film industries were to function.

Commercial Production Policy

This section will focus upon the reasons for the emergence of alternative film endings in Denmark and Russia, again taking an international perspective. Commercial production and the nature of the entertainment industry were to influence the policies of national film companies as they clamoured for a place on the highly competitive international market. Differentiation of the product proved necessary for those companies aspiring to global success. For Nordisk alternative endings were to constitute part of a wider production policy aimed at tailoring films to different national consumers. For Russian companies, they were considered a necessary adaptation to have films sell in the more dominant and institutionalised Western markets. In both cases, alternative endings were produced with the fundamental aim of selling more films in a wider market and increasing revenue.

Money-making

In the early twentieth century, cinema was regarded 'first and foremost as a means of making money' (Taylor and Christie 1994: 19). In order to increase the amount of revenue it was necessary to increase the size of the distribution network and, with it, the audience. In a competitive entertainment industry, film companies needed to demonstrate innovation and differentiate their product in order to succeed. As in America, where happy endings were encouraged as a means of 'increasing the stream of dimes and nickels flowing into the coffers', the endings produced in Denmark and Russia fundamentally served as a means to earn more money (Trumpbour 2002: 19).

For Nordisk, the production of alternative endings was linked to the company's interest in expansion into Russia. The potential of the Russian market had, despite its inherent difficulties, attracted attempts to set up a local branch by several different countries and companies (Malmkjaer 1997: 123). The adoption of alternative endings into Nordisk's production policy coincides with a deal brokered in 1911 with the Russian film company Thiemann, Reinhardt & Osipov. A letter from the time communicates to the new distribution agent that Nordisk 'will always, if possible, make a special dramatic ending for Russia. We have given clear orders about this to our directors and literary employees' (Thorsen 2010a: 14). It appears that the guarantee of unhappy endings made for the market was discussed as part of the deal. In the two years that followed, Russia became Nordisk's second largest export market, only surpassed by Germany, and in 1914 the Russian market became Nordisk's largest (Thorsen 2010a: 13). This would imply that the deal was a success and that film, which Nordisk exported to Russia in these years, answered the demands of the Russian market. This assertion is confirmed both by the lack of complaints from Russian agents and by surveys responded to by the Russian public (Thorsen 2009: 145; Ginzburg 1963: 163). According to records from 1913, for example, answering a question about their favourite film company, 916 of the 1313 inhabitants interviewed in Kharkov answered Nordisk (cited in Thorsen 2009: 145). The quality and quantity of the films produced by Nordisk would doubtless have played a more significant role than the endings (Christensen 2009: 61). Nevertheless, the explicit assurance that special endings would 'always, if possible' be made demonstrates that the endings did play some role, even if only as a marketing gimmick for Nordisk. As such, potential increase in revenue from wider distribution was a significant motivation for their production.

Although there is no such evidence that explicitly links Russian-made alternative endings to deals within a particular foreign market, research done by Tsivian and Jay Leyda would suggest a similar financial incentive. In 1906, Aleksandr Khanzhonkov followed Aleksandr Drankov's lead and broke away from the French-owned Gaumont to set up his own film company. According to Leyda, the successes of foreign films made in Russia for foreign audiences, such as *Smert' Ioanna Groznogo* (1909) which was withdrawn in Russia but enjoyed notable success across the border, made Khanzhonkov 'determined to reach the rich foreign market, too' (Leyda 1983: 38; Lebedev 1965). In addition, Tsivian observes in his work on the early Soviet period that film companies had inherited a belief from the pre-Revolutionary days that 'the death of a hero made foreign sales problematic' (Tsivian 2008: 24). Taken together these observations suggest that the motivation for making happy endings for export was founded in a desire to have those films successfully sell in the West.

The endings made both in Denmark and in Russia were a means of 'ensuring' the appeal of those films abroad, and in theory, therefore 'ensuring' their sale to foreign distributors.

Product Differentiation

In a market so intensely competitive and developing so quickly 'product differentiation' became essential for success. In her work on the Hollywood mode of production, Janet Staiger notes an important tension between standardisation and differentiation: 'standardising - to be known for excellence and to increase efficiency, differentiation to compete in a varied market and as grounds for repeated consumption.' (Staiger 1985: 108) Through the production of alternative endings a film company was able to differentiate its product, in the case of Nordisk even gaining a reputation 'for at levere det, man ønskede' ('for giving [the buyer] what they wanted') (Malmkjaer 1997: 163). Simultaneously, however, the innovations which were to differentiate the film companies were made within a wider standardised context. Film companies in both countries relied upon the foundation of an international reputation and worked within the confines of those standards being consolidated in the 1910s.

This tension between standardisation and differentiation is revealed in the combination of Olsen's international ambitions for his company and recognition that in order to realise these ambitions the company would need to be reliable and respectable. Olsen recognised that just such a company needed to be producing films that were 'acceptable to all cultural groups', writing in his memoirs 'they [the employees of Nordisk] couldn't pay the bills if we shot the wrong picture' (Olsen cited in Thorsen 2010a: 2). Yet, to achieve his dream of Nordisk Films Kompagni becoming 'the biggest in the world', it was necessary to demonstrate innovation and novelty in order to maintain a competitive edge in the market (Thorsen 2010b: 465; Staiger 1985: 97). Nordisk had been amongst the first to make the transition from shorts to feature length films and this was to bring some international recognition (Thorsen 2009: 117). After its being standardised across the industry, however, Nordisk needed new means of standing out. Affirmation for Nordisk came with the emergence of the first international film stars, the quality of the sets and design, cinematic 'finesse', and eroticism (Malmkjaer 1997: 160, 162; Nordisk Film 2011). Included in this oft-cited list should also be the reputation that Nordisk gained for 'providing what was wanted' by its buyers (Malmkjaer 1997: 163). This refers both to the Russian endings and the other adaptations made especially for individual national markets. Whilst making sad endings for the Russians, Nordisk also produced 'discrete' and 'stronger' versions of scenes to suit the censors and avoided certain themes or topics. For example, no spies were to be present in films for the Germans, and in English versions, no man could be seen inviting a woman into a room if the two would be alone with a bed (Malmkjaer 1997: 163; Thorsen 2010a: 19). Any guarantee that a film company could offer to ensure a film would pass the censors would have been a big selling point. Thorsen notes:

> Med en films forholdsvis korte 'levetid' kan producenten ikke med sikkerhed være garanterest at få sin investering igen. Derfor blev brandingen af en film overfor publikum en måde at sikre filmens succes. (Thorsen 2009: 143)

> With a film's relatively short 'lifespan' the producer could not with any certainty guarantee to get his investment back. Therefore the branding of a film to the audience became one way to ensure a film's success.

Having a reputation of satisfying demand, passing the censors and delivering a high quality product was vital to Nordisk's success. Alternative endings as a means of satisfying audience demand were a part of the creation of its brand. The endings, then, in part arose due to the demands of the film industry and the value placed on innovation and differentiation as a means of competing in that industry.

In the case of Russia, Tsivian argues that the alternative film endings are linked to a distinctively Russian style of acting and direction. As such, he describes the Russian endings as forming part of an 'arsenal of cultural tools deployed by national cinema to stake a claim on the map of international filmmaking' (Tsivian 2004: 342). As opposed to giving the foreign market 'what it wanted', the Russian film companies exploited the mystery and exoticism attached to the Western perception of Russia to emphasise the 'Russian' aspect of the films they were exporting and thus differentiating them. The slow pace of the action aimed at complimenting a 'psychological' style of acting, for example, was to be branded 'Russian cinema style' (Tsivian 2004: 342; Anon. 1911: 2).The production of a happy ending for the West, though, cannot be seen as an extension of this policy – if it were a truly Russian product, then why not export the *un*happy endings supposedly so popular amongst its domestic audiences? Here the tension of differentiation and standardisation is revealed. The relatively insignificant output of Russian film companies could not afford to displease the American and European audiences, which as Russian film-makers understood it, desired a happy resolution. As such, the innovations of Russian film style had to occur within the framework of the more dominant American narrative style and with its prescribed happy ending (Staiger 1985: 97). Tsivian's theory explains the Russian endings as if they were intended for export. In fact, Russia pursued the same commercial strategy as Nordisk in producing happy endings for the West, pandering to an internationally more powerful national stereotype.

Russia and Denmark: Export-Oriented

The roots of the commercial strategies of both Russia and Denmark are found in the differing development of the film industries in each country. These film industries were at the mercy of those larger and more influential that were more developed or had more money at their disposal.

Denmark, as a small, peripheral nation, has necessarily always been reliant upon foreign export. When setting up Nordisk in the early 1900s, Olsen's recognition that 'the demand for films exceeded the number of films produced' led him to focus on exportation (Engberg 1993: 63). In conjunction with this he implemented policies within the company that would enable the films to be tailored to the nations to which Nordisk was exporting. As he wrote to a disgruntled British customer, with whom he had misjudged the audience preference, 'we do in all cases always make, if it's possible different endings according to the tastes of different countries' (Thorsen 2010a: 15; 2009: 141). At the end of the war, around ninety-eight percent of Nordisk's income came from its output in foreign markets (Arnedal 2006: 30). The fate of Nordisk was thus closely bound with the export markets. In his thesis Thorsen links the demise of Nordisk to the move away from an international focus after the war (Thorsen 2009: 365). With so much riding on success abroad, it is no wonder that an ambitious man like Olsen would induce orders to his workers to go out of their way to tailor films to the tastes of foreign consumers.

Whilst for Denmark, its size and position on the edge of

Europe made carving out a space on the international market essential for success, Russia was faced with an enormous domestic market and, theoretically, little financial or practical need to expand its market abroad. As was to be seen during the war and after the Revolution with the subsequent restrictions on the import of foreign films, the domestic market alone could provide and sustain a flourishing and profitable film industry. Nevertheless, Russia, too, was engaged in the process of producing alternative endings for export.

Russia's alternative endings find explanation in the situation of its domestic film industry. The Russian film industry was dominated by foreign firms from its outset. Foreign companies had technical expertise, financial support and wide distribution networks that Russian companies could not compete with. In journals of the 1910s many articles are concerned with the inability of Russian film companies to contend with foreign firms. An enduring example is the belief that Russian companies were incapable of making successful comedy films (Leyda 1983: 35; Lebedev 1965). In order to break the stranglehold that foreign companies like Pathé had over the market, Russian film-makers and distributors had to find a means of differentiating their films. Unlike Denmark, Russia had strong cultural connotations in Europe as being 'exotic' and unknown (Leyda 1983: 38; Norris 2008: i). Attempts by foreign film companies to capture 'Russianness' on screen were widely criticised (cited in Tsivian 2008: 41; Leyda 1983: 30). Russia's strong cultural connotations gave it a different position in the world film market and a means of differentiating its films through its subjects and cinematic style. The endings were considered a necessary adaptation in order to have their films sell abroad, enabling Russian film companies to both access the rich foreign film markets and in the process disseminate a defined national style.

The alternative endings, then, serve various purposes for the Russian and the Danish film companies that produced them. In both cases, the alternative ending provided a resolution to the tension inherent to the film industry, occurring as a result of the value afforded to both standardisation and differentiation within it. Companies within Denmark, such as Nordisk, needed to actively carve out a niche in the international market and to make a reputation in order to achieve any level of success within that wider international context. This was achieved in part through the use of the alternative ending as a marketing gimmick, a novelty that could be associated with other features of 'tailoring' that the company was engaged in. Russia, similarly peripheral to Europe, but with a reputation for 'difference', utilised the alternative endings as a means of selling its films abroad and, in the process, standardising its innovative film style. The differing strategies for competing in the international film market, then, can be explained by the positions of individual nations in reference to it.

Conclusion

Alternative endings are the result of film-makers in Denmark and Russia responding to aesthetic and commercial developments within the international film industry, which in the 1910s was going through a period of dynamic change. Although the industries in the two different national contexts have histories of their own, the emergence of alternative endings in each case must not be viewed as two separate phenomena. The practice in both countries arose as means of competing on the international market. Fundamentally, then, alternative endings were produced in order to appeal to new audiences, the success of which would lead to an increase in revenue. The situation of the film industry at the time enabled endings to be manipulated in a process of adaptation to new foreign markets. The fluidity of the times allowed for greater flexibility and experiment in relation to narrative, content and style than later decades would permit. Cultural stereotypes determined the nature of the endings that were produced. The films and their alternative endings then constructed and produced these stereotypes, circulating them in new markets embedded in a new visual medium.

Alternative endings reveal a tension between the global and national existent in the film industry. Assumptions about national markets and audiences found at the core of the practice were drawn from internationally held stereotypes and constructed in accordance with an understanding of a nation's position within a wider global context. The 'new global consciousness' of the filmmaker and cinemagoer meant that perceptions of national culture, be they externally or internally focused, were formed by and understood within this international framework. These perceptions were constructed, mediated and distributed through films released in the international market. The investigation of alternative endings thus exposes how international markets shape the ways in which national identity is produced and consumed.

Author's Comment

The essay here is an edited version of my undergraduate dissertation completed in the spring term 2012. A third section on cultural perception and audience recruitment within the industry has been omitted in order to shorten what was previously a 10,000 word project.

I followed the BA Language and Culture degree programme studying Russian and Swedish languages along with various aspects of Slavic and Nordic cultures. I chose Nordic Cinema in my second year, at which point I was introduced not only to Nordic directors, films, actors and movements, but also more fundamentally to film as an object of study. Previous to this, my interest and understanding of cinema, it has to be said, was rather superficial. This project came about almost totally by chance but the finished product feels to be a culmination of that which I learned during the preceding four years of study.

Reading the essay now, I should have liked to have had the time to watch more films and to have realised my interest in the topic whilst on my Year Abroad in Russia. Research in the Moscow film fund, I am sure, would have been an experience worth having in its own right and would have thrown light upon other curious paths for exploration. I also ought to have discussed the film texts themselves and explored the differing narrative and aesthetic qualities of the films and their endings but given the nature of the period under scrutiny and the lack of surviving materials (especially on the Russian side) this would have been difficult. I would have liked to have got my hands on some of the old journals and programmes themselves instead of being limited to those copies online, but again this would have involved travel, time and money that, unfortunately, I did not have at my disposal. A project for the future, perhaps.

1. *Et Drama paa Havet* dir. Eduard Schnedler Sørensen, Nordisk (1912); *Atlantis* dir. August Blom, Nordisk (1913); *En Fare for Samfundet* dir. Robert Dinesen, Nordisk (1915); *Blade af Satans Bog* dir. Carl Theodor Dreyer, Nordisk (1919) [English ending]; *Evangeliemandens Liv* dir. Holger-Madsen, Nordisk (1914)
2. Examples to be found in *Evangeliemandens Liv* (1914); *Atlantis* (1913); *Rukoj Materi, Drama po Telefonu, Nevesta Ognya* as described in Tsivian 1989: 24-42.

References

Abel R (1994). *The Cine Goes to Town: French Cinema 1896 - 1914.* Berkeley: University of California Press.

Arnedal, P. (2006). *Nordisk Film - en del af Danmark i 100 år* København: Aschehoug.

Berdyaev, N (2012). 'Volya k zhizni I volya k kul'ture' Accessed at: http://cgo.irbis-nbuv.gov.ua/spivb/9_1.pdf

Burch, N. (1990). 'A Primitive Mode of Representation?' In T. Elsaesser, A. Barker (eds): *Early Cinema: Space, Frame, Narrative.* BFI Publishing, London.

Christensen, T. (2009). 'Restoration of Danish Silent Films – in colour'. *Film History* 21:1.

Engberg, M. (1993). 'The Erotic Melodrama in Danish Silent Films 1910 – 1918'. *Film History* 5:1.

Donaldson, L. (n.d.). 'Our Allies and the Cinema. A General Survey of Trade Conditions in the Countries at War with Germany'. *The Bioscope* 11 November.

Franklin, S. and E. Widdis (eds) (2004). *National Identity in Russian Culture.* Cambridge: Cambridge University Press.

Ginzburg, S. (2007; 1963). *Kinematofrag dorevoliutsionnoi Rossii.* Moscow: Agraf.

Grieveson, L. and .P Krämer (eds) (2004). *The Silent Cinema Reader* London and New York: Routledge.

Gunning, T. (2004). '"Now you see it, now you don't": The Temporality of the Cinema of Attractions'. In Grieveson, L. and P. Krämer (eds): *The Silent Cinema Reader* London and New York: Routledge.

Gunning, T. (2008). 'Early cinema as global cinema: the encyclopaedic ambition'. In Abel, R., G. Bertellini, R. King (eds): *Early Cinema and the 'National'*. New Barnet: John Libbey Publishing Ltd.

Hutchings, S. (ed.) (2008). *Russia and its Other(s) on Film: Screening Intercultural Dialogue* Basingstoke: Palgrave Macmillan.

Jarvie, I. (2000). 'National Cinema: A Theoretical Assessment'. In Hjort, M. and S. MacKenzie (eds): *Cinema and Nation*. London: Routledge.

Kostuikhin, E. (n.d.). 'Magic Tales that End Badly'. https://journals.ku.edu/index.php/folklorica/article/viewFile/3670/3514. Accessed 22 April 2012.

Lebedev, N. (n.d.). *Kinematograf v dorevoliutsionnoj Rossii* (1896-1917). http://www.bibliotekar.ru/kino/2.htm

Leyda, J. (1983). *Kino: A History of the Russian and Soviet Film*. Princeton: Princeton University Press.

Low, R. (1949). *The History of British Film 1906 - 1914*. London: George Allen & Unwin Ltd.

Malmkjær, P. (1997). *Gøgler og Generaldirektør: Ole Olsen grundlæggeren af Nordisk Film* Copenhagen: Gyldendal.

Musiał, K. (2002). *Roots of the Scandinavian Model: Images of Progress in the Era of Modernisation*. Baden-Baden: Nomos.

Neergaard, E. (1960). *Historien om dansk film* København: Gyldendal.

Nielsen, J. (1999). 'A Small Danish Player in a Big Market: A/S Filmfabriken Danmark's Output in Russia, 1913 - 1917'. In Fullerton, J., J. Olsson (eds): *Nordic Explorations: Film before 1930* Sydney: John Libbey Publishing Ltd.

Norris, S. (2008). 'Introduction: Insiders and Outsiders in Russian Cinema'. In Norris, S., Z. Torlone (eds): *Insiders and Outsiders in Russian Cinema*. Bloomington: Indiana University Press.

Sandberg, M. (2001). 'Pocket Movies: Souvenir Cinema Programmes and the Danish Silent Cinema'. *Film History* 13:1.

Staiger, J. (1985). 'The Hollywood Mode of Production to 1930'. In Bordwell, D., J. Staiger, K. Thompson (eds): *The Classical Hollywood Cinema: Film Style and Mode of Production to 1960*. London: Routledge.

Taylor, R. and I. Christie (eds) (1994): *The Film Factory: Russian and Soviet Cinema in Documents 1896 - 1939*. London: Routledge.

Taylor, R. and I. Christie (eds) (1994): *Inside the Film Factory: New Approaches to Russian and Soviet Cinema*. London: Routledge.

Thompson, K. (1985). 'The formulation of the classical style, 1909 - 1928'. In Bordwell, D., J. Staiger, K. Thompson (eds): *The Classical Hollywood Cinema: Film Style and Mode of Production to 1960.* London: Routledge.

Thorsen, I. (2009). *Isbjørnens anatomi: Nordisk Films Kompagni som erhvervsvirksomhed i perioden 1906 - 1928* Thesis (Ph.d.-afhandling), Københavns Universitet.

Thorsen, I. (2010a). '"We had to be careful." The self-imposed regulations, alterations and censorship strategies of Nordisk Films Kompagni 1911 - 1928'. *Scandinavian Canadian Studies / Études Scandinaves au Canada* 19, 112-126.

Thorsen, I. (2010b). '"Nordisk Films Kompagni Will Now Become the Biggest in the World"'. *Film History* 22:4, 463-478.

Trumpbour, J. (2002). *Selling Hollywood to the World: U.S. and European Struggles for Mastery of the Global Film Industry, 1920-1950* Cambridge: Cambridge University Press.

Tsivian, Y. (1989). *Silent Witnesses: Russian Films, 1908 - 1919 / Testimoni Silenziosi: film russi, 1908 -1919* Pordenone, London: Edizioni Biblioteca dell-immagine, BFI.

Tsivian, Y. (1991). 'Some Preparatory Remarks on Russian Cinema'. In Christie, I., R. Taylor (eds): *Inside the Film Factory. London:* Routledge.

Tsivian, Y. and R. Taylor (eds) (1994). *Early Cinema in Russia and its Cultural Reception.* Trans. Alan Bodger. London: Routledge.

Tsivian, Y. (2004). 'New Notes on Russian Film Culture between 1908 and 1919'. In Grieveson, L. and P. Krämer (eds): *The Silent Cinema Reader.* London and New York: Routledge.

Tsivian, Y. (2008). 'The Wise and Wicked Game: Reediting, Foreignness, and Soviet Film Culture of the Twenties'. In Norris, S. and Z. Torlone (eds): *Insiders and Outsiders in Russian Cinema. Bloomington:* Indiana University Press.

Tybjerg, C. (997). 'Spekulanter og himmelstormere'. *Kosmorama* 220.

Zharov, S. (n.d.). 'Tsivilizatsiya i kul'tura v istoricheskix sud'bax Zapada i Rossii'. http://phipsy99-04.narod.ru/nauka/zharov.pdf Accessed 22 April 2012.

Masken, 9 March 1916

Russian Journals consulted

Ekran Rossii 15 May 1916

Ekran Rossii 5 April 1916

Iuzhanin 1 November 1915

Elektro-Teatr 29 March 1909

'Nashe natsional'noe bogatstvo' and 'Nashi kustari za granitsei' *Peterburgskii Kinematograf* 8 January 1911

'Kul'tura i eya Plody' *Peterburgskii Kinematograf* 19 January 1911

'Odna' *Peterburgskii Kinematograf* 16 February 1911

Petrogradskii Kino-Zhurnal 1 February 1916

'Otechestvennaya Promyshlennost'' *Kinemo* 15 October 1909

Ėklėr-zhurnal / izdavaemyĭ moskovskim otd. frantsuzskago o-va "Ėklėr" 1913 – 1914

Ėlektro-teatr "Palas." November and December 1914, January 1915

Nation and Identity

The Unknown Soldier in Finnish History

Essi Viitanen

December 1955 saw the release of what was to become the most popular film in Finnish history. The film was based on Väinö Linna's immensely successful novel, which had sold 100,000 copies within six months of its release in 1954, as Jukka Sihvonen (2005) notes. The film was *Tuntematon sotilas* (The Unknown Soldier), which was directed by Edvin Laine. The film brought Finnish film production to a completely new level when the script was bought from Linna for the largest sum in the history of Finnish filmmaking at the time, according to the director (Laine 1983). This grand scale continued as the film drew 2.8 million viewers to the cinemas (Uusitalo 2004), which was well over half of Finland's population in 1955 (Tilastokeskus 2004). From 1967 onwards *Tuntematon sotilas* has been shown on Finnish television every year on Independence Day, each time reaching an average of 1.35 million viewers (Uusitalo 2004). Edvin Laine (1983) states that the film has been screened in 65 countries, which is more than any other Finnish film to date. Its success has extended beyond Finland as well, as Jukka Sihvonen (2005: 141) claims: '*Tuntematon sotilas* remains the most widely seen Finnish film, both in Finland and abroad'.

The setting of *Tuntematon sotilas* is the Continuation War between Finland and the Soviet Union 1941 to 1944. The film shows the war through a machinegun company's first attack and subsequent withdrawal. The film's characters are a diverse set of caricatures of Finnish people. The film has risen to become an important part of the Finnish culture and national heritage. The Minister of Culture, Tanja Karpela (2004: 13), uses the following description: 'Tuntematon sotilas on ollut alusta asti enemmän kuin ensimmäinen ja samalla suurin suomalainen sotaelokuva' (*Tuntematon sotilas* has been more than the first and biggest Finnish war film from the beginning), and continues to praise it as 'tärkeä osa kansakunnan muistia ja kultuuriperintöä' (an important part of the nation's collective memory and cultural heritage). The Finnish Film Foundation's director Jouni Mykkänen (2004: 82) agrees, as he declares, 'Laineen Tuntematon sotilas on ollut 50 vuotta yksi suomalaisista peruselokuvista. Se on muodostunut osaksi kansalaiskasvatusta' (Laine's *Tuntematon sotilas* has been one of the essential Finnish films for 50 years. It has reached the appreciation of a very large audience in Finland. It has become a part of its citizens' education). This adoration is taken even further by a Finnish representative in the European Parliament, Lasse Lehtinen (2004: 85):

> Edvin Laineen Tuntematon sotilas on osa kansakunnan kollektiivista muistia, useamman sukupolven yhteinen kokemus. Se on kansallinen hartaushetki jokaisena itsenäisyyspäivänä, suomalaisille samanlainen riitti kuin koko kristikunnalle jouluevankeliumin lukeminen.'

> *Tuntematon sotilas* directed by Edvin Laine is a part of the collective memory of the nation, a shared experience of several generations. It is a spiritual moment for the nation every Independence Day, a rite to Finns, like the reading of Christmas gospel for the entire Christendom.

Minister of Defence Seppo Kääriäinen (2004: 15) explains the military legacy of the film:

> Tuntematon sotilas on erittäin isänmaallinen teos. ... Se korostaa erityisesti kansallista yhtenäisyyttä, sitä että jokainen panos yhteiseksi hyväksi on arvokas ja yhtä tervetullut. ... Se isänmaallisuuden henki, joka elähdytti vanhempiamme ja isovanhempiamme raskaina sotavuosina, toimii tänäkin päivänä perustana sille vahvalle maanpuolustustahdolle, joka on ollut leimallista meille suomalaisille. Tuntemattoman sotilaan perintö velvoittaa meitä vaalimaan tuota tahtoa myös tulevaisuudessa.
>
> *Tuntematon sotilas* is a very patriotic film. It underlines national unity, that every person's contribution for the common goal is as valued and welcome. That spirit of patriotism, that filled the hearts of our parents and grandparents in the difficult years of war, works today as a foundation for the strong national defence spirit that has marked us Finns. The legacy of *Tuntematon sotilas* obliges us to cherish that spirit in the future as well.

If the film was made after the lost Continuation War to justify the war and polish up national pride, it still seems to work. Jukka Sihvonen (2005) writes that the Defence Forces even purchased copies of the film to use as teaching material. It seems strange that a war film that ultimately tells the story of a small nation losing to the Soviet Union is now used in the army as an example for Finnish soldiers.

What makes *Tuntematon sotilas* such a unique film, besides its status as a national treasure, is how the time in which it was made has left a mark on it. In the forty years before 1955, when the film was released, Finland had been through four wars, one of which was a civil war. The tense political climate in Finland after the Second World War had a major role in shaping the way *Tuntematon sotilas* portrays the nation, its inhabitants and their place in the world.

Inkeri Ahvenisto and Katariina Järveläinen (1999) published the results of a research project in the magazine *Wider Screen*. Ahvenisto and Järveläinen (1999) had been interviewing 15 year-old Finns about their attitudes towards history and historical film. The conclusion from Ahvenisto and Järveläinen's (1999) work was that historical films give information, help students identify with and understand information they had received from other sources. One part of the study left out in the article, which was quoted by Jari Sedergren in an YLE television 'Poliittinen elokuva' interview on 10.3.2006, affirmed that the most important source of information about the Second World War for Finnish 15 year-olds is Laine's film, *Tuntematon sotilas*.

The film is regularly shown on television, is used for education in the army and is a major influence on the way young Finnish people perceive their history. Yet the film was made under strict political censorship, even if it was mostly self-inflicted, that alters the film's historical outlook. This is of course natural, for as Robert Rosenstone (1995: 43) writes, 'History does not exist until it is created. And we create it in terms of our underlying values.' This is very appropriate in the case of *Tuntematon sotilas*. The film, like all historical films, should be viewed critically. Knowing more of the political and social context of the film might give reason to re-examine its accepted role as merely reflecting and chronicling the Finnish war effort.

Historical context

Anatole Mazour (1956: 168) states that 'a personal appeal from Marshal Mannerheim to the Generalissimo Stalin for a cease-fire order was accepted, and orders to that effect were issued to all forces beginning at 7:00 a.m., September 4, 1944'. Mazour (1956: 168) notes that, only 'ten days later, on September 14, negotiations opened in Moscow and the armistice agreement was signed on the 19th'. Although this was the end of the war between Finland and the Soviet Union, it was not the end of all armed conflict in Finland. As Mazour (1956: 170) writes in his book *Finland between East and West*, Finland 'had hardly signed the armistice when the country was compelled to plunge into another phase of the conflict, nothing short of a true war against the German forces in northern Finland'. It took 224 days for the Finns to regain the land in Lapland, as Mazour (1956) states. Mazour (1956: 170) claims that, the 'retreating Germans left Lapland a totally devastated area', leaving houses and churches all levelled to the ground. Mazour (1956: 171) also describes this new war as, 'one of the strangest turnabouts of the war took place, when the German army laid waste a country to which only a few months before it was pledged a loyal ally'.

The war in northern Finland was not the only challenge the nation was facing after the armistice. Olli Vehviläinen (2002: 152) recounts how an Allied Commission, working under the Soviet High Command, came to Finland to supervise 'the implementation of the armistice conditions'. Vehviläinen (2002: 152) argues that 'the task of the Control Commission was to ensure that Finland remained within the sphere of influence of the USSR, that is, in the words used at the time, to pursue a foreign policy that was friendly towards the Soviet Union'. Finnish internal politics were also going through a change at the time. As Vehviläinen (2002: 154) claims, 'the workers' organizations attracted many new members ... the trade union movement demanded a say in deciding about working conditions ... [and] for the first time in Finnish history there was a Communist in the government'. Vehviläinen (2002: 154) writes that the Communists were gaining support, 'by taking advantage of the people's weariness with war, the dissatisfaction of the underprivileged and the bitter memory of 1918'.

In February 1948, 'a communist government took over in Czechoslovakia, which had been regarded as a country likely to retain its multi-party system within the Soviet sphere because of its strong Western affinities', as Anthony James (1994: 113) describes the situation. James notes that it was 'only three days after these events in Prague, President Paasikivi received a letter from Stalin proposing that Finland should sign a mutual assistance treaty with the Soviet Union similar to those which Stalin had signed with Hungary and Romania' (133). Lauri Puntila (1975: 190) describes how the Treaty of Friendship, Cooperation, and Mutual Aid was 'approved by parliament with considerable misgiving in April 1948'. The agreement 'requires the contracting parties to develop friendly relations and work together to maintain international peace and security in accordance with the principles and objectives of the United Nations', according to Puntila (1994: 190). The treaty also states that, 'in the eventuality of Finland, or the Soviet Union through Finnish territory, becoming the object of an armed attack by Germany of any state allied with the latter, Finland will, true to its obligations as an independent State, fight to repel the attack'.

The treaty also has a separate article, to 'give assurance of their decision to act in a spirit of co-operation and friendship towards the further development and consolidation of economic and cultural relations between Finland and the Soviet Union.' Anthony James (1994: 133) notes that 'it is sometimes pointed out that anti-Soviet books, articles and films were discouraged and even on occasions suppressed in Finland during the Kekkonen period,' which began when he was elected Prime Minister in 1950. This is the very restrictive political context in which *Tuntematon sotilas* was produced. The film was produced under the supervision of a government obliged to please a foreign nation. Its self-inflicted political correctness and self-effacing manner is very much in line with Finnish foreign and domestic politics of the time. As Anthony James (2002: 133) writes of the Soviet Union's power over Finland, 'behind the scenes they exerted complete control over the Finnish government, while the Finns in the interests of their survival could only respond with docile compliance'. He goes on to present the term 'finlandisation', which was invented 'to describe this arrangement ... [as] a term of political abuse'.

Class Division

Tuntematon sotilas was released in 1955, thirty-seven years after the Civil War and only fifteen years after the Moscow peace treaty ended the war between Finland and the Soviet Republic. This historical context has strongly influenced the way in which the film portrays the society, politics and tensions of the time. The film's technical merits are few, and rather than following a traditional narrative pattern, 'the film is constructed around a collection of episodes', as Juha Sihvonen (2005: 142) states. Conversely, the long spanning popularity of the film does not lie in its story or cinematic innovation, but in its characters and their relations.

'Instead of a few individual protagonists, the description concentrates on a *group* of men', as Juha Sihvonen (2005: 142) describes the film in the book, *The Cinema of Scandinavia*. *Tuntematon sotilas* portrays the common soldiers of a Finnish machinegun company headed by Lieutenant Koskela (Kosti Klimelä) as they fight the Soviets in the Continuation War of 1941-44. The film does not focus on the experiences and growth of a few central protagonists, but treats the individual and rather shallow characters as pieces that form the more important unit of the machine gun company. The soldiers are caricatures, whose actions or feelings are not explained or explored. What makes the soldiers significant, besides the exaggerated uniqueness of their personalities, is their involvement in and contribution to the unit.

There is a broad spectrum of social backgrounds and personalities in the machine gun company. Lahtinen (Veikko Sinisalo) openly expresses his atheism, communism and resentment towards the capitalists. Rokka (Reino Tolvanen) is an exceptional and witty soldier, who is fighting to protect his farmland, which lies close to the Soviet-Finnish border. Lehto (Åke Lindman) portrays the heroic and self-sacrificing Finnish combatant, who is not only brave, but also stubborn and rebellious to the point of stupidity. Riitaoja (Olavi Ahonen), on the contrary, is a cowardly and useless soldier who abandons his fellows at the sight of danger. These are a few of the most overstated representations of Finnish soldiers. Juha Sihvonen (2005: 142) argues that 'as a type each figure represents the part of Finland the character was born in, epitomising the manifold nature of the Finnish folk'.

This multiplicity of origins is displayed not only in the personal traits, but also more strongly with the use of dialects. 'One of the most evident means of distinguishing the soldiers from each other is the use of speech dialects', as Juha Sihvonen (2005: 143) notes. Or, as Roger Manvell (1974: 329) claims, 'the soldiers talk (as the subtitles more than hint) with unfettered bluntness, and are characterized with a lively reality'. The soldiers have strong dialects that are specific to regions of Finland and make frequent references to the areas they come from. This creates an impression of a unified yet diverse country brought together by the war. James and Lesley Milroy (1985: 98) describe the differences between working-class dialects and standard language in their book *Authority in Language: Investigating Language Prescription and Standardisation*:

> it has already been emphasised that there is no obvious linguistic reason for this stigma: working-class dialects operate within working-class communities as efficiently as any other linguistic system, sometimes including useful distinctions which are not present in the standard forms of the language.

The use of dialects in *Tuntematon sotilas* distinguishes not only the origins, but also the social status of the soldiers. The regional dialects range from Hietanen's (Heikki Savolainen) west coast to Rokka's Karelia, but all of them are socially marked. When the soldiers choose to speak in their own dialects, instead of trying to use the official tone of speech, they also choose to carry the working-class stigma that comes along with it. This creates an impression of a company that is proud of its working-class background. Through the dialogue, *Tuntematon sotilas* portrays the Finnish army as a culturally varied nation of workers uniting to fight a common enemy.

The officers, in contrast with the soldiers, speak in an exaggeratedly official manner that is usually restricted to written language. This way of speaking removes all links to their past or place of origin. Whereas the soldiers' identity is built on the colourful ways they express themselves verbally, the officers are stripped of their individuality by communicating in an unnatural and restricted way. As James and Lesley Milroy (1985: 59) claim:

> a standard language is additionally maintained in an official and institutional way. It is the official language, used by government; it is codified in dictionaries and grammar-books; it is appealed to as the norm in the educational system. These facts give it a *legitimacy* that other varieties do not usually have.

Therefore, the language of the officers is not neutral or impartial, but represents the institutions and social structure as much as the working-class dialects of the soldiers. This is natural, of course, when showing a strongly hierarchical system such as the army. *Tuntematon sotilas* takes this symbol of status further by juxtaposing it with such an unusual wealth of working-class dialects. The use of language to reinforce social status in *Tuntematon sotilas* not only cuts off the soldiers from the officers socially, but also complicates their communication, as Rokka bluntly states to officer Lammio:

'No fancy words, OK? I'm only a farmer and don't understand those words'.

There is a strong division between the soldiers and officers that is crossed only by Lieutenant Koskela. Koskela leads the machinegun company with an altruistic and equal attitude, which strongly differs from the other lieutenants; the other officers are shown as rigid and small-minded. Lammio (Jussi Jurkka) epitomizes this self-righteous and hated authority. He and his strict reign are more hated than the enemy they are at war with. When the colourful and individual soldiers are contrasted with the strict and impersonal authority, it is clear which side the viewer identifies with. As soldier Susi (Kale Teuronen) puts it: 'Boy was he stuck-up. We don't like that kind'.

Officer Lammio, despite being logical and only acting within his jurisdiction, is depicted as a small-minded tyrant. By all logic, a high-ranking clean-shaven army officer should be admired as he leads the troops to battle the enemy. Lammio's speech is accent-free, his clothes always clean and his behaviour flawless. Within these strengths lie the character's weaknesses. He symbolizes a totalitarian leader, who does not comprehend the realities of war from behind his rigid leadership. This is revealed as Rokka bellows to him, 'Don't you see where we're heading? Soon we'll be in real trouble! Half of us are gonna die and you nag about discipline!'

While Lammio should be the heroic leader, the soldiers are portrayed as the real, if reluctant, heroes of the film. They are the ones who resent the war and the government that has sent them to fight it. The soldiers disobey their orders, steal and avoid work. They make their own alcohol in a stolen kettle and leave the company without permission. Yet when they talk their way into additional food portions, they give the bread away to the children of the country they have come to occupy. This ideal of solidarity and sharing is not far from the politics of the Finnish socialists of the time.

Red soldiers and White officers

Olli Vehviläinen (2002) explains in his book *Finland in the Second World War: Between Germany and Russia* how Finland, after declaring its independence in December 1917, was constantly between nations. Vehviläinen (2002) affirms that the rise to power of the Bolsheviks in Russia, and the Soviet government's agreement to separate national minorities, set Finland's pursuit of independence in motion. This was the setting that led Finland to its civil war, which started only one month after its declaration of independence. Vehviläinen (2002: 4) identifies the causes of the division of the nation in how 'the Bolshevik revolution had increased social agitation and when the old order collapsed the workers began to form units called "Red Guards", while the non-socialists created their own "Civil Guards"'. This meant that the newly independent country was crudely divided into left-wing Reds and right-wing Whites. Vehviläinen (2002: 4) describes how 'the presence in the country of Russian revolutionary military units encouraged the workers, who increasingly began to take matters into their own hands,' which led to 'the desire of the non-socialists to sever the country altogether from revolutionary Russia'.

Vehviläinen (2002: 6) argues that 'the Red forces were

composed almost entirely of the urban proletariat and the poor of the countryside ... [who] obtained all their arms from Bolshevik Russia, and a few Russians fought alongside them in the war ... The Whites, for their part, had the support of Germany, which supplied them with weapons.' Germany also allowed the *Jägers*, who had been fighting there as volunteers, to return home to join the government forces (Vehviläinen 2002: 6). These Finnish Jägers had been in military training in Germany since 1915 and 'the majority clearly had a so-called "bourgeois" background', according to Puntila (1975: 92). Mazour (1956: 47) confirms that 'most of the Civil Guards came from the upper and middle classes'. This shows that the Civil War was not only between political parties, but also between social classes.

It is in this context that *Tuntematon sotilas*' characters were created. The scenes in which the soldiers and officers celebrate the seventy-fifth birthday of their Commander-in-Chief, Mannerheim, emphasise this in a direct way. The company is outside their tent drinking their homemade alcohol and listening to the Russian song 'Kalinka'. Rokka asks 'Koskela, aren't you going to the headquarters?' and gets the answer, 'I belong here'. After a few drinks, officer Koskela, who is portrayed as an equal and sincere leader of his company, goes to confront the other equally drunken officers.

In contrast to the 'Kalinka', the officers are singing German marches in the headquarters. Koskela greets the officers in Russian as he walks in and continues to speak in Russian, even mentioning the United Soviet Republic. He then goes on to sing Finnish children's songs and bellow about Finnish folk heroes. An officer finishes his German song and warns

Koskela, 'Yes, I know Finnish too, and it might be best that you keep to it as well'.

The symbolism of this scene is not restricted to dialogue. Koskela is the tallest of the officers and, with his blond hair, is the most traditionally Finnish-looking. His shabby, but sturdy appearance is set against the physically weaker buttoned-up officer wearing glasses. The scene shows how the Red working-class hero that speaks Russian stands up against the White, well-groomed upper-class officer speaking German. It is not without meaning that, after the Red hero punches the White officer, he is tied up and taken away.

Tuntematon sotilas plays with the old political division of the Civil War which, as Olli Vehviläinen (2002: 6) writes, 'has taken much time to heal.' Even though the film differentiates the working-class soldiers from the upper-class officers, it shows through lieutenant Koskela that there can be a way to have the best of both sides. Koskela shows 'a different style of command that appeals to the men and suits the Finnish backwoods warriors better', as Timo Hirvonen (2002: 62) writes. Koskela is a figure that represents the Reds but is of the same status as the Whites. His character embodies the country's need to unite in the face of a common threat.

The supposed roots of Lammio's strict control is revealed when he orders the company to clean up and walk in formation and Lahtinen comments: 'The German way. That nut has lost what little brain he ever had'. Lammio is thereby established as a White officer, whose dictatorship is not only hated, but also flawed. The only time he is shown in battle with his troops, he orders his solders into a coup and gets his

The Unknown Soldier in Finnish History

best soldier killed. He is a loathed and incompetent authority, but even though there are fierce objections, his orders are always followed. This pressuring presence of unwanted authority is not very different from the German military presence in Finland during, and especially after, the Continuation War.

This pressure of a White authority against the Red soldiers is made evident in a scene where the soldiers are told to be ready to leave within an hour. The soldiers unanimously refuse to leave, while Määttä (Pentti Siimes) yells, 'What the hell? We're not leaving!' The situation escalates to the point of a threatened death penalty but the soldiers' reactions remain rebellious: 'Shit, let's have it! Hit us with your best shot!' This is when Lammio hits a nerve and silences the company by stating, 'This is not the Red Guard, where you elect the officers. Is that clear?' This conflict between the undisputed but hated authority and the Finnish soldiers is again reminiscent of the Finnish political situation being stuck under the authority of their Western ally, Germany, that towards the end of the war becomes the enemy. Lieutenant Koskela, whose gentler command gives the soldiers an excuse to obey without losing face, once again saves the situation. His character continues to work as a catalyst between the officers and soldiers, allowing the latter to keep their stubborn pride.

The relationship between the officers and soldiers in *Tuntematon sotilas* is one that reflects the political tensions of the time it was made. In 1955, when the film was released, the Germans had lost the war and Finland was struggling to maintain a friendly relationship with the Soviet Union. This was also only ten years after the last Germans withdrew from the Lapland war against Finland that started straight after the Continuation War. The dislike for White officers has its roots not only in the Civil War, but also in the Continuation War and its aftermath. *Tuntematon sotilas* differentiates the German-sympathising officers from the Soviet-orientated soldiers, and naturally sides with the working-class soldiers. In the light of the discussion between Lieutenants Kariluoto (Matti Ranin) and Koskela, it seems understandable for a nation that has lost the war to seek vindication.

> Koskela: All is lost.
>
> Kariluoto: Hard times. Wonder what'll happen to us? Us all. And Finland.
>
> Koskela: What happens to losers. Finish.
>
> Kariluoto: I can't stand that. Anything but that.

Tuntematon Sotilas does not show a triumphant nation in battle, but it does show a nation torn apart by a Civil War reunite to face a common threat. Even if the attempt is not victorious, the film does serve a unifying function as it shows the diverse soldiers of Finland in the trenches. Although the White officers are not included in the team, it does not seem to matter as it is the working-class soldiers who are the representatives of the Finnish nation in *Tuntematon sotilas*. Thus, in the beginning of the film, the priest asks the soldier to pray, 'to bless our nation and make it unanimous'.

Differentiating Finnish culture

The film *Tuntematon sotilas* is based on Väinö Linna's book by the same name published in 1954, barely a year before the film was released. As Jukka Sihvonen (2005: 140) writes, 'the book became an immediate success among the reading public.' Sihvonen (2005: 140) continues to argue that even though the book received much attention from the press, 'the critical reception was not unanimously positive', but its commercial success proves 'that the "common people" in Finland loved it'. Or, as the film's director Edvin Laine (1983: 37) describes the time of the book's publication, 'Tuntematonta sotilasta luettiin, siitä puhuttiin, siihen otettiin kantaa. Teosta pidettiin suurenmoisena saavutuksena, jota ylistettiin pilviin, mutta oli niitäkin, jotka loukkaantuivat ja moittivat kirjailijaa isänmaan petturiksi ja pyhäin häpäisijäksi' (*Tuntematon sotilas* was read, talked about, debated. The book was considered an extraordinary achievement, and praised, but there were also those who were offended and criticized the writer for being unpatriotic and blasphemous).

Controversy surrounded the book *Tuntematon sotilas*, even though it was strongly censored. Jukka Sihvonen (2005: 139) claims that 'several of the cuts testify to the ideologically radical aspects of Linna's text, and also of the issues that the conservative "public sphere" of mid-1950s Finland still suffered when having to deal with anti-war criticism'. The novel's pacifist ideology was toned down, just as the film is self-censored into a masterpiece of political correctness towards the threatening eastern neighbour in the spirit of finlandisation.

Even though *Tuntematon sotilas* is a portrayal of the war between Finland and Soviet Union, it does peculiarly little to antagonize the Soviet soldiers or nation. This is of course understandable for a film made by the defeated country under the strict supervision of the victorious opponent. The negative feelings towards the enemy are only shown while in battle and, even then, the comments stay very impersonal. The dialogue shows the soldiers reluctance to fight their 'kindred nation' and often comments on the German involvement in the war. Considering the film is of a nation at war with the Soviet Union and allied with Germany, this dialogue seems bizarre.

> Lahtinen: That German looney's on the move, and we'll be following. Wonder how it'll turn out, our neighbour's well equipped.
>
> Hietanen: They're afraid the Russians will come here if Germany attacks them.
>
> Lahtinen: What for? The Russians never attacked anybody. But the Germans are here.

Lahtinen's argument about Russia not attacking any nation in the Second World War can be seen as a fundamentally distorted view of world politics at the time. Or, alternatively, as severe self-censorship in an attempt to work under the Treaty of Friendship, Cooperation, and Mutual Aid. *Tuntematon sotilas* very much accommodates the request for the 'spirit of co-operation and friendship' in cultural relations described in the treaty. This political pressure made the film walk a tightrope of political correctness trying to maintain some national pride. There are very few subjects on which the film dares to criticize the Soviet Union, but Karelia, which Finland lost to the Soviet Union in 1940, is one of these. This attitude is apparent in Rokka's comment: 'We don't give a damn about Europe. We'll take Karelia back and go home'.

When crossing the old border, Lahtinen comments: 'This is where our rights end. From now on, we're plundering.' This sparks one of the few adverse comments: 'Oh, so we're crooks when we cross borders? The others are protecting national security when shifting borders'. The apologetic approach to the war is then revised as the company reaches Petrozavodsk and, instead of satisfaction and celebration, the company's reaction is contrary.

> Lahtinen: We fought for that?
>
> Rokka: Forget that, I wish that I were home.
>
> Susi: You said it.

There are only a few times when the Soviet soldiers are given more of a personality than distant voices behind gunfire. Keeping the enemy faceless helps to portray the war as impersonal and impartial. One of the times when the Soviet solders are given a face is when Rokka takes a Soviet officer prisoner. Rokka takes the prisoner Baranow (Veikko Uusimäki) to the officer's headquarters on the same visit when he himself is going to be disciplined. Rokka says to Baranow as they approach the headquarters, both as delinquents, 'Don't worry. We'll go to prison together. We'll be OK. I'll teach you how to make lamp stands'. This strange setting again places the Finnish soldiers on the same side with the Soviets.

The relationship between the soldiers and occupants illustrates the schizophrenic situation of the Finnish soldiers fighting against a nation they supposedly respect and whose hatred towards the capitalists they share, at least in the wisdom of the aftermath of the war. The company arriving in the occupied town of Petrozavodsk could have been a victorious march of liberators reuniting the oppressed Karelian people with their fatherland. The political climate of the times with Finland's remorse over the war and the self-censorship demanded by Treaty of Friendship, Cooperation, and Mutual Aid, make this sequence more complex. The soldiers bring food for the children like saviours and court the Karelian women but are met with rejection. Though the Karelians still speak Finnish, they do not welcome their liberators. The scene in which the soldiers visit a Karelian woman openly addresses the strenuous subject of war. Instead of defending Finnish politics and appraising the Soviet Union, *Tuntematon sotilas* settles for the always constructive approach of blaming a third party, Germany.

Veerukka's confrontational questions 'Why did you come? Why not let us be alone?' are answered by Rokka: 'Come on, Veerukka. You started this. You took my farm. That's why we're here.' This is the only defence or justification the soldiers try to give their actions. There is no nationalist speech or standing up for the validation of the Finnish war effort. The potential argument is solved by laying the blame on Germany, as Veerukka says: 'Who came? Hitler!' This accusation is met by a very diplomatic Hietanen, 'I know that war only hurts people on both sides. There's always suffering. The innocent ones suffer most. Like the kids.' After settling that war is a horrible thing and Germany is to blame, the soldiers watch Veerukka perform an ecstatic Kalinka. No one gets their feelings hurt and all the participants enjoy a traditional Russian dance to get into a better mood. This scene is reminiscent of what Olli Vehviläinen (2002: 168) describes in his book *Finland in the Second World War* as Finland taking 'refuge in a policy of Scandinavian neutrality' after the Second World War.

If *Tuntematon sotilas* is hesitant to discuss the political issues between Finland and the Soviet Union, it does not hesitate to show differences in culture. Differentiating Soviet and Finnish cultures must have seemed a safer way to add to the feel of Finnish independence than dealing with political tensions. If finlandisation demanded censorship of the political issues in the film, it did not deny the existence of cultural differences. At a time when the nation is under severe pressure from a stronger nation, *Tuntematon sotilas* highlights the cultural separation of Finland.

As the soldiers reach Petrozavodsk, there is a shot of an Orthodox church, something unfamiliar to the Finnish population, of which ninety-six per cent was of the Lutheran faith at the time of the war, according to Harri Heino (1997). The Lutheran faith remains a staple of the army throughout the film. There is praying before war and when injured, and the last words of a young soldier are those of a familiar Lutheran prayer. A military priest follows along and consoles the soldiers in times of fear.

Karelia, despite being lost only four years previously to the

Soviet Union, has no indication of Finnish culture. Veerukka's house has a balalaika on the wall. She also has a picture of Stalin on her wall, which gives an indication that she is not missing Finnish rule. When she dances Kalinka to a song sung in Russian, she is exotic and far from Finnish. These symbols of Russian culture do not only create an impression that the Finnish soldiers are now abroad, but they also create a cultural gap between the Finns and Soviets. If these paintings and dances are evidently Soviet, it means that Finnish culture must be something else. This gives the film some space to distance the Finnish from the Soviets in a politically inoffensive manner.

Tuntematon sotilas shows the company singing Finnish ballads, Koskela referring to mythic Finnish folk heroes and discussions about what they had heard on the Finnish radio. These are small indications of an autonomous and special culture that lies behind the façade of a nation at war. The film recognises that Finland has a religion, music and past of its own not governed by the previous rulers, the Soviet Union or Sweden. This is a small acknowledgement that, even if the country's politics is practically under foreign rule, the national spirit has not been lost.

Even if *Tuntematon sotilas* is careful not to mention Soviet-Finnish politics, it is not afraid to express its disappointment with the government that has sent it to war. Getting news from the country's leader is treated with indifference. The information that 'some minister's going to speak' initiates only an uninterested response from Hietanen: 'The news is alright, but I don't care much about them ministers. I don't give a hoot what he's saying. He can't do nothing about them mosquitoes anyway'. This dismissal is not very strange considering the film was made after the war and these were the ministers that had lead them to a defeated battle. The minister on the radio bellows nationalist propaganda: '...and the success of our defence is guaranteed. Our hardened defence forces as brave and as willing but better equipped than in the last war, will fight for our freedom, the integrity of our borders, the faith of our fathers and our free democracy'. This inspirational speech does not keep the interest of the soldiers for long, as they turn their attention to watch artillery passing by. Hietanen's line about the mosquitoes gains deeper meaning as one of the soldiers slaps a mosquito off his neck as the minister continues his fervent speech in the background.

When *Tuntematon sotilas* critiques Finnish ministers, it is not only an attack on the government, but also against the authority that forces them into war against the Soviet Union. Instead of being patriot heroes fighting for the freedom of their fatherland, the soldiers show their disapproval of the government and war. This way the Finnish civilians are not held responsible for participating in the war. Honkajoki (Tarmo Manni) makes this view clear as he prays: 'Keep our leaders from banging their heads against the Karelian pine again'.

On several occasions, it is made clear that the soldiers hate the capitalists and would not be in the trenches if it were not for the actions of those foolish politicians. This dislike of capitalists is demonstrated in Lahtinen's bitter comment: 'They fool the simple ones to keep them humble to the capitalists,' or by Hietanen's defiant, 'I won't be humbling myself to no capitalist on my land!' The reasons for the war are declared by Lahtinen's mocking line, 'Give us strength to defend the capitalists' purse'. This sides the soldier ideologically with the Soviet Communists. Unlike the proud patriots, who are ready to defend their homeland, *Tuntematon sotilas*' company is full of grumbling reluctant soldiers. Korpela embodies this unwillingness to fight when he answers Lieutenant Lammio's enquiry about his name: 'You got my papers right there. Hell, you should know my name, as you came to my home to bring me here!' As it becomes clear that Finland has lost the war, one of the soldiers remarks very unpatriotically, 'Who cares! As long as this foolishness ends'.

Tuntematon sotilas holds the government fully responsible for the lost war, in which the soldiers are only the capitalists' pawn. This is taking the self-censorship of finlandisation to an extreme. It is not enough to avoid accusing the Soviet Union for the war, but the film assaults the country's own government for allowing this unfortunate quarrel with the Soviets who, to quote Lahtinen, 'never attacked nobody'. *Tuntematon sotilas* walks a thin line between totally degrading Finland in the interest of not insulting the Soviet Union and keeping up some national pride. The film condemns the Finnish involvement in the war by accusing it of being led by capitalists or Germany. Alternatively, there are some subjects in which *Tuntematon sotilas* dares to stand up to the Soviet Union. These involve differentiating the Soviet culture as foreign and admitting to wanting the lost territory of Karelia back.

Use of documentary footage

The structure of *Tuntematon sotilas* is marked by documentary sequences that break up the fictional plot. Jukka Sihvonen (2005: 145) argues that 'in the film the shifts between major episodes are marked by images of soldiers marching attached to sequences of documentary footage inserted between the fictional material'. This archive material gives the film a sense of reality and credibility beyond the autobiographical context of Väinö Linna's novel. Sihvonen (2005: 145) suggests that this 'might be seen simply as the director's input into discussions of Tuntematon Sstilas as a documentary reportage'. As the director, Edvin Laine, explains in his autobiography (1983: 46): 'se on kuvattava asiallisesti, ei mihinkään suuntaan liioitellen eikä paisutellen' (it had to be filmed in a factual way, not elaborating in any direction). The documentary footage gives the film an air of reliability and authority, as if validating the fictional parts.

Jukka Sihvonen (2005: 145) also argues that the archive footage has other functions 'in the rhythm of the film.' Sihvonen states (2005: 145) that, 'as documentaries[,] they are reminders of the "real" events of the war', and, 'the documentary footage aims at increasing the level of credibility in general'. This is a parallel to Laine's (1983) comment on the film's factual approach. Sihvonen (2005: 145) continues that the documentary sequences work 'as if using citations from a historical event ... [that] participates in the film's entire operation as a "documentary recording" of the lines of speech, characters and episodes of the novel'. The archive footage is not only a convenient way to add explosions and impressive artillery to the film. As Sihvonen (2005: 145) states: 'this material not only 'fills the breaks' when moving forward together with the platoon from one episode to another; the "documents" establish another level entirely, the level of reality, in relation to which the rest of the film is to be seen'.

When watching *Tuntematon sotilas*, it seems as if the documentary footage is giving a context to the novel's narrative. Even though, as Sihvonen (2005: 145) notes, the archive footage's visual outlook 'clearly diverges from the fictional material', one feels as if the characters of the film might just be there among the other marchers. The fictional material deepens and brings a human face to the soldiers of the newsreels. When the film came out in 1955, the viewers had surely seen lots of similar footage on the news and had first-hand experience of war. Now *Tuntematon sotilas* gave the nation's war efforts a face and a voice. Robert Rosenstone (1995: 52) notes of the use of archive material in fictional films: 'all those old photographs and all that newsreel footage are saturated with a prepackaged emotion: nostalgia'.

Producing *Tuntematon sotilas*

Tuntematon sotilas was produced and distributed by Suomen Filmiteollisuus SF Oy, as the Finnish Film archive's ELONET database states. At this time, in 1955, Finnish film production was working under a studio system, as Hannu Salmi (1999) states in the book *Kriisi, Kritiikki ja Konsensus*. Salmi (1999) writes that Suomen Filmiteollisuus, along with Suomi-Filmi and Fennada-Filmi, dominated the markets. As this was a time of financial independence for the film industry, the government attempted to exercise control using surveillance and censorship, as Salmi (1999: 7) notes. This was before what Salmi (1999) describes as the crisis and bankruptcy of the studio system in 1963, which was followed by government-funded filmmaking. *Tuntematon sotilas*, however, was produced under the studio system, in which funding had to be found either from within the studio or from external investors.

The film's director Edvin Laine (1983: 82) explains how producer Toivo Särkkä needed to take out an enormous loan to pay for the preparations of *The Unknown Solder*. As Laine (1983) recalls, they received no financial aid from the government. 'Kun kaikki talvikohtaukset oli kuvattu, materiaali leikattu ja otokset asetettu peräkkäin, Yhdyspankin johtokunta kutsuttiin elokuvaa katsomaan. Koko johtokunta noudatti kutsua. Kun tämä pätkä oli katsottu, johtokunta yksimielisesti ilmoitti meille rahoittavansa elokuvan' (When all the winter scenes were shot, and the material edited, the board of Yhdyspankki was invited to watch the film. The entire board accepted the invitation. After watching the excerpt, the board unanimously agreed to finance the movie). Laine (1983: 50) thus explains the additional backing. This financing from the bank explains how the then exceptionally expensive film could be made. However, money was not the only thing that was required for a large-scale war film. *Tuntematon sotilas* needed access to military equipment including guns and tanks for the battle scenes. This was to prove difficult.

Laine (1983: 44) recalls how the Minister of Foreign Affairs, Johannes Virolainen, 'sanoi jyrkästi, ettei laske meitä edes leikkisotaan maamme rajojen sisäpuolella!' (said firmly, that he would not let us into even a pretend war within the borders of our nation!') when asked for assistance with the military supplies. Then the Minister of Defence, Emil Skog, had to withdraw his promises after the Generals at the ministry had disagreed, as Laine (1983) notes. Laine especially recalls how general Olenius, who was then chief secretary, had strongly been opposed. Jukka Sihvonen (2005: 146) writes how 'the Ministry of Defence caused one of the big problems in the production of the film in 1955 when it refused its military co-operation, preventing the filmmakers from borrowing the materials utilised by the military. The reason for this unwillingness was probably Linna's controversial representation of the "military order" in the source novel'. Sihvonen (2005: 146) also lists a previous film produced by Suomen Filmiteollisuus in 1954 as contributing to the lack of support, writing: 'a more crucial reason might have been that the head of the Defence Forces, General K.A.Heiskanen, was "deeply hurt" by a military farce, *Majuri maantieltä* (*The Major off the Highway*)'.

Starting to lose faith, Laine (1983) remembers turning to his good friend Home Secretary Väinö Leskinen who had the border guard under his command. In his autobiography, Laine (1983: 44) recalls how Leskinen had happily obliged to help supply military equipment for the filming. Laine (1983: 45) then comments on the hesitance of ministers: 'Kyllähän me tiesimme, että aihe oli arkaluontoinen, mutta olisi pitänyt herrojen ministeriössä luottaa meihin. Emme kai me hienosta aiheesta aikoneet tehdä sellaista suurelokuvaa, josta aiheutuisi naapurillemme ja meille itsellemme haittaa!' (Of course we knew the subject matter was delicate, but the gentlemen in the ministries should have trusted us. We wouldn't have made a big film that would have caused harm to our neighbours and ourselves, from such a great subject). His acknowledgement of the need to avoid offending the neighbours is very expressive of the political policies of the time. Laine (1983) writes with pride about the number of high-ranking Russian officers and politics who have given recognition to the film for its factual and unbiased style of depiction. This, however, was not the only time the production of *Tuntematon sotilas* had to convince politicians to assist in the making of the film.

The next obstacle that required help from politicians to overcome was finding the tank that Hietanen destroys in the film. This it was not possible to get through Leskinen, as the border guard did not have any tanks, as Laine (1983) recalls. Laine (1983) writes how he eventually decided to turn to Prime Minister Urho Kekkonen. The Minister agreed that 'Jospa sisäministeri Väinö Leskisen kanssa katsomme tähän asti otetut valmiit otokset, niin päätetään sitten' (maybe if we watch the finished footage you have shot so far, with the home secretary Väinö Leskinen, and then we'll decide) as Laine (1983: 47) writes. Laine (1983) remembers how, after viewing the footage shot for the film so far, Urho Kekkonen gave access to the tank brigade in Parola to film all the necessary scenes. So, even if *Tuntematon sotilas* was produced by an independent studio and received its funding from a commercial bank, it still needed the assistance of the government to complete the film.

Interestingly enough, the politicians who offered their help in the production of *Tuntematon sotilas* were of the same political stance. Väinö Leskinen, who according to Laine (1983) gave access to military equipment for the film, was the president of the Finnish Social Democratic Party, as Jukka Nevakivi (1996) notes. Nevakivi (1996) also recalls how Leskinen convinced the Soviet ambassador that the party's management had a positive attitude towards the Soviet Union. He was also one of the few Finnish politicians who visited Moscow in 1954, as Nevakivi (1996) states. Emil Skog, who Laine (1983) recalls as having promised to help with the military supplies for the film, was also a member of the Finnish Social Democratic Party, according to Jukka Nevakivi (1996). In 1955, when *Tuntematon sotilas* was filmed, Skog was the president of the party, as Jukka Nevakivi (1996) notes. More interesting is Urho Kekkonen, who was Prime Minister for the Agrarian Party, as Nevakivi (1996) confirms, at the time of the production of *Tuntematon sotilas*. He gave permission to use the Parola tank brigade for the filming, as Laine's (1983) biography states.

This was also at the time that he was running for president. Nevakivi (1996) reminds readers that Kekkonen had the complete support of the ex-KGB agent Vladimirov in his presidential campaign. Kekkonen was tending towards finlandisation, as he described the phenomenon 'pelkästään myönteisesti eikä nähnyt Neuvostoliiton Suomi-suhteita alistushakuisina vaan luottamuksellisina ja rakentavina, rauhanomaisen rinnakkainelon politiikkana.' (solely positive and did not consider the Soviet-Finnish relation oppressive, but a confidential and constructive, politically peaceful coexistence), as Nevakivi (1996: 11) recounts. In a nation that was under such strict political surveillance, it was crucial for the presidential candidates to maintain a good relationship with the Soviet Union, Nevakivi (1996) argues. Nevakivi further describes how Kekkonen had begun to advise more inexperienced politicians on how to further their careers with the help of Moscow. Kekkonen's presidential campaign demanded that he gave off a positive image of the Soviet Union to his voters. Kekkonen's support of *Tuntematon sotilas* and his public presence at the premiere of the film might have assisted the presidential campaign. Timo Hirvonen (2004: 19) describes the premiere of *Tuntematon sotilas* in Helsinki on the 21st of December 1955: 'Vasta kun silloinen pääministeri Urho Kekkonen nousi ylös kutsuvierasaitiostaan vaimonsa Sylvin kanssa osoittamaan suosiotaan elokuvalle, elokuvan tuottaja, maisteri T.J. Särkkä, kohottatui helpottuneena ylös' (It was only after the then Prime Minister Urho Kekkonen stood up with his wife Sylvi in their guest stall to applaud the film, that the producer T.J. Särkkä stood up relieved). It was two months after the premiere that Kekkonen was elected president.

Tuntematon sotilas' political correctness was still not sufficient for the Soviet Union. Nevakivi (1996) claims that the film received fierce criticism in the Soviet Embassy. The Embassy's Counsellor Loginov (1955) wrote a report of the film stating that, as a whole, the film was aimed against the Soviet Union and thought that the film exaggerated the Soviet Union hostility towards Finland. He found it strange that Kekkonen had personally read the script and approved of it, as Nevakivi (1996) confirms. Loginov also wrote in his 21.12.1955 report to the Soviet Union that he 'wondered if it would be possible to notify Kekkonen that considering Finland and the Soviet Union's good relations ... the film is not appropriate to be shown'.

Conclusion

Tuntematon sotilas is a reflection of the political and social tensions of the time. Even though the film is about the Continuation War between Finland and the Soviet Union, it represents Finnish history in a broader sense. *Tuntematon sotilas* shows the effects of the Civil War on the nation. The officer's spiteful references to the 'Red Guard' demonstrate how the division of the Civil War has not yet been forgotten. The soldiers are still shown as members of the working class, who hate the 'capitalists' and listen to Kalinka. The officers are still buttoned-up representatives of 'the German way'. Their separation has roots in the Civil War of 1917, but is brought to the surface again by the Continuation War, where the Finnish nation is once more stuck between Germany and the Soviet Union.

Tuntematon sotilas has these unique interests as it was produced under a very strict political rule. The terms of the Treaty of Friendship, Cooperation and Mutual Aid had a major influence on how *Tuntematon sotilas* was able to treat political issues. The self-censorship of finlandisation affected the ways in which the film presented Soviet-Finnish relations during the war. This political climate meant that the film could not show the Soviet Union or its participation in the war in a negative light. What makes the film interesting is how it weaves its way through a minefield of restrictions and censorship to produce a politically correct film that would not damage the peaceful coexistence with the neighbouring country.

Besides the crippling demand not to antagonize the enemy in a war film, *Tuntematon sotilas* has to show a depressing end to the war, which the heroes lose. Since the film is unable to build up the national spirit on victory or mocking the enemy, it emphasises the characteristics and guts of the Finnish soldiers. The stubborn bravery of the Finnish soldiers is depicted throughout the film. On many occasions, ridiculous

The Unknown Soldier in Finnish History

courage is illustrated. At one point, for example, an injured soldier is taken away and he says, 'Lost a leg, but I'm not crying over one leg!' If they cannot win, at least they do not cry.

Tuntematon sotilas is a better illustration of the time it was made in than of the war it attempts to represent. The historical accuracy of the war and its causes, despite the credibility of the archive footage, is questionable. The way the film portrays the political climate of 1955 may be unintentional, but it is more truthful. Robert Rosenstone (1995: 11) states '[t]hat all history, including written history, is a construction, not a reflection. That history (as we practice it) is an ideological and cultural product of the Western World at a particular time in its development.' This is very true of *Tuntematon sotilas*.

Whiteclay and Culbert (1996: 3) write, 'war films – including antiwar films – have established the prevailing public images of war in the twentieth century.' This is equivalent to *Tuntematon sotilas*' status as a part of Finnish national heritage. It is important to be aware of the reasons why the film depicts the war and its politics in the way it does. Whiteclay and Culbert (1996: 6) claim that 'the public memory of war in the twentieth century has been created less from a remembered past than from a manufactured past, one substantially shaped by images in documentaries, feature films, and television programmes'. This is crucial to acknowledge with a film that, as Ahvenisto and Järveläinen (1999) learned, is the most important point of reference for young Finns about the Second World War. A critical and informed perspective on the film can allow *Tuntematon sotilas* to be seen not only as

315

reflecting or chronicling Finnish history, but as a product of that history itself.

Author's Comment

This paper was written as a final dissertation for a BA degree in Media Arts at Royal Holloway, University of London, in 2007. It was written under the supervision of Dr Jacob Leigh, who helped it find a balance between film history and critical analysis. Choosing a Finnish film for the paper came partially from my own background as a Finn, but more from a curiosity towards the film itself. In 2006 the Finnish newspaper *Helsingin Sanomat* published a series of articles on the characters of *Tuntematon sotilas*, reigniting the debate around the book and film. I was curious to find out why the film's popularity had endured so long. Looking back at the essay now, I would further explore the questions it opens up about cinema's role in developing national identity and history. It would be interesting to find out more about the process of film production and censorship during this period to better understand the role of film as national project and political tool. These questions about the multifaceted relationship between film and the society that it reflects, develops and reimagines continue to preoccupy my research.

The Unknown Soldier in Finnish History

I am currently working on a PhD on Finnish film and the welfare nation in the Department of Scandinavian Studies at UCL.

References

April 6, 1947. *Agreement of Friendship, Co-operation and Mutual Assistance between the Republic of Finland and the Union of Soviet Socialist Republic.*

Ahvenisto, I. and Järveläinen, K. (1999). 'Huvia vai Hyötyä?' *Wider Screen.* http://www.widerscreen.fi/1999-1-2/huvia-vai-hyotya/. Accessed 18 December 2006.

Culbert, D. and Whiteclay, J. (1996). *World War II, Film and History.* Oxford: Oxford University Press.

Elonet, (2006). 'Tuntematon Sotilas (1955)'. *The Finnish Film Archive.* Available from: http://www.elonet.fi/title/tt4481/muut. Accessed 18 December 2006.

Heino, H. (1997). *Mihin Suomi tänään uskoo.* Porvoo: Wsoy.

Hirvonen, T. (ed.) (2004). *Koko Kansan Tuntematon.* Helsinki: Alfamer Kustannus Oy.

James, A. (1994). 'A Northern Paradox: How Finland Survived the Cold War'. *Contemporary Review,* 264 (1538): 113.

Karpela, T. (2004). 'Tuntematon Sotilas, elävä klassikko'. In Hirvonen, T. (ed.): *Koko Kansan Tuntematon.* Helsinki: Alfamer.

Kääriäinen, S. (2004). 'Tuntemattoman Sotilaan perintö velvoittaa'. In Hirvonen, T. (ed.): *Koko Kansan Tuntematon.* Helsinki: Alfamer.

Laine, E. (1983). *Tuntematon Sotilas ja Pylvässänky.* Helsinki: Kustannusosakeyhtiö Tammi.

Lehtinen, L. (2004). 'Osa kansakunnan kollektiivista muistia'. In Hirvonen, T. (ed.) *Koko Kansan Tuntematon*. Helsinki: Alfamer.

Logonov (1995). Letter nr. 436 to S. G. Lapin. 21st October.

Manvell, R. (1974). *Films and the Second World War*. South Brunswick: A. S. Barnes and Company.

Mazour, A.G. (1956). *Finland between East and West*. Princeton: D. Van Nostrand Company, Inc.

Milroy, J. and Milroy, L. (1985). *Authority in Language: Investigating language prescription and standardisation*. London: Routledge.

Mykkänen, J. (2004). '1900-luvun Seitsemän veljestä'. In Hirvonen T. (ed.) *Koko Kansan Tuntematon*. Helsinki: Alfamer.

Nevakivi, J. (1996). *Miten Kekkonen Pääsi Valtaan ja Suomi Suomettui*. Helsinki: Otava.

Puntila, L.A. (1975). *The Political History of Finland 1806-1966*. London: William Heinemann Ltd.

Ray, R. (1985). *A Certain Tendency of the Hollywood Cinema*. Princeton: Princeton University Press.

Rosenstone, R.A. (1995). *Visions of the Past: The Challenge of Film to Our Idea of History*. Cambridge: Harvard University Press.

Salmi, H. (1999). *Kriisi, kritiikki ja konsensus: Elokuva ja suomalainen yhteiskunta*. Turku: Turun yliopisto-Kulttuurihistoria.

Sihvonen, J. (2005). 'Tuntematon Sotilas/Tuntematon Sotilas'. In Soila, T. (ed.): *The Cinema of Scandinavia*. London: Wallflower Press.

Soini, T. (2004). 'Tuntematon tuntuu ytimissä'. In Hirvonen, T. (ed.): *Koko Kansan Tuntematon*. Helsinki: Alfamer.

Tilastokeskus (2004). *Väestorakenne 2004*. Helsinki: Tilastokeskus.

Uusitalo, K. (2004). 'Tuntemattoman Sotilaan kesä'. In Hirvonen, T. (ed.): *Koko Kansan Tuntematon*. Helsinki: Alfamer, pp.22-25.

Vehviläinen, O. (2002). *Finland in the Second World War: Between Germany and Russia*. New York: Palgrave.

YLE Teema (2006). *Poliittinen elokuva*. Helsinki, YLE Teema, 10th March.

Globalisation and National Identity in Transnational Nordic Cinema

Rebecca Spaven

> ...displacement, diaspora, exile, migration, nomadism, homelessness, border-crossing and tourism (Mazierska and Rascaroli 2006: 1)

The Nordic region is a curious case of the formation of several distinct nations, each with a specific identity, despite historically liquid borders and boundaries, constantly shifting ownership and huge geographical distances. The term 'Nordic' is becoming a troublesome one, always adjusting to fit the political and cultural changes within the European north. Thus recent Nordic film reflects this liminality, collecting influences and portraying those pushed to the margins of such nomadic, transitory societies. This essay will study various representations of sensory and emotional experiences of the transnational North by focussing on three films in particular: *Mies vailla menneisyyttä* (The Man without a Past, Aki Kaurismäki, Finland, 2002), *Zozo* (Josef Fares, Sweden, 2005) and *Á köldum klaka* (Cold Fever, Friðrik Þór Friðriksson, Iceland, 1995). The films deal with identity in very different ways, with the protagonists facing the dilemmas of being forcibly removed from their old lives and thrust into alien environments, each coming from a distinct background, which shapes the way they behave in their new environments. The films also portray the influence of different cultures on each other and what happens when they collide. In particular, this essay will discuss the rendering of the sensual experiences of taste, smell, touch and sound and their importance in shaping the characters' perception and participation in their new surroundings.

The change in population and culture of the Nordic countries in the last century has been a focus for many modern filmmakers, both immigrant and native. The Nordic nations have often been considered relatively homogeneous, but increasing immigration is changing the cultural landscape and producing many films documenting life in the new multicultural cities. The films of Kaurismäki, portraying life in Finland, with both its Scandinavian and Soviet history, have often been described as unmistakably 'Finnish', yet teem with American cultural references and imagery. Films such as *Leningrad Cowboys Go America* (Aki Kaurismäki, 1989), with its curious mix of Russian undertones, Finnish language and American obsession, explores 'the difficulties of conceptualising Finnish culture and identity in relation to its constantly fluctuating geopolitical position in an integrating *Western* Europe' (Kääpä 2010: 206).

American Rock 'n' Roll music plays a significant part in many of Kaurismäki's films. In *mies vailla menneisyyttä*, M manages to get hold of a jukebox, which he gives pride of place in the storage container in which he lives, immediately transforming it into a home-like space, as the music accompanies many of M's pivotal moments. In *Zozo*, the protagonist has to deal with a cold reception from his fellow schoolmates when he arrives in Sweden, laughing at his mention of salted apples, and jokingly suggesting adding salt to berries, as if trying to protect the essence of their Swedishness. The directness of his grandfather's dealings with any opposition, be it Zozo's bullies or the owner of the apples he picks, is a sharp contrast to the typical Swedish reserve and formality. *Á köldum klaka's* Japanese protagonist has the opposite problem, as he struggles to come to terms with the exuberance of the Icelandic welcome and the pungency of the food.

Hirata's bodily experience of Iceland is fascinating to watch. In our first introduction to him, we see him in Tokyo, at a fish market in the early hours of the morning. He is freezing, trying to protect himself against the cold, and looking forward to a holiday in Hawaii, yet instead is obliged to visit the icy wastes of Iceland to commemorate the seventh anniversary of his parents' death. His lack of knowledge of Iceland's climate and landscape is obvious in his dress, which leaves him utterly unprepared, but allows the audience to participate in his sensory experience of the cold, as we watch him trek through the wilderness, shivering and red-faced. The contrast between Iceland and Hirata's native Tokyo is important because of both the similarities and the differences in landscape. The countries' shared volcanic topography, although in Tokyo it is hidden by the 'flux' of the 'city of screens' (Thomson 2006: 162), connects them, and when Hirata visits the graveyard with his grandfather, we gain a sense of the spiritual culture behind the technology of modern Japan. The repetition of the graveyard, on Hirata's journey across Iceland, forges links between his homeland and this strange new place. However the shift in aspect ratio from 1:66 to 2:35, although allowing the viewer to 'enjoy' the experience of seeing the Icelandic landscape in widescreen, provides us with a problem concerning the authenticity of the space and the invasion of technology in 'coding' the Icelandic landscape as mediated through the screen. Cinematising the Icelandic landscape in

Nation and Identity

Towards the end of *Á köldum klaka* (Á köldum klaka, Friðrik Þór Friðriksson, 1995), Hirata performs a Shinto ceremony in the Icelandic snow, honouring his dead parents.

such a way enforces the film's ability to 'convey experience through an appeal to embodied and nonvisual cultural knowledge and memory' (ibid: 156) by presenting the viewer with a haptic landscape in which to participate.

The use of the topography to play visual tricks on the viewer, specifically with the white-outs, is visually stunning with the lone figure of Hirata burnt onto the retina with his red scarf, dark hair and coat. His inappropriate clothing, the trappings of a sober businessman, ensure he stands out vividly from the vast snowy landscape. In one instance, where we see him walking towards the camera, a vast truck suddenly appears over the brow of a hill behind him, packed with singing men. The vehicle and the figure of Hirata are our only ways of mapping the geography of the scene in the complete uniformity of the landscape under a heavy blanket of snow. As such our sensory connection to the scene is amplified, as our eyes struggle to organise the scene. Often, the wilderness takes on a more haptic nature, when rows of jagged rocks appear out of the snow, and we watch Hirata struggling to climb around them. These endlessly imposing panoramas evolve into a far more intimate space, when Hirata finally arrives at the site of his parents' death. The river and the snow become tools in his ritual as he floats the candles downstream on blocks of ice and pours *sake* into the water. By taking part in the landscape he injects it with his own cultural significance, and his bodily performance of the ritual unlocks a series of sense memories in both the character and the viewer. The smell of the incense, for instance, and the burning match. The sound of the glug of sake, as it is poured out and the palpable feeling of cold as we see Hirata's bare hands carving out the snow. Hirata's resigned bafflement that has so far been the extent of his performance as a character is replaced by a confidence, for the moment Hirata has found a comfort in this foreign place.

The intercultural elements of the film do not end with Hirata. Also imposing themselves on the Icelandic landscape are two Americans, with whom Hirata is forced to travel. I use the word 'impose' because they act like a sign for the American dominance that finds its way even to the most remote service station, and the hot dog with ketchup that Jack lets off a round of bullets for. The dissemination of American culture and globalisation is something that is dealt with often in the films of the Kaurismäki brothers, particularly in Aki's *Leningrad Cowboys* trilogy, and *Ariel* (1988). Kaurismäki once said that 'Finland is the most American country in Western Europe.' He simultaneously bemoans and celebrates the cultural hegemony of the 'spiritually poorest nation in the world' (Kääpä 2010: 79), a sentiment that runs through his films in the obvious aesthetic pleasure he takes from the use of old American cars and his parody of the American road movie. In *Ariel*, the car takes on a fetishistic, transformative quality. The American glamour it injects into the wastes of Finnish countryside proves to be visually powerful. Laura Marks discusses the interculturality of fetishes, suggesting that if we understand them as 'properly the product not of a single culture, but of the encounter between two, then we see how fetishes are produced not only in the course of built-up time, but also in the disjunctive movement through space' (Marks 2000:89). Andrew Nestingen outlines how the road movie might be identified, by 'images of the car, shots of dialogue in the car's interior, contrasts between rural and urban spaces, sweeping panoramas with fast panning shots' (2005: 286).

However, he also recognises the problems that arise when trying to categorise Kaurismäki as a genre filmmaker, especially considering his apparent contempt for American cultural hegemony. Kaurismäki exploits the Americanised images of classic cars, yet does not see any intrinsic worth in them. They are merely a tool in 'structuring the gaze of the protagonists and the audience' and a way of furthering the 'narrative and depiction of the characters' (Mazierska & Rascaroli 2006: 20). In *Ariel*, Taisto's Cadillac represents his journey through Finland, using the vocabulary of the American road movie, but also uses 'specifically Finnish/Scandinavian and Eastern European perspectives of the road' (ibid). Taisto adheres to the image of the star of an American road movie, with his leather jacket and cowboy boots, and the collapse of the shed in which the car was parked symbolises his departure from the Finnish countryside. Yet his inability to operate the car's sun-roof, his consequent wrapping of a scarf around his head and the unmistakably Finnish landscape he drives through, avoids the cliché from establishing itself by adding a both a humorous element and a postcard-like rural sentimentality to the scene.

Pietari Kääpä emphasises the issues of globalisation versus national identity:

> The Kaurismäkis' films are concerned with the notion that, in times of increasing globalisation, redefinitions of existing identity formations both cause insecurity and widen the horizons within which people imagine their own sense of belonging...the national in the Kaurismäkis' films is a topic of constant negotiation, not a self-evident fact. (Kääpä 2010: 31)

When the mine in which Taisto worked was closed down, he was forced to move to Helsinki, where neo-liberal corporatist values were beginning to take hold and both the national and global circulation of people, money and images cannot be avoided. *Ariel* and *Man Without A Past* both deal with what happens when one is excluded from the circuit of wealth distribution, and the identity problems that arise from this. Andrew Nestingen highlights this, suggesting that because 'national spaces are increasingly woven into planet-spanning networks of circulation, such rejections of circulation become increasingly problematic' (Nestingen 2004: 100). The nameless protagonist in *Mies vailla menneisyyttä*, unable to remember anything, is dismissed as a time waster by the cold bureaucrats in charge of the job centres and banks. His anonymity begins when his assailants cover his face with his welding mask and leave him to die in the park. This is the one remnant of his past, however, that he remembers, as he encounters some welders at the docks, and his muscle memory allows him to pick up a torch and perform the task. The docks where M settles can be seen as a 'liminal non-space' (Koivunen 2006: 136). This existence of those who have somehow slipped through the welfare net, although meagre, is strangely optimistic.

The problem of Finnish identity is a recurring one in Kaurismäki's films, as he uses marginalised characters for whom personal and national identification is an issue. This is particularly prevalent in *Leningrad Cowboys go America*. The cowboys' ambiguous heritage and culturally confused dress sense symbolise a Finland in transition away from the spectre of the Soviet Union but into the clutches of another superpower: the USA. The film uses landscape imagery typical of traditional Finnish films (ibid: 172), yet refrains from branding them as particularly Finnish, allowing the viewer to wander in the imaginary Fenno-Siberian wilderness. This use of landscape is in contrast to Friðriksson's employment of the Icelandic landscape in *Á köldum klaka,* which functions as a plot device, dominating the film aesthetically, and unmistakably Icelandic. The comparison between the national identification of *Leningrad Cowboys* and *Á köldum klaka* is an interesting one when considering their differing histories. Although, like Finland, it has for much of its history been ruled by another power, Iceland has, probably through its isolation and small population, regained a strong national identity. Indeed, *Á köldum klaka* was criticised by Icelandic audiences for its 'catalogue of Icelandic curiosities and clichés' (Thomson 2006: 150) and its globally conscious presentation of the nation's image. However it also highlights the West's view of Japanese culture by introducing Hirata's world as one of supermodern technology and karaoke machines. The American hitchhiker's comedy Japanese accent and proposition that the radio would not have broken if it had been manufactured in Japan portrays the ready-made Western view of Hirata's homeland, yet Jack and Jill's constant failure to remember his name properly betrays the underlying ignorance and lack of real attention to the culture of Japan. Although Hirata does not allude much to his life in Japan during his stay in Iceland, the opening sequences suggest an insular, technology and business driven life, and there is an implication that he had previously not given his parents' funeral much thought. However the fluency with which he performs the ritual and the emotion that eventually breaks his neutral exterior indicates the power of the intercultural experience of the Icelandic environment, the place of his parents' death and the spiritual significance of the objects he has brought with him from Japan to create a (both cinematically and emotionally) potent scene and a renewed connection to his parents and the Japanese culture.

Fares' portrayal of Zozo's identity is similar in a way, to Hirata's, in that the film begins with his life in Beirut, and it is a family tragedy that brings him to his new home. Zozo's identification with Lebanese culture is mediated through his grandparents, who represent an island of family warmth in the formal and alien culture of Sweden. There is a paradox in his memories of home, with its juxtaposition between the comfort and familiarity of his mother's embrace and the constant threat of danger. Sweden represents safety, but loneliness. This is personified in his new friend Leo, whose drunken father appears to be his only family, and who leads a solitary life at school. His grandfather's aggressive defence of his grandson and his own pride in the face of the inability of the headmaster to recognise a problem between Zozo and the school bully provides Zozo with a conundrum. His calm nature won't allow him to rise to the fight like his grandfather expects him to, which obviously distresses him, culminating in the dramatic scene in which he loses control and the playground in his imaginary world is bombed, just like his hometown.

The Lebanese music playing while Zozo drives through the idyllic Swedish countryside for the first time and the flute his grandfather plays as they sit surrounded by bemused, sunbathing Swedes, offers a reminder of their identity as immigrants. For Zozo, as he will soon find school a less than welcoming place; it is a reminder of the value of his national identity in the face of intolerance and coldness from his fellow pupils. The music returns whenever he imagines his mother or Rita appearing before him, a dream world to which he often escapes. Music often accompanies pivotal moments in Aki Kaurismäki's films, such as in *Mies vailla menneisyyttä*, when M's assailants turn on the radio they find in his suitcase, just before they begin beating him. The stirring classical music is unique to this scene, however, as throughout the film, the music played on M's jukebox is predominantly blues or rockabilly. M's jukebox provides the soundtrack to M's first kiss with Irma, and continues into the next scene as he sits surveying his healthy-looking potato patch, a symbol of his success and happiness in his unorthodox new home. The music that pervades Aki Kaurismäki's films, specifically *Mies vailla menneisyyttä*, also signifies Finland's hybridity as a nation, and also its power to bring people from different backgrounds together. The Finnish tango and R&B, played by the newly invigorated Salvation Army band, brings together the community, creating bonds and giving the formerly liminal space a legitimacy. After witnessing the gang who beat him up being chased off by his neighbours, M comes to realise the value of his new home. This recognition clearly dawns on him when the security guard refers to the disparate crew as 'us'. His identity within the society of outcasts is one of solidity and solidarity, despite his lack of past. His new role as band manager, the architect of the new bonds between the members of the community, also gives him an authority that allows him to stand up to the once dominant security guard.

In his discussion of the road movie, Andrew Nestingen uses the arguments of David Laderman and Timothy Corrigan to propose that 'by dislodging the subject from an immanent social context, journey narratives imply that a transcendental distance (cultural, economic, political, religious) can be attained, which leads to deeper understanding and perspective' (Nestingen 2005: 292). Kaurismäki, by removing his characters from the ordinary social sphere, allows them to 'become more able to critically observe social mores' and, despite often being seen as criminals in the eyes of the law, uphold strict moral codes and live fulfilling lives. His films are a protest against the reality that, in an evolving capitalist welfare state, those on the peripheries are often left there, and attempt to 'create alternative possibilities for individual identities to face up to these wide-ranging forms of societal metamorphosis' (Kääpä 2010: 254).

The preparation and eating of food is another interesting theme in the film. The warmth of the Nieminens' hospitality and the kindness behind the rather thin and unappealing stew that they feed M is a buffer against the coldness of life outside his community, and when he first locks eyes with Irma, there is a bowl of hot soup between them. Food becomes a symbol of the kindness of strangers and a step on the way to normality. When M tries to return the favour and cook for Irma he burns the meat and pours half a box of salt on top of it, yet the evening is successful and Irma praises him for cooking the peas properly. Another example is when M receives the jukebox and the three men sit eating in silence, save the music playing. The solidarity and friendship of receiving and giving something for nothing is a sharp contrast to the greed and selfishness society that forced M to board the train to Helsinki in the first place. The storage container village may be dysfunctional in the eyes of normal society, but by having its own rules it upholds a moral code and gives its members an identity that is far more cohesive and it is telling that he makes no attempt to return to his old life after discovering his real name and meeting his attractive ex-wife. Even in the credits he is named 'M', rather than his 'real' name of Jaakko Antero Lujanen.

In *Á köldum klaka*, Hirata receives many gifts of food. Although unappealing to his untrained palette, they represent the abundance of hospitality in Iceland. The farm he stumbles upon in the middle of a snowy wasteland provides vital warmth, and with it the Icelandic delicacy of boiled sheep's head. The viewer can almost taste the salty tang of the liquorice that Hirata finds in the car and resorts to eating after it breaks down. The violent reaction it prompts seems to cause him to descend into despair at the alienness of this country and its strange-tasting food. However when he meets Siggi, the man who will eventually take him to where he needs to go to perform the ritual, he embraces the strong taste of 'Brennivin', otherwise known as 'Black Death' and drunkenly, yet happily, bites into the sheep's head he clutches in his hand. Like his initiation into the landscape by performing the Japanese funeral ritual, by eating the food, and enjoying it, he creates a multi-sensory, intercultural memory that will inevitably be shaped by his Japanese taste, and therefore unique to him.

In *Zozo*, the young protagonist also has to rely on the kindness of strangers after his family is killed. The flatbread he receives from Rita signals the beginning of their friendship, and without her he would have been unable to travel to Sweden. When he arrives in Sweden to the home of his grandparents, he sits by a lake with his grandfather, who gives him salted apples to eat. He then relays this to the class later, who react in derision and bafflement, suggesting berries with salt, or bananas with pepper might be good to eat. This reaction appears to be a kind of defence against a threat to their own 'Swedishness', an attempt to protect the traditional Swedish berries from this strange Lebanese custom. Zozo insists it is not a typical Lebanese delicacy, yet one can imagine the taste of it, along with the exciting tale of fist-fighting told by his grandfather, creating the kind of sensory shock that remains in the mind for a long time, as, according to Marks, 'senses that are close to the body, like the sense of touch, are capable of storing powerful memories that are lost to the visual' (Marks 2000: 130). Zozo's transition from the war-torn yet familiar environment of Beirut to the serenity of Sweden is an uneasy one. The homogeneity of culture in the small town where he lives ensures that he stand out as an easy target, particularly in the scene where he introduces himself, and the fact that he mentions the salty apples is pivotal. Marks writes about the importance of gustatory and olfactory memories to immigrants and those on the outskirts of society. She states that 'often the sensorium is the only place where cultural memories are preserved. For intercultural cinema, therefore, sense experience is at the heart of cultural memory' (195). She asks 'can the mere audiovisual representation of a gustatorial act successfully arouse lost memories; or... must one physically carry out the act oneself? And what are the intercultural limits of such memory: can one identify with sense memories one has never had?' (198). Although the viewer will not have had exactly the same sensory experiences as shown in a film, one can impose ones own visual and sensory memories on to those on screen, replacing the salted apples with a figment of one's own childhood, in order to participate more fully in the scene. In *Zozo*, we are clearly able to see this kind of sense memory in the process of being created.

The films discussed are interesting when discussed in relation to national identity due to the plurality of their themes. Images of travel pervade the films, and all throw up fascinating questions about the nature of the road movie, in the case of *Á köldum klaka, Leningrad Cowboys* and *Ariel*, and about crossing borders both personally and physically in *Zozo* and *Man Without A Past*. Hirata's journey to Iceland, when the woman says to him, 'You'll love Iceland. Everybody does' and his patriotic taxi driver reeling off the country's various accolades, provides him with a picture of a country with a wealth of culture, yet many of his initial experiences are unhappy ones. The film deals with the idea of xeno and auto-stereotypes brilliantly, exoticising both Icelandic and Japanese culture and the intercultural, emotional and sensory encounters between human, vehicle and landscape. M's train journey in *Mies vailla menneisyyttä* symbolises his transition from rural working-class living to an urban future as well as a total departure from his old life in the rat-race of capitalism to a more fulfilling, community-driven life in the shanty town. Unlike in the the other two Kaurismäki films discussed, the American car is not a way out: instead, M has his jukebox and the music played by the Salvation Army band to take him away from the drudgery of everyday working life. The unshakeable influence of globalisation, prevalent even in this most marginal of communities, underlines Nestingen's point that 'although the films certainly appear Finnish in many ways, they derive a great deal from circulation: of images, of money, of people' (Nestingen 2004: 99).

The quote at the beginning of this essay relates to the changing culture of populations in Europe and how films attempt to describe this. What it highlights is the human need for a home, and the identity that flows from it, whether this be found through music, ritual or travel. The films discussed prove that the nomadic nature of the world provides us with problems to overcome when our personal or national characteristics are questioned, whether this be by ourselves or by others, be they bureaucrats, questioning our right to be in a particular place, or those close to us. The constantly changing idea of what it means to be Nordic, particularly in the case of Finland and Sweden, gives these films an interesting perspective. In the case of Sweden, with its large population of immigrants, it is a country renegotiating its political identity, as the equal, tolerant society is rocked by xenophobic parties. Josef Fares' films provide an instructive insight into being on the receiving end of Swedish hospitality. The role which the senses play in forming our memories and giving us a visual vocabulary with which to describe the things we go through is vital in these films. Zozo's flashbacks and imaginings are very physical encounters, as he remembers embracing his mother and the vision of Rita, with the sun shining down on her. The way Hirata remembers his parents in the ceremony is by performing a series of rituals which connects him and his culture to the landscape through the smell of the incense and the cold feel of the snow against his hands. In *Man Without A Past*, M only remembers his past as a welder when he puts the mask on and feels the torch in his hands, as his body allows him to perform the task he has done so many times. This suggests the power of the subconscious senses over memory to take us back to past times. Our memories are at the heart of our identity, as they allow us to relate personally to every environment we are in, and all the films discussed highlight this, whether it be the Leningrad Cowboys' heavily accented music or Zozo's salted apples.

Author's Comment

This essay was written over the Christmas holidays of my second year as a student of Scandinavian Studies & History of Art. It was the longest essay I had written up to that point, and completed while on holiday in Cuba, which provided an interesting sensory contrast to the wintry scenes I was watching and writing about! I found the longer length a great opportunity to discuss at length what I found to be fascinating issues, and which, after now having spent a year in Gothenburg, Sweden, are still present in my mind.

My experience in Gothenburg of the nature of immigration in Sweden has made me wish I had more time to re-write this essay (although the word count would doubtless have to be doubled), and has given me more of an insight into the issues dealt with, particularly in *Zozo*, of the problems of integration that Sweden has faced, and dealt with somewhat heavy-handedly.

This being the first time I have read my essay since writing it nearly two years ago, I found many things I wanted to revisit, and am now looking forward to embarking in my final year as a Scandinavian Studies student with the opportunity to do an extended essay, in which I am strongly considering continuing my study of Nordic film.

References

Koivunen, Anu (2006). 'Do You Remember Monrepos?' Melancholia, Modernity and Working-Class Masculinity in *The Man Without a Past*'. In Thomson, C.C. (ed.): *Northern Constellations: New Readings in Nordic Cinema*. Norwich: Norvik Press

Kääpä, Pietari (2010). *The National and Beyond:* The Globalisation of Finnish Cinema in the Films of Aki and Mika Kaurismäki New Studies in European Cinema 12. Oxford: Peter Lang.

Marks, Laura U. (2000). *The Skin of the Film. Intercultural Cinema, Embodiment, and the Senses.* London and Durham: Duke University Press.

Mazierska, Ewa, and Laura Rascaroli (2006). *Crossing New Europe: Postmodern Travel and the European Road Movie.* London and New York: Wallflower Press.

Nestingen, Andrew (ed.) (2004): *In Search of Aki Kaurismäki: Aesthetics and Contexts.* Special issue of the Journal of Finnish Studies, University of Toronto / Aspasia Books.

Nestingen, Andrew and Trevor Elkington (eds) (2005). *Transnational Cinema in a Global North: Nordic Cinema in Transition.* Detroit: Wayne State University Press.

Thomson, C. Claire (2006). 'Incense in the Snow: Topologies of Intimacy and Interculturality in Friðriksson's *Cold Fever* and Gondry's *Jóga*'. In Thomson, C. Claire (ed.): *Northern Constellations: New Readings in Nordic Cinema.* Norwich: Norvik Press

Nation and Identity

The Father Figure in Swedish 'Immigrant' Films

Linda Blank

> It is much easier to become a father than to be one.
> Kent Nerburn, *Letters to My Son: Reflections on Becoming a Man*, 1994

Millennium cinema: Swedish Film in the first decade of the new millennium

The development of Swedish film has been marked by waves of success, interchanging with years of stagnancy. The Golden Age of the 1920s was followed by years of limited production, which again was succeeded by the international success of Ingmar Bergman in the 60s and 70s. 'For decades [his] name [...] has been synonymous with Swedish cinema' (Bono and Koskinen, 1996: 5). However, cinema in Sweden has undergone a rather immense change since the Bergman era, as has its perception within, as well as outside, Sweden. Critics, academics and cinephiles have been trying to understand the evolution of the Swedish film and to identify the 'new big deal'. In the book *Swedish Film*, Larsson establishes that there are several greater trends within the newest Swedish cinema. First of all, there is the long-lasting tradition of crime fiction as demonstrated by the success of the Wallander series[1] as well as the Millennium Trilogy[2]. Secondly, there are internationally successful films based on best-selling literature, such as *Låt den rätte komma in* (Let The Right One In, Alfredson, 2008) and – again – the Millennium Trilogy. Another 'small wave' is Lukas Moodysson's work, which has gained global success as his recent film *Mammut* (Mammoth, 2009) shows. Finally, there is the wave of the 'swiftly dubbed "immigrant films"' as demonstrated by the success of Josef Fares' films (Larsson, 2010: 284ff.). Within this group of films, I want to argue, there seems to be a recurring theme of fathers as symbols of patriarchal authority, which will also be the topic of this analysis, as explained in more detail below.

Fathers and other family disasters: Introduction to the changing dynamics of the father role

The father-son relationship may seem an overworked and worn-out topic at first glance. Doubtless, generational conflicts have been going on for a far longer period of time than they have been documented.

> Från grekerna, över Shakespeare och framåt är historien full av uppgörelser mellan män och pojkar. Fäder som stället hårda krav och utsätter barnet för svåra prov för att utröna om det kan bemästra sin (kvinnliga) rädsla. (Hagman 1992: 14)

> From the Greeks through Shakespeare and onwards, history is full of tensions between men and boys. [There have been f]athers with high expectations, putting the child through severe trials in order to determine whether it can overcome its (female) fears.[3]

However, in spite of the recurring theme of the generational conflict, the circumstances surrounding it have changed immensely, thus also affecting its nature and its representation on screen. Traditionally, as Hagman points out,

The Father Figure in Swedish 'Immigrant' Films

the son struggled with becoming a man under the dictator-like regime of his extremely authoritative father, who expected too much from a young boy. Dealing with the conventionally patriarchal male figures, ranging from priests to powerful and pushy fathers in bourgeois society, was also a way of dealing with religion, social norms and other issues within society.

Moreover, the two world wars have changed the demographics of European states, thus also affecting the themes of the films. In his analysis of the changing image of the father in Swedish film, Dahlén (1994: 379) points out:

> en aspekt som belyses tydligt av jämförelsen mellan 50-talet och 70-80-talen är den normativa förändringen från en på 50-talet dominerande "auktoritär, patriarkalisk" familjetyp till en tillåtande familjetyp, där fadern antingen "försvunnit" och överlämnat normbildande och gränssättande till modern eller utvecklat en mer demokratisk fadersroll.

> an aspect that is clearly illustrated by the comparison between the 1950s and the 70s - 80s is the normative change from the "authoritative, patriarchal" family type of the 50s, to a permissive type, where fathers have either "disappeared" , thereby transferring the normative and limiting role to the mother, or developed a more democratic father role.

Although I tend to disagree with Dahlén's claim that fathers in contemporary cinema have a more 'democratic role', a lot of evidence can be found in favour of his 'missing father' theory. In reference to the 1980s and 1990s, Koskinen (1996: 27) claims that 'many critics have noted [that] a remarkable number of Swedish films in recent years have dealt with the theme of fathers and sons[, m]ore specifically, with missing fathers'. Similarly, Hagman (1992: 15) also points out that the theme of the missing father dominated Swedish film in the 1990s. 'Samtliga filmer berättar om pappor som är frånvarande, antigen kroppsligen eller själsligen, och om sönernas stumma längtan efter dem. Om små pojkar som tidigt lär sig att tygla sin kärlek, tiga om sin längtan, svälja sin sorg' (All films deal with fathers who are absent, either physically or spiritually, and the sons' silent longing for them. With small boys who are taught early to control their love, be silent about their longing, swallow their sorrow). There are numerous examples of films that support this claim, for instance *Min store tjocke far* (My Big Great Daddy, Andersson, 1992), *Änglagård* (House of Angels, Nutley, 1992), *Mitt liv som hund* (My Life as a Dog, Hallström, 1985).

'Immigrant film': definition, problems and solutions

While the above might be true for the 1980s and 90s, the films of the new millennium have wrought another change upon the landscape of the Swedish cinema. Another trend can be distinguished in recent Swedish cinema that has been carried on from the cinema of the past century: the one dealing with dysfunctional families and authoritative fathers, who sometimes are abusive, too. Within this trend two rough groups of films can be identified: the second generation films dealing with an immigrant family living in Sweden; and contemporary films dealing with families in Sweden in the 1970s. In the frame of this essay (it being written in 2011), the term **'new** Swedish films' will refer to films produced in the first decade of the new millennium. The films that fall under the two categories stated above share their interest in the representation of fathers within the frame of their community and the effects of their behaviour on the family as a whole, and/or on individual members in particular. Due to the complexity of both trends, I have decided to focus my analysis on the so called 'immigrant films'. Naturally, there are many films that could be included in limited analysis of this kind. I have chosen to focus on the following films: *Hus i helvete* (All Hell Let Loose, Tsalimi, 2002), *Vingar av glas* (Wings of Glass, Bagher, 2000), *Jalla! Jalla!* (Fares, 2000), and *Farsan* (The Dad, Fares, 2010). They all depict fathers clinging on to the patriarchal structure of their family, albeit to differing extents. Firstly, I will investigate the portraits of fathers in the films stated above. Secondly, I intend to demonstrate that the continuous focus on father figures in contemporary film is more than just a reference to generational conflicts, but rather also a reflection of and commentary on social change and issues in modern Swedish society. These films give a portrayal of immigrant families that have grown significantly in number in the recent past, thus reflecting social changes in Sweden. They also demonstrate the cultural clash between 'immigrant' and Swedish cultures. Finally, they deal with the changing concept of male identity and consequently the necessity to re-negotiate the father role.

Additionally, I feel the need to point out that a different definition of 'immigrant films' applies to my analysis. Most scholars use this as an umbrella term to describe different kinds of films made by 'immigrant directors'. For instance, Wright (2010: 292) connects the notion of 'immigrant films' to 'three directors with roots in Lebanon or Iran', such as Josef Fares, Reza Bagher and Reza Parsa. While this is truly a new phenomenon on the landscape of Swedish cinema, I believe it is also disputable to combine these directors into one cluster merely on the basis of their ethnic origin. What differentiates 'my' films from other films about immigrants is that their narrative is an inside perspective of the family, thus allowing them to move away from the usual setting of films covering the same topic. In contrast to films like, for example, *Tic Tac* (Alfredson, 1997) that deal with racism within Sweden directly, the films of this analysis show people from different cultures co-existing and dealing with their problems, as well as intrafamilial problems. Therefore, in terms of this essay, 'immigrant films' should be understood as a thematic grouping of the films discussed rather than being linked to directors' personal backgrounds.

Generational conflict: An analysis

The daughters strike back: The father-daughter relationship

The cook, the tyrant, his wife and his daughters: *Hus i helvete*

Hus i helvete is a drama released in 2002 directed by Susan Taslimi that centres on the Iranian family of Mr. Serbandi and 'his women'. It is a story of Minoo, his oldest daughter, who comes back from exile in the USA for the wedding of her younger sister and this is when the actual drama begins to unfold. Serbandi is not a patriarch in the usual sense, as, for instance, in the Dogme film *Festen* (Celebration, Vinterberg, 1998)[4]: an imperturbable leader, superior and secure in his power. Rather, he seems to be emasculated by each of the family members around him. His wife is the primary source of family income and does not shy away from flirting with the

The Father Figure in Swedish 'Immigrant' Films

Swedish sewing machine repairman Leif. Moreover, Minoo disregards him openly, while his younger daughter Gita 'maintains the pretense of playing by the household rules but is in fact already sexually involved with her fiancé' (Wright, 2010: 301). Furthermore, he operates a catering company and cooks himself, which is traditionally seen as a rather feminine type of work. This applies especially to the Arab community, as pointed out by Serbandi's mother, who criticizes both her son for taking care of the household and his wife for letting him do so. 'Are you a master or a housewife? Housework is women's work!' she says. Serbandi himself repeats to clients 'It's my wife who cooks', thus revealing his own attitude towards gender specific standards and his job. Ironically, when he says 'I'm the boss', in the background we can hear and see his mother and wife fighting, thus proving the exact opposite of what he says. This scene, along with many others, is shot with a handheld camera, which reveals the chaos in Serbandi's 'empire'. As Doxtater points out: 'Serbandi [as … the] supposed head of the household, […] comically struggles to maintain his position of patriarchal authority amid steam, tensions, and seemingly endless familiar bickering' (Doxtater, 2006: 66). He wants to hold the family together by controlling it through violence, but simultaneously does not have the ability to succeed.

Herr Serbandi is portrayed as an eccentric and aggressive man throughout the film, as demonstrated in several scenes. However, I want to concentrate on two particular consecutive scenes that show him as an abusive father – visually and in terms of the narrative. One of the scenes that demonstrate Serbandi's aggressiveness and inability to control his irrational rage outbreaks is when he locks Minoo in her bedroom. First he tries to get to his son, who is hiding under the bed, then he tries to take out his anger on Minoo, but she closes the door. The shot switches from her younger sister, who comes in between Serbandi and the door, trying to protect Minoo, to the final scene when his wife tries to attack him, but he overpowers her and throws her on the bed. Notably, the sequence of these specific shots is filmed with a particular camera setting. We follow the action on screen from an over-shoulder perspective, shot from a high angle, thus emphasizing Serbandi's (physical) superiority over the ones he abuses. Furthermore, the last shot of this scene visually resembles a rape scene, which is the climax of Serbandi's outbreak of rage. Serbandi throws his wife Nana on the bed and holds her arms while lying on top of her. Again, a high angled shot enables us to see Nana's scared gaze directed at her husband, thus emphasizing her inferiority even more by letting us witness her reaction. This episode is supported by the use of a hand held camera, which continuously adds a sense of chaos and disorder to the family's life.

Notably, the tension of the scene resolves when the audience sees the scared children standing behind the bed from Serbandi's point of view, which is shot with a static camera, thus putting an end to Serbandi's outbreak and the impression of chaos created by the handheld camera. Then, in a medium close up, we see Serbandi in the foreground, which makes him appear even bigger, while his wife is lying still, unable to move in her state of shock. However, although the scene itself ends at that particular moment, we no longer know where Serbandi's limits lie and what he is capable of. Paradoxically, his aggressiveness and physical superiority do not demonstrate the superior position that he claims to have. On the contrary, the viewers are led to believe that Serbandi tries to overcompensate for his weak position within the family and lack of masculinity by his attempts to overpower 'his women'. In her analysis of the film, Wright (2010: 301) makes a significant point: 'The harder Serbandi strives to assert his dominance, the less actual control he is able to seize and the more frantic he becomes'.

This scene is followed by a flashback to Minoo's past in the USA. Already at the beginning of the film Serbandi aggressively attacks Minoo when she tries to leave the house. He tries to control her and take her freedom by locking her in his apartment – the only limited space that he seems to be able to control. Taslimi plays with visual associations by juxtaposing Serbandi and Minoo's abuser. We clearly see Serbandi's figure: a rather corpulent dark-haired man with a beard, who just locked Minoo into a room of his apartment. Several seconds later we are introduced to a scene from Minoo's past as a stripper (or perhaps even a prostitute), shot with a hand held camera. We see her half naked on a bed, again, with a corpulent dark-haired man with a beard. He throws her on the bed when she clearly states that she wants to leave. By the means of this particular type of editing, a parallel emerges between the two men we see in two shots close to each other. As the French film theorist Bazin says '[montage is] the creation of a sense or meaning not proper to the images themselves but derived exclusively from their juxtaposition' (quoted in Barsan and Monahan, 2010: 329). Thus the American man, who clearly abuses her and possibly even rapes her, is directly compared to her father, who most probably did not rape her, but certainly does not shy away from physical abuse, traumatizing his children.

Although there is no indication of sexual abuse from the side of the father, the mistreatment that Minoo faces from him is compared to her experience in the US, thus adding to Serbandi's portrayal as an abusive patriarch, especially taking into account that her father was the reason why she left in the first place.

Interestingly enough, the suspense built up by the scene when Serbandi locks up Minoo continues to increase at Gita's wedding. Scared by Serbandi's action from the previous night, the family is forced to proceed with the wedding ceremony despite Minoo's absence as Serbandi orders everyone to do. On the one hand, viewers do not believe in his capability to overpower his family because his behaviour is interpreted as signs of weakness. On the other hand, he gets intoxicated and 'experiences a complete meltdown' at the wedding (Wright, 2010: 301). His almost insane dance creates a sense of fear because we await some form of outrage from him, as prepared by the scene before the wedding. These ambiguous feelings serve to build up suspense since we no longer know what to expect from him. Furthermore, suspense is also built up by Minoo's dance and Serbandi's reaction towards it. The handheld camera changes between Minoo's and Serbandi's point of view with increasing speed, supported by the similar speed of the drums that accompany Minoo's performance. This scene resembles a fight between two people and not surprisingly Serbandi finally thrusts towards Minoo. However, 'Gita leaps on stage and defends her sister by wrapping her in the folds of her wedding dress, in response to which Serbandi stammers out his own retaliatory performance', thus indicating that he has lost his physical superiority (Doxtater, 2006: 68). Therefore, he verbally abuses his family and, being denied support for his accusations from the wedding guests, he only succeeds in putting himself and his family in a humiliating position.

After Minoo's public striptease in front of the guests, the roles seem to reverse and Serbandi can no longer preserve the image of being in control of his family. This is demonstrated by the final 'Last Supper-esque, mid-length' (ibid.) shot of the film that shows the family dining at the festive table, especially if contrasted to a similar shot in the beginning of the film. While in the beginning of the film we see a dinner table with traditional seating arrangements - at the kitchen table Serbandi as the patriarch of the family is seated opposite his wife - this is no longer the case in the last shot. At the wedding we see the women of the family seated centrally with Gita's husband and brother seated at the ends of the table, while 'the patriarch Serbandi is relegated off-screen where he remains invisible and excluded' (ibid.). This shows that his position in the family is lost and the women have finally obtained some sort of independence, although it is unclear to what extent it will apply to them in the future. Serbandi's position is also emphasized by the fact that his presence at that particular moment is confirmed only after his mother addresses him, thus showing that he has lost his 'commanding voice' in the family. All in all, the film ultimately shows the complete breakdown of a patriarchal authority because Serbandi's authority has been compromised and will never be re-established.

Minoo's rebellion symbolizes two different things that are significant for the understanding of the film. First of all, both her escape from her imprisonment in the room and her striptease at the wedding are 'the visualization of escape and constriction', as Doxtater (ibid.) claims. Minoo's physical escape can be read as a metaphor for her final emancipation and independence from her father and patriarchal authority in general. The film thus aims at transforming gender roles and power relationships as they are implied by society and in this particular cultural community. Furthermore, it challenges the stereotypical concepts of behaviour and dress codes that are considered appropriate for '"traditional" societies', as opposed to Swedish norms (ibid.) The conflict between Minoo and her father is not simply an intergenerational one as, for instance, could be claimed for *Vingar av glas*. Their conflict is also constituted by the power struggle between patriarchal authority and the oppressed group. In addition, as the oppressed group is almost exclusively female, at least in terms of resistance, it also raises gender related questions. Thus, 'the film works to bring women's desire out into the open to be acknowledged, affirmed, and flaunted in the face of a male position capable of disowning a daughter' (ibid.).

Secondly, Minoo's rebellion can also be regarded as the symbol of the struggle between two different cultures. Like most of the 'immigrant films', *Hus i helvete* shows a family caught in between two different cultures – their own and the 'host' Swedish society. Along with other films of this analysis, *Hus i helvete* does not suggest the complete rejection of one culture in order to be able to live in another, but rather shows the difficulty of combining them. There is neither any preference for either of the two, nor any evaluation of them, but simply the statement that these cultures are different, which makes their co-existence somewhat problematic. This is supported by the fact that not only the oppression by the patriarchal father is criticized by the film, but also the 'objectification and exploitation to which exposed female bodies can be subjected in hypocritically "free", "Western society". This position is represented by the American world of erotic dancing and figured in Sweden by Minoo's deadbeat Swedish boyfriend' (ibid.). Therefore the film challenges both cultures by representing them partly in a negative light. Instead of criticizing one another, it suggests that members of a culture should reflect upon their own and realize the values of the other one.

Caught in between: Vingar av glas

Vingar av glas is a drama directed by Reza Bagher in 2000. It shows a family of three people – Nazli, her sister and their father – trying to manage their lives in a small Swedish town. While facing the usual problems of the teenage years, eighteen-year-old Nazli also struggles with finding a job, her father's overprotective authority and the over-affectionate cousin who tries to rape her. The film deals with the 'generational conflict within her family and her own struggle for self-definition as she straddles two cultures' (Wright, 2010: 298). The representation of the father in this particular film is, similar to other films included in this analysis, of an ambiguous nature. On one hand, Abbas is shown as a caring and loving father who puts his daughters before his own interests. On the other hand, he is also portrayed as an authoritative father who tries to exercise control over his daughters, sometimes even in a violent and aggressive way. In the following paragraphs, I will explain how these two aspects represent the family's struggle with their cultural identity and their inner problems.

The ambiguousness of the father figure is established quite early in the film. In the very beginning, we see a scene in the kitchen showing the family doing the dishes and clearing the table together. As the handheld camera bounces between Abbas and his daughters in their small kitchen, we get an image of a unified family. As seen later on in the film, there is no division of 'female' and 'male' labour in this household, despite the expected stereotypes. On the contrary, doing the dishes in this family is a collective task, which portrays Abbas as quite a modern man. However, this image is not completely correct, since his intentions to arrange 'comfortable marriages for them' are entirely traditional and patriarchal (ibid.: 299). Furthermore, Nazli is supposed to marry her cousin, which is considered appropriate for the Middle Eastern culture, while being very unusual for Swedish standards, as pointed out in a conversation between Nazli and her Swedish girlfriend. This ambiguous representation of a father is comparable to the picture painted in *Hus i helvete*: the father verbally confirms his male authority, while contradictory actions are shown on screen. Despite this similarity, Abbas is not comparable to the almost insane abusive authority of Serbandi in *Hus i helvete*. While Serbandi tries to seize power because he feels emasculated by his family, Abbas is portrayed as a father who pursues his daughters' interests. This is further emphasized by the fact that he 'has chosen Mahin's [the older daughter's] partner knowing that she is already in love with him', thus demonstrating that he takes his daughters' wishes into account (Wright, 2010: 299).

Furthermore, there are several scenes that show Abbas taking care of the household, which is traditionally considered to be the female sector of life (Hagström, 1999: 41). In contrast to Serbandi, who denies that he is the one cooking when asked on the phone, Abbas completely takes over all tasks concerned with the home. For instance, in a succession of shots Abbas is shown, equipped with rubber gloves and a mop, cleaning the kitchen floor, the windows and then setting the festive table. Another (quite comic) example is when Abbas hangs up the laundry, which is mostly female underwear. On one hand, the lingerie, in a sense, reminds us of the female aspect of taking care of a household, but on the other hand, it emphasizes Abbas' willingness to do well by his daughters, even things that are unusual for his culture. This applies especially because this shot is followed by the contrasting one of Nazli resting on the couch, while her father does the laundry. All together this shows that Abbas

> has assumed the traditionally female role in the absence of his deceased wife. A more culturally consistent pattern would be for him to expect his daughters, who after all are adults, to take over all the domestic chores, yet neither Nazli nor her more compliant and traditional sister are assigned or have assumed primary responsibility for such tasks.' (Wright, 2010: 299)

Despite this positive portrayal of Abbas as a father that makes it difficult to view him as a patriarchal tyrant, he is still 'the product of a culture that asserts patriarchal control over female members of the household' (ibid.). There are two particular scenes that envisage this image of Abbas as a patriarch similar to other films mentioned here. The first one is when he locks Nazli in their apartment after seeing the Swedish boys who came to pick her up. In an aggressive argument, Abbas tries to impose his parental control over Nazli by preventing her from leaving. Similar to the situation in *Hus i helvete*, having failed to control Nazli's behaviour on a psychological level, Abbas attempts to impose physical restrictions by confining Nazli to his apartment. However, this is more than merely an act of abuse and the restriction of someone's freedom. The space of their house is the only place that Abbas (and comparably Serbandi) seems to be able to exert control. This is opposed to the outer world, where he feels like a failure due to his job situation and language problems, as made clear by children laughing at his performance. Therefore, both Abbas and Serbandi logically assume that by locking their daughters into the space of their homes, they can gain control over their lives. This act of physical control over their daughters can be regarded as a desperate attempt to establish his authority, at least within the family. Surely, this asserts the patriarchal authority of the fathers, but only for the limited period of the 'imprisonment' of the daughters. Both Nazli and Minoo manage to break out of the apartment, thus overthrowing their fathers' authority and undermining the established power positions.

The second scene portrays Abbas even more as a patriarch who disregards his daughter's opinion. At Mahlin's wedding, Nazli publicly insults her cousin, who attempted to rape her, to the surprise of the guests and anger of her father. Again, confined in the claustrophobic space of her room, Nazli faces her father's anger and attack. While she tries to shed light on her cousin's true nature, Abbas slaps her in the face and throws her on the bed, thus establishing physical superiority over her. The handheld camera and dark lighting visually add a sense of chaos to the situation and emphasize that the shaky relationship between Abbas and Nazli is on the verge of breakdown. The camera quickly changes between Abbas', Nazli's and Mahlin's points of view, thus also adding a distorted feeling to the claustrophobic situation Nazli finds herself in. Tired of Nazli's teenage misbehaviour, Abbas does not believe Nazli's rape accusations and continues to lecture her. This scene depicts Abbas as a patriarch, almost abusive, who, to the audience's surprise, is reluctant to listen to Nazli. This is also emphasized by the low angle camera perspective whenever Abbas is shown from Nazli's point of view, thus visually establishing the power positions. However, the fact that 'despite the family's dependency on and a personal financial obligation to Hamid, Abbas eventually believes Nazli's version of events' again restores Abbas' image as a loving father. This ambiguous portrayal of the father figure, lays the groundwork for the narrative. While 'making Abbas a largely sympathetic figure', it simultaneously allows the conflict to develop and most significantly allows for a happy ending (ibid.).

At the reconciliation Nazli confronts her father about the origin of their problems: she feels misunderstood and not listened to. This can be interpreted as a usual intergenerational conflict that millions of teenagers and parents face. In her analysis Wright (2010: 300) points out that:

> Whether or not Abbas' [acceptance of Nazli's rape accusations] is believable in the context of this particular subculture, the nuanced portrayal of both father and daughter makes it possible for the Swedish audience to view Nazli's rebellion, her struggle to achieve autonomy, as typical for most teenagers' rejection of parental authority and search for a coherent

identity rather than as motivated solely by cultural and ethnic differences.

However, while Wright's claim might be correct in dismissing ethnical background as a primary motivation for the conflict, it is still a significant backdrop upon which the father-daughter conflict unfolds because it involves aspects specific to their culture, such as arranged marriage. Furthermore, although there are several points mentioned above that 'make [...] it more difficult for the viewer to regard [Abbas] solely as a patriarchal tyrant' (ibid.), the two scenes described above should not be overlooked in the portrayal of him as an, at least partially, patriarchal father.

The silence of the sons: The father-son relationship

The other love triangle: Lisa, Roro and his father in *Jalla! Jalla!*

Analysing the father figure in the context of comedies, such as Josef Fares' films, is quite different to dramas such as *Hus i helvete*. This is simply because the film belongs to the genre of 'feel good films'[5] that has established itself in Swedish cinema in the new millennium (Lindblad, 2002: 33). Being comedies both *Jalla! Jalla!* and *Farsan* primarily serve the purpose of entertaining the audience by amusing them. Therefore, the image of the father painted by these films is, naturally, not as excruciating as it is in dramas such as *Hus i helvete*. Even the atmosphere of the films is very different: while *Hus i helvete* is shot in dark colours matching its dramatic elements, *Jalla! Jalla!* literally opens on a positive note with the reggae song *Know My Line* by Daniel Lemma.

Nonetheless, both *Jalla! Jalla!* and *Farsan* still offer a glimpse of patriarchal fathers who dominate their sons' lives and are thus relevant to this analysis.

> I såväl Fares som Baghers filmer finns en mörk undertext som för första gången i svensk långfilm, och dessutom inför en månghövdad publik i hela landet, talar klarspråk om den social and familjepolitiskt utsatta situation. (Lindblad 2002: 33)
>
> In both Fares' and Bagher's films, there is a dark subtext which, for the first time in Swedish cinema and before a large audience nationwide, speaks clearly about the socially and politically vulnerable situation of the family.

Moreover, in *Fucking Film,* Koskinen (2002: 10) claims that Josef Fares in particular relies more on traditional film making, in terms of both narrative and technology, instead of indulging in the possibilities that technological progress offers. 'Fares står med fötterna tryggt förankrade i den filmhistoriska myllan utan att på minsta sätt visa tendenser att flippra ut i total regellöshet, som ny teknik inte sällan frestar till.' (Fares stands firmly with both feet in the film-historical ground without showing any tendency to flip out in a total absence of rules, which new technology might tempt one to do.) Therefore, despite the fact that it gives less space for the analysis of the visual text, it is still legitimate to claim that these films aim at representing society in a realistic way. Hence they reflect upon society and attempt to deal with contemporary issues: family relations, immigrants and integration. Although there are several similarities between *Jalla! Jalla!* and *Farsan,* the two paternal characters are fundamentally different. As will be demonstrated later, Roro's father can be regarded as more of a dominating patriarch than Sami's, while *Farsan* possibly shows a way of dealing with the authority of the father. Thus, the two films will undergo separate analyses.

Jalla! Jalla! was released in 2000 and was the film that triggered off a wave of the so called 'immigrant films' that followed as the first decade of the millennium progressed. It is 'both a romantic comedy that concludes with two pairings that cross ethnic barriers and a buddy film in which ethnic background is irrelevant to friendship' (Wright, 2010: 296). It deals with the relationship between Roro, a young man of Lebanese ancestry, and Lisa, his Swedish girlfriend. Their 'emotionally and [...] physically satisfying relationship' is threatened by his family's attempt, 'unaware of Lisa's existence, to marry him off to Yasmin, a member of their own group' (ibid.). Roro is an adult still under the major influence of his father, who seems to be willing to control his every move, which is characteristic of all films within this analysis. There are two major aspects in their relationship. On one hand, it is his father's authority and dominating hand that controls Roro. On the other hand, Roro seems to be in need of his father's protection and, possibly even, dominance.

Firstly, Roro's inferiority toward his father is demonstrated by making him appear as a teenager. For instance, when he visits Lisa at home, he gets a call from his father asking where he is and whether he is with a girl, which is conventionally associated with teenage behaviour by the Western audience. The fact that Roro is playing a video game with his girlfriend only underlines his portrayal as an immature young boy. In a match cut between Roro and his father talking on the phone

The Father Figure in Swedish 'Immigrant' Films

with each other, his posture portrays him as a scared guilty teenager, caught by his parents doing something he should not do. The match cut only enhances the positions that Roro and his father hold. Obviously fearing his father's authority, he immediately follows his father's orders. Lisa, quite correctly, points out 'Damn it, Roro, you aren't a child anymore. [...] It's time for you to break free', thus emphasizing that he is still under the absolute control of his father. The fact that Roro behaves like a teenager in relation to his father is quite ironic because he seems to be very confident and self-assured in terms of his masculinity, as opposed to Måns, his friend, who struggles with his fading masculinity.

Another example of his father's superiority and control of Roro's life is demonstrated by the fact that he arranges a wedding for him without asking Roro about his feelings or wishes, as in other films included in this analysis. In the scene when Roro meets his wife-to-be, we are introduced to Yasmin and her brother Paul, who takes on the authoritarian role in the absence of her father. Both Yasmin and Roro do not want to get married, however, have little say in this, as the marriage is decided by Paul and Roro's father. On screen, this is demonstrated by contrasting medium close up shots of the bride and the groom-to-be as opposed to Paul and Roro's father. The initial long shot of the room showing all the people gradually zooms in on Jasmin and Roro. Both of them are shown looking down without saying a word, while the surrounding voices discuss their future. Therefore at first glance we are under the impression that Yasmin and Roro are the centre of attention, but as the perspective of the camera changes the focus is set on Paul and Roro's father[6], who decide upon the details of the marriage, leaving the two children quietly accepting their destiny without even looking at each other. Thus, a very stereotypically patriarchal picture of Roro's father is painted: as the highest authority of the family he decides how Roro is to live his life, without taking into account that Roro could have made his own plans already.

Furthemore, there is a notable contrast between Roro's and Lisa's family and their attitude towards this relationship. First of all, while Lisa is free to choose her own partner, Roro is forced into a marriage with a Lebanese girl. Roro's family does not even know about Lisa's existence, the reason for which seems to be that they would not accept a Swedish girlfriend, which raises the inevitable question of cultural and ethnic differences. However, 'Lisa's father pays no attention to Roro's ethnic heritage and facilitates the couple's union' (Wright, 2010: 298). On one hand this gives room for the obvious comparison between Lisa's father, who seems to be open-minded and welcoming, in contrast to Roro's father, who controls and dominates his son. This attitude is supported by their parents' houses, which symbolically stand for the different situations Lisa and Roro are in. While Lisa's parents live in an 'idyllic house in the countryside [which] is as iconographically Swedish as a painting by Carl Larsson', Roro lives in a small flat with his extended family (ibid., 297). The physical space and freedom is as limited as Roro's freedom of choice and decisions. Therefore, this disparity contributes to the image of Roro's father as an authoritarian patriarch. On the other hand, this also points out that 'the obstacle to [Roro's and Lisa's relationship] is not her parents, but the well-intended effort of Roro's extended Lebanese family' (ibid.). Thus it sheds a different light on the issue of integration. According to the film, it is not Swedish society which refuses to accept immigrants, but rather the immigrants who refuse to adapt and become integrated into Swedish society.

The second aspect that is characteristic of the relationship between Roro and his father is Roro's dependence on him. The reason why Roro cannot break free from his father is simply because he needs him. However, Roro's need for his father goes beyond the basic social need, rather he requires his father to save him. An example of this is the scene when Roro is chased and beaten up by the 'testosterone-induced' (ibid.) and aggressive group of men who seek revenge on Måns, Roro's best friend. While Måns manages to escape the consequences, Roro is pinned down to the ground by two men, who disregard the fact that he is not involved. Interestingly enough, Fares plays with stereotypes here: he avoids the picture of a physical confrontation between an immigrant and a group of strong Swedish men. Instead, this situation is used to portray the relationship between Roro and his father. When his father hears Roro scream, he comes to his help and pushes the two men away with his comic 'stomach bump' move. Therefore, Roro's father is portrayed as physically superior to both the men and Roro, which is underscored by his overweight figure as opposed to Roro's. The fact that his father saves Roro also puts him in the position of a vulnerable teenager who needs protection from his father, thus reinforcing the authoritarian figure of Roro's father, but at the same time also showing that their relationship is beneficial for Roro.

Furthermore, the aspect of an arranged marriage naturally falls into the highly stereotypical representation of a Middle

Eastern family as seen in today's society, and accompanies every film in this essay. However, the stereotype is broken when Roro's father actually takes his son's side by letting him leave the wedding with Lisa. He even aids him to do so by giving him the keys to his car, thus, fully demonstrating his support for his son's decision. Still, this scene cannot be regarded as a reversal of roles as seen, for instance, at the end of *Hus i helvete*, because Roro does not escape his father's authority. Certainly, Roro speaks up and introduces his girlfriend to his family, thus escaping the imposed marriage, but he also seeks his father's approval. Before actually leaving, he asks his father 'Säkert?' [Are you sure?] when his father offers him his keys, indicating Roro's continuing dependence on his father. The car, as the ultimate symbol of freedom of movement, seems more like a 'wedding gift' than means of escape. Consequently, the father's authority is re-enforced through this scene. However, simultaneously through the acceptance of the constellations of the two couples, films like *Jalla! Jalla!* try to avoid ethnic stereotyping, as Wright claims. Hence, although this particular scene does not demonstrate Roro's emancipation from his family, it is more important in terms of showing Roro's father coming to terms with his son's decision. He declines his own cultural norms in favour of the norms of 'Western' society. Similarly, as described in the analysis of *Hus i helvete*, Fares' film aims at reconciling the two cultures by bringing two ethnically-mixed couples together. Furthermore, the film shows that the relationship between Roro and his father is not entirely based on authoritative patriarchal hierarchy, but rather that it is two-sided, as in *Vingar av glas*. Therefore, Fares moves away from the stereotype of Middle Eastern fathers as authoritative and abusive, showing that they are also caring and helpful.

When Farsan met the baby

As pointed out before, it is slightly problematic to analyse such serious topics as generational conflicts and gender related issues in Josef Fares' comedies. Nonetheless, *Farsan* (2010) gives room for a critical portrayal of a patriarchal father and raises questions about masculinity. The film deals with a middle-aged man, Aziz, who works in a bicycle repair shop and wishes for nothing more than a grandchild from his son Sami. However, Sami, married to a Swedish young woman, Amanda, is infertile and, fearing his father's reaction, the couple conceals a planned adoption from Aziz.

Sami and his father seem to care about each other deeply, which is partially the reason why Sami keeps the truth from him. Already in the beginning of the film, this mutual caring is established: while Farsan brings food for his son, Sami and Amanda attempt to set him up with one of Amanda's female colleagues. Sami and Aziz seek each other's advice. For instance, Sami helps Aziz with shopping when the later decides to find a date. Furthermore, they are portrayed as being on the same level, almost as friends, which makes Aziz a likeable character as opposed to the other fathers presented in this analysis. 'Han lever uteslutande för sin son och det oerhört efterlängtade barnbarn som hans svärdotter bär i magen' (Lövenlid, 2011) (He lives exclusively for his son and the long-awaited grandchild his daughter-in-law is carrying). For instance, when Aziz visits Sami and Amanda, they end up playing video games. In a medium shot, we see both of them on a couch sitting next to each other, thus emphasizing their close relationship, which is based on mutual love. This particular shot is especially interesting if compared to, for instance, the low angle shots of Serbandi, which visually support his superior position within the family. As a comedy *Farsan* naturally needs to create likable characters for the audience to sympathise and laugh with them. Therefore, Aziz is portrayed as an amusing father, who is also a good friend to the people around him. For instance, he attempts to help Jörgen deal with his masculinity issues and comforts Juan when he loses his dog.

This being said, the issue of grandchildren becomes absurd and sheds a different light on Aziz's and Sami's relationship. Despite their close bond, Sami still does not dare to tell his father that he cannot have children himself, but instead decides to deceive his beloved father. This issue becomes even more interesting when related to the question of masculinity, although this is not raised directly in the film. It is left open as to why Sami fears his father: whether it is because he is afraid of his authority, or because he is afraid of failing as a man in the eyes of another man. By leaving this question open, Fares creates an ambiguous portrait of Aziz, simultaneously hinting at these issues. Further, the ambiguity is underscored by Aziz's portrayal as a likeable character, while revealing his immense, rather negative impact on his son's life, which seems illogical given their relationship. Moreover, Aziz still holds patriarchal worldviews, ranging from specific family matters to the role of women in general. The family tree that he presents Sami and Amanda with demonstrates this quite clearly. Aziz, as the patriarch of the family, is placed on top, followed by Sami and Amanda, and then their children. Despite the fact that the scene has a comic undertone and Amanda jokingly accepts Aziz's demand for four grandchildren, it reveals Aziz's control of Sami's life.

'[Relationen] är således upplagt för många trassliga nödlögner och genanta situationer i väntan på att den ofrånkomliga sanningen ska krypa fram' (ibid.) ([The relationship] is therefore prone to many tangled white lies and embarrassing situations in anticipation of the inevitable truth to emerge).

A further aspect of Aziz's character and the theme of the film, as with other films of this analysis, is masculinity. Considering what Aziz says and how he behaves, his character is quite ambiguous. On one hand, he is portrayed as a man who shares his feelings because he shows affection for his son and daughter-in-law and also visits his wife's grave to tell her that he still loves her. Furthermore, there are several scenes that present him to us as lonely and nostalgic, thus making him a likeable character. For instance, there is a shot of him at home, where the camera, in a slow pan shot of his apartment, shows Aziz lying on the bed and thinking. This is supported by nostalgic and melancholic music, adding up to an image of Aziz that demands compassion rather than rage. On the other hand, there are several aspects that reveal Aziz's traditional and patriarchal worldview as far. For instance, when he decides to help his boss Jörgen to overcome marital problems, he clearly says that men should have the upper hand in a marriage, not paying attention to the desires of the woman, even contradicting her. Aziz 'är obändigt trygg i sin libanesiska machismo och med en världsbild där män tar tag i saker, dealar och fixar, medan kvinnor antingen är respektingivande husmödrar eller åtråframkallande "snigga brodar"' (ibid.) (is firmly secure in his Lebanese machismo and holds a world view, which expects men to take care of things, deal and fix, while women are either respectful housewives or desirable pretty women).[7]

Surely, his attempt to make 'a strong man' of Jörgen by tying him to the roof of a fast driving car cannot be taken seriously by the watching audience. However, this still marks a trend in Aziz's patriarchal worldview. Especially since no one seems to contradict the points he makes, rather, both Juan and Jörgen agree with him. Jörgen even seems to aspire to Aziz's knowledge and hyper-masculinity. Thus, the image of masculinity is not limited to Aziz's ethnical background; it is personified by him. Johan Croneman (2010) criticizes Fares for this portrayal of men: 'Farsans världsåskådning skulle väl beskrivas – inte befästas?' (Farsans' worldview should be described – not confirmed?). In addition, while as an audience we are introduced to Aziz's inner world and are aware of his loneliness and feelings, in the diegetic world of the film his feelings remain hidden from others. His loneliness and vulnerability remain covered by his 'libanesiska machismo' (Lebanese machismo) whenever he is around the people he knows. Therefore, instead of breaking the stereotypes of male and female roles, they are being enforced over and over again, which is also emphasized by the passive role women are given in Fares' films.

An aspect that distinguishes *Farsan* from the other films in this analysis is that Sami is both a son and a future father. Interestingly enough, Sami's relationship with his future child is immensely affected by his relationship to his own father. At a baby shop, Sami tries to persuade Amanda to tell Aziz another white lie about the baby, but Amanda correctly points out: 'Det är alltid Farsan, Farsan, Farsan. *Du* och jag ska skaffa familj! *Du* ska bli papa!'. (It is always Farsan, Farsan, Farsan. *You* and me are starting a family! *You* are going to be a dad!) Instead of concentrating on his child and wife, Sami is preoccupied by how his father is going to take the adoption news. On one hand, this reveals the extent of Aziz's impact on Sami's life because, even if he is not actively suppressing him, as opposed to *Hus i helvete* for example, Sami still feels his authority. On the other hand, this aspect also demonstrates that Sami himself puts his father's satisfaction over his own and that of his family. This being a comedy, a happy end is inevitable, thus, both fathers accept the current situation and begin to appreciate what they have. Furthermore, the reconciliation of the family can be regarded as a hint at a resolution for this generational conflict: one should not hold on to traditional values, stereotypes and prejudices, if they stand in the way of one's happiness, which is the simple message of the 'feel good' films. This is also emphasized by the fact that Aziz seems to have successfully combined two cultures. He seems to be fully integrated into the Swedish society, while still keeping his own habits. Generally, in contrast to other films included in this essay, *Farsan* shows a rather healthy and good-natured relationship between a son and his father. This could be seen as a recent development in the representation of immigrant families in film. Such a statement, however, demands a close observation of films in the next couple of years to see if this becomes a new trend in cinema or in family relations within immigrant communities.

Summary and Conclusion

All things considered, one can clearly state that these films represent a man – a father – struggling with his role in society and his family. But why are immigrant films any different to other films based on the father-son relationship, of which there have been so many throughout the history of cinema?

Firstly, these films reflect upon changes and demographics within Swedish society. As pointed out by many academics, there are other ethnic groups living in Sweden, who also fight, write and film. Secondly, it is notable that these films demonstrate a stereotypically patriarchal perception of fathers from the Middle East within the Western 'civilized' society of Sweden. But more importantly, it shows a very complex generational conflict. In addition to showing the traditional issue of children growing up under a seemingly authoritative paternal regime, this conflict also represents the tensions between different cultures when they come into contact. Rather than portraying this conflict as an issue of old versus new, these films show both children and parents with immigrant backgrounds being caught between two cultures: the original culture, as both symbolized and imposed by the family, and the host culture. Thus, their conflict is not only generational, but also touches upon problems of integration: while fathers hold on to their traditions and thus struggle to merge with society, their children, nurtured in an environment of different norms, become part of it. This is also emphasized by the fact that these films are products of the 'second generation': they are made by children of immigrants who grew up in Swedish society but were raised with the values of their parents. Therefore, these films deal with far more than simply 'the missing father' or other kinds of generational conflicts; they deal with social problems, integration and inner and outer conflicts.

Fathers re-negotiating masculinity

The portrayal of men and masculinity seems to have been a *leitmotif* in Scandinavian cinema for the past decade, ranging from abusive fathers (e.g. *Festen)* and violent young men (e.g. *Evil*, Håfström, 2003) to successful men 'moving from the big world and fast life to the small, quiet village' (Marklund, 2008: 56). As Marklund (ibid.) argues in his article '"Can anyone help these men": A Portrait of Men in Successful Contemporary Scandinavian Cinema', there are men who are uncomfortable with 'be[ing] measured against old standards of masculinity', implying that these standards have changed. Undoubtedly, the role of the father is an important part of male identity, no matter if a man denies or embraces it. Therefore, departing from the view that the concept of masculinity has been transformed, understanding how the role and perception of the father has changed is an important issue.

In a recent article 'Why We Need to Re-imagine Masculinity', Romano and Dokoupil (2010) write that the concept of masculinity has been transformed globally according to what had been demanded from men at a particular time of history. They claim that, according to Michael Kimmel, a historical sociologist, before 1776 the male ideal was 'still a genteel patriarch, a dandified landowner steeped in the codes of the Old World'. However, by the early 19th century the image of the perfect man was replaced by 'the heroic artisan, the rugged individualist [...] who might lead a caravan west' (ibid.). As time shaped the modern society, the ideal man became 'the self-made man, a restless, competitive breadwinner, whose masculinity depended on success in an industrial, materialistic society. It is clear that we have arrived at another crossroads — only today the prevailing codes of manhood have yet to adjust to the changing demands on men' (ibid.). Therefore, it is obvious that men are at a stage of re-defining themselves and their roles in society, which is reflected by themes evident in cinema. While Romano and Dokoupil's claim is made upon their notions about men and society in the US, the same aspects apply, and perhaps even more so, to Sweden, as I shall explain.

This is especially interesting in terms of immigrant films, for two reasons. Firstly, these fathers need to re-negotiate their whole identity, including their masculinity, while trying (or being forced) to adapt to Swedish society. Secondly, the role of the father in their home culture might be very different to the Swedish one, thus adding pressure on immigrant fathers and contrasting their behaviour with the Swedish 'ideal'. The generational conflict automatically becomes a question of a cultural clash because, in addition to their parental worries, fathers also struggle with the different values that their children seem to demand. All films initially portray fathers as the patriarch of the family, who need to take care of the family and arrange their lives. From the fathers' point of view, their interference in their children's lives is considered a duty, not authoritative control or abuse. Both Serbandi and Abbas attempt to control their daughters' actions and even their clothing style, and the question of arranged marriages is raised in all of the films. Even in *Farsan,* a film that shows the least authoritative father of them all, Aziz tries to impose his own values upon his son, while Sami strives to make his own life choices concerning his family plans.

As suggested by the films, in this particular cultural group, the patriarchal position that the men try to hold is part of their role as a father, as well as their masculine identity. Therefore, what their children consider freedom of choice, these fathers consider as disobedience that undermines their authority, and even masculinity, which is defined by the family structure. Consequently, in order to keep the family together, they feel the need to re-enforce their authoritative regime and constrain their children. However, this proves to be problematic against the backdrop of the 'Western values' or, in this particular case, Sweden. Immigrant films, therefore, show cultural and ethnic collisions in families where children and parents live in different worlds, stresses Helena Lindblad (2002: 33).

Swedish society in general is a significant example for how the role of the father has changed, especially since the 'simple but revolutionary' paternity-leave legislation in 1992. 'Now [there are] more than 80% of Swedish fathers [who] take four months off for the birth of a new child', thus, demonstrating how the traditional gender roles have shifted (Romano and Dokoupil, 2010). Many academics and journalists seem to praise Sweden as the example of genius social engineering that is causing the emergence of a new definition of masculinity (Bennhold, 2010). Generally, in today's Western societies, including Sweden, it gets

> allt svårare för dagens fäder att rent konkret fylla den traditionella rollen som förmedlare av samhälleligt accepterade normer och värderingar, d. v. s. att vara en social [...] instans.(Dahlén, 1994: 359)

> increasingly difficult for today's fathers to completely live up to the traditional role of suppliers of socially accepted norms and values, i.e. to be a social institution of authority.

However, it is even more difficult for those trying to form a symbiosis of different cultural norms. Therefore, the films discussed above show not only men struggling with their children, but men struggling with their changing role in society.

In this society, equality and freedom of choice seem to be more important than the façade of purity and respectability that the patriarch feels the need to protect. However, instead of adapting to the new situation for the sake of harmony in their family, these fathers try to impose their own values and desires on their family and children. Both Serbandi and Abbas feel emasculated because their daughters try to escape the imposed rules, as explained earlier. They, thus, attempt to restore their masculinity by emerging as a patriarch and call upon stereotypes of Middle Eastern men. The aggressiveness, or even abuse, however, only point to the fact that they are struggling with their role as a father and with their masculinity, which are part of their role as a provider and protector of the family. Both *Jalla! Jalla!* and *Farsan* show similar issues that the fathers are struggling with, although they are not as authoritative as Abbas and Serbandi. This is partly because these are comedies and partly because they feature a father-son relationship, which has different dynamics to the daughter-father relationship. However, it is important to point out that *Farsan* comically depicts a hyper-masculine father, which has two different effects. On one hand, it obviously adds a comic element to the film, as a substantial part of the amusing scenes and dialogue are coupled to masculinity. On the other hand, it points out that masculinity is a significant issue for today's men and in need of re-defining, especially for those groups who have more traditional views on it. In the films discussed, immigrant men face the need to re-negotiate their identity, not only as part of the society, but also against its values and norms. In a way, these films offer advice, or at least show possible ways, for male roles and behaviour, similar to the magazines. As David Gauntlett points out in his study of masculinity:

> The existence and popularity of male magazines shows men rather insecurely trying to find their place in the modern world, seeking help regarding how to behave in relationships, and advice on how to earn the attention, love and respect of women, and the friendship of other men. (Gauntlett 2002: 189)

Two types of generational conflict

As mentioned before, there are differences in the illustration of the generational conflicts amongst the discussed films. While *Jalla! Jalla!* and *Farsan* depict a conflict between father and son, *Vingar av glas* and *Hus i helvete* show the relationship between father and daughter, which adds a different taste to the authoritarian father figure. Tackling the issue of a father-daughter relationship inevitably raises the question of gender roles and gender appropriate behaviour. As opposed to the sons, daughters seem to face more struggle and confrontation from the side of their fathers. They experience violence from their fathers, who try to control the way they look and the men they interact with. Therefore, a daughter's struggle with the authoritative patriarch automatically becomes a battle of the sexes. In both *Hus i helvete* and *Vingar av glas*, the generational conflict is illustrated by pointing out gender inequality. In Sweden, the newspapers still occasionally report on women being mistreated by Muslim men, such as Fadime Sahindahl, a victim of an honour crime in 2002 (Wright, 2010:

301). Although both *Jalla! Jalla!* and *Farsan* are comedies and therefore less tragic in their mood, gender specific stereotypes seem to be symptomatic in these films, too. Despite the fact that they do not contribute substantially to the development of the generational conflict, in both films women are not shown as being equal to men. As Wright (ibid.: 298) correctly points out, *Jalla! Jalla!* touches upon but does not elaborate on the

> difficult situation of young women from Middle Eastern backgrounds whose opinions, even in Sweden, are limited by family pressure and prevailing cultural norms. [...] Thus although the narrative plays on ethnic stereotypes to call into question conventional standards of masculinity, overall it reveals a conventional perspective on appropriate male and female roles.

This is no different in *Farsan*, as Johan Croneman (2010) points out: 'Det är inget riktigt fräscht kvinnoporträtt. [...] Tjejerna ser mest ut som staffage, portar som pojkarna kan åka slalom emellan i all sin briljans.' (This is not a very modern portrayal of women. The girls mostly look like decoration, gates between which boys can zigzag in all their brilliance.) Although this issue is not exclusive to immigrant cinema, immigrant films in this analysis show that a father-daughter conflict stress the gender stereotypes to a greater extent than Fares' films, which portray a father-son relationship.

Clash of the cultures

Through the generational conflict within an immigrant family, these films also highlight the situation of immigrants. The so called 'immigrant films' are not a mere 'depiction of various immigrant subcultures', but also 'mirror [...] and comment [...] on social change' (Wright, 2010: 293). Harald Runblom (1995: 310), an historian concentrating on Nordic migration, claims that '[t]he greatest cultural challenge to the Nordic countries concerns Islam and the immigration from Muslim countries, [which] is a new phenomenon'. While Sweden has experienced ongoing change in the population constellation in the 20th century, it was still 'ethnically and linguistically [one] of the most homogeneous countries in the world' (ibid.). However, from the 1960s on, several waves of Muslim immigration have reached Sweden, thus bringing significant changes to the ethnic constellation of Swedish society. The United Nations report (1996) that 'in 1995, more than 10% of the population was born abroad and first or second generation immigrants comprised nearly 20% of the population'. Suddenly, Swedish people were forced to deal with immigrants, facing the 'intrusion' of different cultures and developing integration policies.

Runblom also points out that knowledge of the immigrant Muslim culture is still low, thus occasionally leading to misconception and misunderstanding of their behaviour and cultural conduct by different parts of the population. Moreover, '[t]he rapid transformation of Sweden [...] has only become visible and integrated into aspects of popular culture since about the year 2000, reflecting the slow pace of Swedish reconciliation with an unrelenting globalization process that it can no longer pretend to ignore' (Westerståhl Stenport, 2007: 2). Certainly, the emergence of 'immigrant films' and their increasing number in the past decade mirror Sweden's modern-day multi-ethnicity. The directors of these films are mostly second-generation filmmakers, who grew up in immigrant communities in Sweden and offer the audience a window into the life of other ethnicities in the country. This claim is also supported by the fact that many Swedish contemporary directors aim at depicting everyday life of real people instead of concentrating on the Hollywood-esque 'rich and beautiful' (Koskinen, 1996: 34). Following this trend, immigrant films show simple people with their personal problems, which, however, are symptomatic of society. These films 'delineate a personal view of Swedish society that incorporates the experiences of characters who, like their creators, are immigrants from the Middle East' (Wright, 2010: 301).

This is also supported by the rather simplistic use of camera and editing, seen especially in Fares' films (Koskinen, 2002: 109). Many academics claim that new Swedish film has little stylistic experimentation, and rather it relies heavily on narrative and dynamics between the characters, thus portraying society in a more realistic way, without distorting the image by technical experimentation. While this might be true, it is also important to remember that these films were made for a Swedish audience, which has contributed to the nationwide success of these films. Therefore, one could also claim that the portrayal of the immigrant families is realistic in the eyes of the audience, which is the host society itself. Yet still, these films provide an insider view of the communities, thus aiming at achieving a balance between the different points of view.

For this reason, it is crucial to recognise that these films do not solely mirror the social situation, but also comment on it and give space for the re-negotiation of the immigrant-host relationship. On one hand, they attempt to break down prejudices and stereotypes of the immigrant families on different levels. Firstly, all films provide resolutions for conflicts and the successful co-habitation of the two cultures. Secondly, both *Hus i helvete* and *Vingar av glas* challenge gender roles and stereotypes in terms of clothing and appropriate behaviour of women in their respective cultures. On the other hand, they show both positive and negative aspects of both cultures, thus inviting the audience to reflect upon themselves, instead of simply keeping a hostile attitude towards 'the Other'. As I already pointed out in the analysis of *Hus i helvete*, the 'Westernized' 'free' society is not depicted as an ideal state, it is rather criticized for its objectification and exploitation of the female body. Similarly, *Jalla! Jalla!* touches upon issues such as violence from the side of the testosterone-driven men, while in *Farsan* we see a comical representation of the pressure on men and masculinity from within Swedish society, as exemplified by Jörgen. Therefore, these films allow the audience to witness the confrontation of two cultures, thus hinting at the fact that cultural integration should be approached from both sides.

Summary

All things considered, these so-called 'immigrant films' portray a complex web of issues through their depiction of the father. First of all, they show a generational conflict that is set against a cultural backdrop that is being re-defined at the same time. These films also reflect upon the changing role of men in the modern society, especially in Sweden, and the reluctance of men to keep up with it. The changing role of men in the host society adds pressure on immigrant men since they need to adapt to values, which are often different to their own and, at the same time, in the process of change. Moreover, all four films reflect social changes within Swedish society, which emerges as a multi-ethnic community. Through the conflict between fathers and their children, these films show the cultural clash between the 'imported' culture and that one of the host society. However, instead of favouring one or the other, it invites the viewer to form a symbiosis of both and simultaneously for each side to reflect upon its own values and norms.

Author's Comment

This project is an undergraduate dissertation and a result of long and persistent research. Being a dedicated admirer of Ingmar Bergman, perhaps the most dominant father figure in Swedish film, it is not surprising that my dissertation was on Nordic cinema, especially with the focus on Sweden in particular. After months of thorough research and what felt like a million DVDs, I discovered that there are two topics which a lot of contemporary Swedish films seem to have in common: immigrant culture and father figures. Being a student of BA Language & Culture I knew that there must be a correlation between these two trends, which I attempted to discover in the course of my essay. It turned out to be a very complex but interesting web of issues and ideas. Yet, in order to understand how Swedish society influences these directors one could also explore the background of the so called 'immigrant films': how are films made and funded, how committees make decisions about which films are promoted.

After graduating in August 2012, I retired from my professional career as a film critic and started working in a London-based film productions company. Up until this day, I remain a cinephile and a secret admirer of Lars von Trier's work.

1. From 2005 a TV Show based on Mankell's novels about the detective Wallander has been successfully released on DVD and TV, but also shown at theatres in Sweden. Simultaneously the BBC released an adaptation as well, which has gained popularity in the UK.
2. *The Girl With the Dragon Tattoo* (Arden Oplev, 2009), *The Girl Who Played With Fire* (Alfredson, 2009), *The Girl Who Kicked the Hornet's Nest* (Alfredson, 2009)
3. This and all following translations are mine.
4. In her essay 'In my father's house there are many mansions' Ellen Rees concludes that the first Dogme films (*Festen*, *Idioterne*, both 1998) deal with a dysfunctional family, showing how the children overthrow the patriarchal bourgeois authority of the father by occupying their houses.
5. This is an expression that has established itself within the frame of contemporary Swedish cinema. 'Feel good films' refer to light comedies that have a happy ending, as opposed to dark themes of loneliness and isolation typical for Scandinavian cinema.
6. Swedish for father and the only way Roro refers to his father.
7. The expression 'snigga brodar' is a collocial way of saying 'pretty women' in Swedish with a Lebanese accent.

References

Barsan, Richard and Monahan, David (2010). *Looking at Movies.* New York: W.W. Norton & Co.

Bennhold, Katrin (2010). 'In Sweden Men Can Have It All', *The New York Times.* http://www.nytimes.com/2010/06/10/world/europe/10iht-sweden.html. Accessed 9 May 2011.

Bono, Francesco and Koskinen, Maaret (1996). 'Foreword', in *Film in Sweden.* Smedjebacken: Smegraf.

Dahlén, Peter (1994). "Fadersupproret som kom av sig. Om generationsklyftan i svensk efterkrigsfilm". In Johan Fornäs et al. (eds): *Ungdomskultur i Sverige,* FUS-report no. 6. Stockholm/Stehag: Brutus Östlings Bokförlag Symposion.

Doxtater, Amanda (2006). 'Bodies in Elevators: The Conveyance of Ethnicity in Recent Swedish Films'. In Thomson, C. Claire (ed.): *Northern Constellations: New Readings in Nordic Cinema.* London: Norvik Press.

Croneman, Johan (2010). 'Farsan'. *Dagens Nyheter.* http://www.dn.se/kultur-noje/filmrecensioner/farsan. Accessed 9 May 2011.

Gauntlett, David (2002). *Media, Gender and Identity: An Introduction.* London and New York: Routledge.

Hagman, Ingrid (1992). 'Den frånvarande fadern'. *Chaplin* 241, 4.

Hagström, Charlotte (1999). *Man blir pappa: föräldraskap och maskulinitet i förändring*. Lund, Sweden: Nordic Academic Press.

Koskinen, Maaret (2002). 'Konsten att förena gammalt med nytt. Form och berättande i Jalla! Jalla!'. In Björkman, Stig, Helena Lindblad, and Fredrik Sahlin (eds): *Fucking Film: Den nya svenska filmen*. Stockholm: Alfabeta Bokförlag.

Koskinen, Maaret (1996). 'The Swedish Film of the Eighties and Nineties: A Critical Survey'. In Bono, Francesco and Maaret Koskinen (eds): *Swedish Film*. Smedjebacken: Smegraf.

Larsson, Mariah (2010). 'A Renewal of Swedish Film: Introduction'. In Larsson, Mariah and Anders Marklund (eds): *Swedish Film: An Introduction and Reader*. Lund, Sweden: Nordic Academic Press.

Lindblad, Helena (2002). 'Det Nya filmlandet'. In Björkman, Stig, Helena Lindblad and Fredrik Sahlin (eds): *Fucking Film: Den nya svenska filmen*. Stockholm: Alfabeta Bokförlag.

Lövenlid, Björn (2010). 'Lättsmält och kul med pappa Fares'. *Upsala Nya Tidning*. http://www.unt.se/kultur/film/laumlttsmaumllt-och-kul-med-pappa-fares-108412-default.aspx. Accessed 9 May 2011.

Marklund, Anders (2008). '"Can Anyone Help These Men?": A Portrayal of Men in Successful Contemporary Scandinavian Cinema'. *Film International*, 6.5.

Romano, Andrew and Dokoupil, Tony, (2010). 'Men's Lib.'. *Newsweek*. http://www.newsweek.com/2010/09/20/why-we-need-to-reimagine-masculinity.html. Accessed 9 May 2011.

Runblom, Harald, (1995). 'Immigrantion to Scnadinavia after WWII'. In Tägil, Sven (ed.): *Ethnicity and Nation-Building in the Nordic World.* London: Hurst & Company.

United Nations (1996). Committee on the Elimination of Racial Discrimination. *Twelfth periodic reports of States parties due in 1995. Addendum. Sweden.* http://www.unhchr.ch/ tbs/doc.nsf/0/971eaa155731875980256442005a1b38? Opendocument. Accessed 9 May 2011.

Westerståhl Stenport, Anna, (2007). 'Bodies Under Assault: National and Immigration in Henning Mankell's Faceless Killers'. *Scandinavian Studies* 79.1.

Wright, Rochelle, (2010). '"Immigrant Film" in Sweden at the Millennium'. In Larsson, Mariah and Anders Marklund (eds): *Swedish Film: An Introduction and Reader.* Lund, Sweden: Nordic Academic Press.

www.ingramcontent.com/pod-product-compliance
Lightning Source LLC
Chambersburg PA
CBHW050512170426
43201CB00013B/1928